OR. F. S

Cape Colony

TRANSUAAL

THE BRITISH EPIC

A History of the
English-Speaking Peoples,
from the Earliest Times
to the Present Day,
for Intermediate Grades

The Background of our Times

GENERAL EDITORS:
KENNETH MAWSON, M.A.,
Assistant Superintendent of
Secondary Schools,
North York Board of Education

JOHN T. SAYWELL, PH.D.,
Professor of History,
Dean of Arts and Science,
York University, Toronto

BOOK I
Bold Ventures

BOOK II
Nation of the North

BOOK III
The British Epic

BOOK IV
The Modern Era

Toronto   Vancouver

THE
BRITISH EPIC

JOHN C. RICKER, M.A.,
Professor of History,
The College of Education,
University of Toronto

JOHN T. SAYWELL, PH.D.,
Professor of History,
Dean of Arts and Science,
York University, Toronto

A. EARLE STRONG, B.A.,
Formerly Head of the History Department,
Lawrence Park Collegiate Institute,
Toronto

HUGH J. VALLERY, M.A.,
Academic Director,
Metropolitan Toronto School Board,
Study of Educational Facilities

Illustrated by LEWIS PARKER
Maps by ROBERT KUNZ

CLARKE, IRWIN &
COMPANY LIMITED

8 9 10 11 12 JD 79 78 77 76 75 74 73 72 71 70

Printed in Canada

CONTENTS

Book IV—TOWARDS DEMOCRACY

LIST OF MAPS

LIST OF CHARTS

PREFACE

The British Epic has been written with the Canadian student in mind. It emphasizes those important facts in British history, particularly the development of democratic government and the evolution of the Empire and the Commonwealth, which have profoundly affected the lives of Canadians.

In the belief that history should be enjoyed as well as learned, the authors have sought to tell their story in a lively manner and have kept dates and dry facts to a minimum. At the same time, however, they have included study aids which will make the student's task of assimilating essential facts much easier. The pupil would do well to become familiar with these devices—maps, charts, genealogical tables, time lines, time charts, index—and make use of them in every possible way.

At the beginning of every section there is a vertical line indicating the segment of time covered in that book. At the head of every chapter there is a horizontal time line indicating the portion of that segment dealt with in the chapter to follow. Consider Chapter Seven, for example. Book I deals with the period from 100 B.C. to A.D. 1485. Chapter Seven deals with the period from 1154 to 1199. During the first part of that period, from 1154 to 1189, Henry II was on the throne. His reign, as you will learn, was marked by the development of common law, one of England's outstanding achievements. As soon as he came to the throne in 1154 Henry set out to restore law and order to a country torn by civil strife. In 1170, after Henry had quarrelled with Thomas à Becket, the Archbishop was murdered, an event which affected Henry and the country deeply. In 1189 Henry was succeeded by his son Richard who reigned until 1199. If you study the other time lines you will see that they are all constructed on the same principle. The top line shows the portion of the book-period to be covered in the chapter; the bottom line shows the principal events that occurred during that time.

PROLOGUE

Why study history? Every student asks the same question. Think for a moment of a man suddenly stricken with loss of memory, or amnesia. He is little more than a physical object occupying space. He does not know who he is, where he has come from, or where he is going. History is society's memory. It tells man where he has come from and therefore what he is. History cannot tell us where we are going, but of all studies it provides the most reliable guide. That is why successful diplomats and statesmen place a high value on the study of history. Without history human society would be just as lost as a man with amnesia.

Why study *British* history? For a Canadian, the language in which the question is asked immediately suggests one answer. Yet there is more to it than that. In history curricula throughout the world British history is perhaps the only subject studied everywhere. Library shelves hold books on British history by Canadians and Americans, Australians and South Africans, Russians and Germans, Indians and Chinese. In one way or another Britain has had a powerful effect on every part of the world. For centuries London was the world's commercial and financial centre and for much of the globe it still is. British merchantmen dominated the sea lanes and Glasgow-built ships and British seamen were found in every port from Canton to Vancouver, from Rio de Janeiro to Murmansk.

Until recent times Britain's Empire lay sprawled across the globe. From that Empire has emerged the modern Commonwealth of Nations, in the making of which Canadians played a large part. Here Indians and Australians, Africans and Malayans, English and Canadians meet on terms of complete equality and independence, each recognizing Queen Elizabeth as head of the Commonwealth and the symbol of their unity. This Commonwealth of Nations is one of the miracles of modern statesmanship.

To the outposts of empire British missionaries carried the Christian message and British settlers planted British institutions and laws. Wherever they went—settler or missionary, explorer or trader—the

English language went with them. Today, wherever educated men meet, English is likely to be the only language they have in common. That English is spoken in Great Britain, the United States, and the Commonwealth may yet prove to be one fact that will save the western world from disaster. It provides a basis for the unity of much of the free world.

Moreover, in Canadian eyes British history is part of Canada's history. It is not just that we were once a colony in the Empire and are now an independent state within the Commonwealth. Our Parliament is modelled on the English Parliament. Our political parties have adopted English names and have frequently borrowed the ideas of their trans-Atlantic counterparts. Our entire legal system had its beginnings in England over a thousand years ago. Such fundamental individual rights as trial by jury, freedom from unjust arrest, and freedom of speech are part of our British inheritance. These cherished rights provide yet another foundation for the unity of the English-speaking world.

We Canadians must peruse the rich pages of British history and gain a firm grasp of the history of Empire and Commonwealth and the growth of free institutions in England before we can fully understand the developments of our own institutions. We believe that *The British Epic* will lead to this understanding and we hope that in reading it you will have a pleasant and rewarding experience.

BOOK I

THE MEDIÆVAL FOUNDATIONS

1. The Dawn of British History
2. The Invasions
3. Anglo-Saxon England: The People
4. Anglo-Saxon England: Government and Law
5. The Norman Conquest
6. The Norman Monarchy
7. Henry II and the Common Law
8. King John and Magna Carta
9. The Great Experiment: 1216-1327
10. The Sunset of Mediæval England: 1327-1485
11. Country and Town in the Late Middle Ages
12. The Spirit of the Late Middle Ages

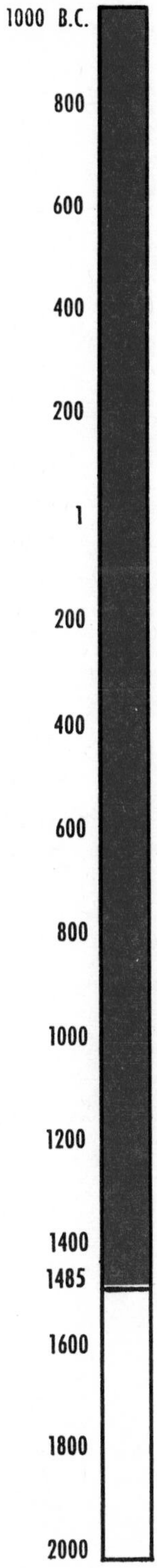
1000 B.C.
800
600
400
200
1
200
400
600
800
1000
1200
1400
1485
1600
1800
2000

KINGS OF MEDIAEVAL ENGLAND

1066-1087	William I	
1087-1100	William II (Rufus)	Norman
1100-1135	Henry I	
1135-1154	Stephen	

1154-1189	Henry II	
1189-1199	Richard I (The Lion-heart)	
1199-1216	John I	Angevin
1216-1272	Henry III	
1272-1307	Edward I	
1307-1327	Edward II	Plantagenet
1327-1377	Edward III	
1377-1399	Richard II	

1399-1413	Henry IV	
1413-1422	Henry V	Lancastrian
1422-1461	Henry VI	

1461-1483	Edward IV	
1483	Edward V	Yorkist
1483-1485	Richard III	

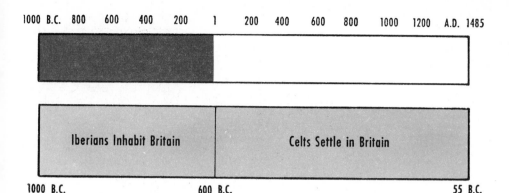

1000 B.C. 800 600 400 200 1 200 400 600 800 1000 1200 A.D. 1485

Iberians Inhabit Britain | Celts Settle in Britain

1000 B.C.   600 B.C.   55 B.C.

CHAPTER ONE

THE DAWN OF BRITISH HISTORY

Thousands of years ago, long before men left any written record of their activities, the British islands were part of the mainland of Europe. The Thames and Trent rivers flowed into the Rhine, which itself ran north towards the Arctic through a marshy plain which now lies beneath the stormy waters of the North Sea. Savage beasts moved freely from Europe into the dense forests of England, pursued by skin-clad hunters who were little more than savages themselves.

The first great event in British history was the gradual physical change which cut the islands adrift from the continent of Europe. Scientists say that the melting of the huge polar ice-cap that once extended over northern Europe caused the seas to rise and flood the lowlands where the English Channel and the North Sea now lie. This geographical circumstance had a tremendous effect on the future of Britain. Free from constant strife with their neighbours on the Continent, the island peoples were able eventually to develop their own political institutions and way of life. At the same time their nearness to Europe made them a part of European civilization.

For many centuries after Britain became an island, however, wave after wave of wandering peoples reached her shores. Separated from the mainland of Europe by only twenty-one miles of water, the island lay invitingly open. The flat coastline of the east and south enabled ships to be easily beached, and deep rivers provided easy access to the fertile lowlands of the interior. These early invaders were hunters and valued the wild game which swarmed in the British forests. Later, there came others who were interested in the tin, copper, and iron for which

3

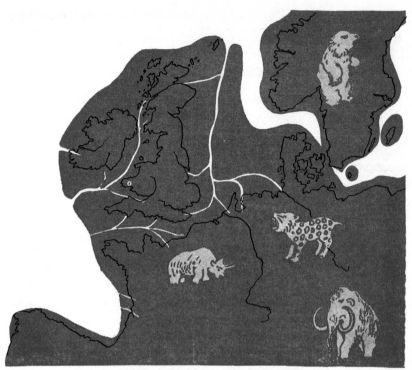

THE BRITISH ISLES BEFORE THE GLACIAL AGE

early Britain became famous, and in the rich agricultural lands of the southern and eastern plains.

As each group of migrant peoples pressed into the island, it killed or enslaved the previous inhabitants or drove them into the less fertile regions of the north and west. When invaders tried to advance into these areas, they found their way blocked by the rugged mountain ranges of Wales, north-west England, and Scotland. But for these natural fortresses, each wave of invaders might have swept over the entire country, destroying all before it. As it was, remnants of several peoples survived to give Britain the racial variety still found there today. From the valleys of Wales have come a people whose love of music is the envy of the world. From the Highlands of Scotland have come men who have carried the bagpipe and the kilt to the far corners of the earth.

Iberians   At the dawn of British history the inhabitants of the islands were the Iberians who, from being savage hunters using stone tools, had grown, over many years, into a fairly civilized people. They had learned how to weave cloth and fashion pottery, how to domesticate animals, and

4

cultivate the soil. Perhaps from distant Mediterranean traders they learned how to smelt copper and tin together to make bronze. It was probably the Iberians who erected the massive circle of standing stones, some over twenty feet high, which can still be seen at Stonehenge.

About six hundred years before the birth of Christ, the Iberians faced a group of invaders from northern Europe known as the Celts. Celts Armed with weapons of iron, successive waves of the Celtic warriors, usually tall and fair-haired, established control over most of the island. In time the language of the Iberians disappeared from Britain and the mixed peoples looked upon themselves as Celts.

The Celts were organized in primitive family units known as tribes or clans. Although their great love was fighting and hunting, they came to rely more and more on grazing and farming. They also became expert in metal working and their weapons and armour often demonstrated great skill and artistry.

Like most primitive peoples, the Celts were superstitious and worshipped many gods and goddesses. Their priests, known as Druids, had

EARLY BRITONS

Many of the Celts were large limbed, with long, reddish, curly hair. They lived in huts in clearings surrounded by a palisade of felled trees. Usually they were more interested in grazing cattle than in raising crops and lived mainly on meat and milk. Some Celts used brass and iron rings or bars for money. They shaped clay pottery and fashioned a variety of tools and weapons from iron.

ATLANTIC OCEAN

NORTH SEA

IRISH SEA

Severn
River

Thames River

English Channel

FRANCE

	Fertile Land
	Hills
	Mountains

PHYSICAL GEOGRAPHY OF THE BRITISH ISLES

great power and influence, just as the medicine men did among the Indians, and the price of disobedience to them was exile or execution. Although many of the Druids' practices, such as the use of the mistletoe

A DRUID CEREMONY

Some Druids spent as long as twenty years in training for their position and in memorizing the long verses chanted in their religious ceremonies. At certain times of the year Celtic clans met at holy places where the Druids held religious ceremonies and settled legal cases, for they were also the judicial and police authorities, with power to banish or execute those who did not obey them. The Druids were not required to pay taxes or go to war. The oak tree and mistletoe were their sacred symbols.

in magic, were harmless, some of their religious rites were extremely cruel. The practice of burning victims alive in wicker baskets to appease the gods shocked even the hardened Roman legionaries when they appeared in Britain 55 years before the birth of Christ.

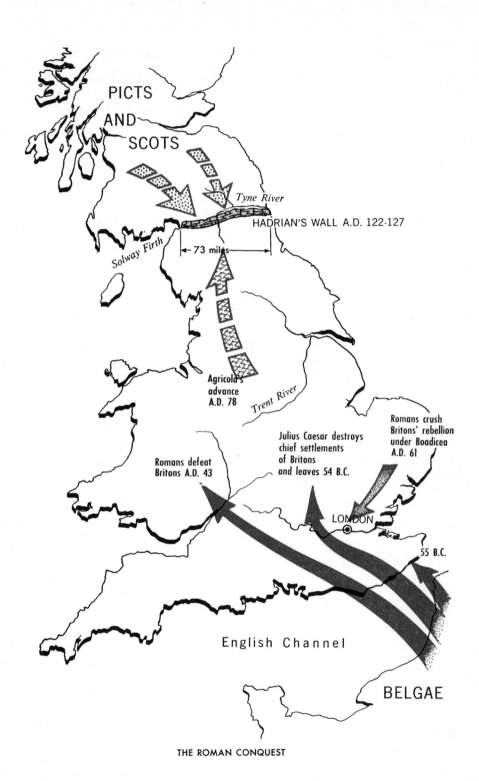

THE ROMAN CONQUEST

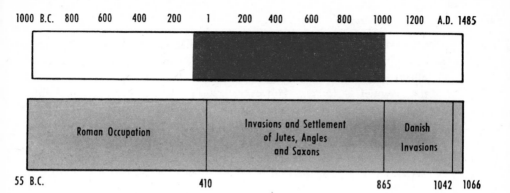

| 1000 B.C. | 800 | 600 | 400 | 200 | 1 | 200 | 400 | 600 | 800 | 1000 | 1200 | A.D. 1485 |

| Roman Occupation | Invasions and Settlement of Jutes, Angles and Saxons | Danish Invasions |

55 B.C.   410   865   1042   1066

CHAPTER TWO

THE INVASIONS

The Romans first invaded Britain under the great general Julius The Romans Caesar in 55 and 54 B.C. The wild heroism of the undisciplined Celts was useless against the organized legions of the best fighting machine the

HADRIAN'S WALL

This defensive wall, which stretched for 73 miles, was built between A.D. 122 and 127. It was twenty feet high and eight feet thick. Twenty thousand legionaries manned the area and detachments constantly patrolled the flat walk along the top. The wall had seventeen great forts, as well as a "milecastle" each mile and a turret or signal tower every 500 yards. On the northern side of the wall was a thirty-foot ditch and on the southern side was a road to permit the rapid movement of troops to areas where the Picts and Scots attacked.

9

world had yet seen. The spectacular charges of the Celtic chariots caused momentary dismay in the Roman ranks, but as weapons of effective warfare these chariots were, in the long run, as obsolete as the bayonet is today. However, Caesar's first expeditions had little permanent effect on the island, for after moving a short distance inland he returned to the Continent to attend to problems more important than the conquest of an island on the fringe of the known world.

It was almost a century later, in the reign of the emperor Claudius (A.D. 41-54), that the real Roman conquest began. It was a story of savage fighting and unspeakable torture, but in spite of the heroic resistance of Queen Boadicea in A.D. 61 the issue was never really in doubt. Under the famous general Agricola the Romans advanced steadily northwards between A.D. 77 and 84. However, the stubborn Picts who inhabited Scotland would not submit and in A.D. 122 the

CELTIC CHARIOTS

Julius Caesar described his first meeting with the chariots of the Celts as follows: "At first the charioteers ride in all directions, usually throwing the ranks into confusion by the very terror caused by the horses, as well as by the noise of the wheels; then as soon as they have come between the squads of horsemen, they leap from the chariots and fight on foot. The drivers of the chariots then withdraw a little from the battle and place the chariots together, so that if the warriors are hard pressed by the number of the enemy, they have a safe retreat. . . . Their horsemen possess such activity . . . that on steep and even precipitous ground they are accustomed to check their excited horses, to control and turn them about quickly, to run out on the pole, to stand on the yoke, and then swiftly to return to the chariot."

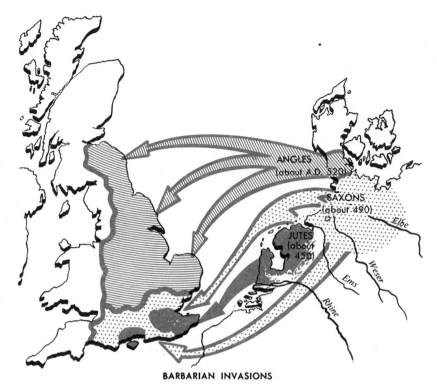

BARBARIAN INVASIONS

Roman emperor Hadrian ordered a great fortified wall to be built from Solway to the mouth of the Tyne. This wall marked the permanent northern frontier of Rome's great empire. The Romans did not colonize Britain, but remained there essentially as an army of occupation.

Much has been written about the elaborate civilization which the Romans brought to Britain. Their political organization, their famous walled towns, their sumptuous Italian villas and baths, their famous military highways and skilfully engineered bridges have all been described in endless detail by generations of admiring historians. The brilliance of their achievement cannot be denied, but when the Romans had to withdraw to defend their homeland in the fourth century, they left little of permanent value behind them. The flame of Christianity which they had kindled flickered bravely in some isolated valleys of Wales and their well-laid roads continued to be the best in England until 1750. For the real foundations of British civilization, however, we must look to the accomplishment of less highly developed peoples than the Romans.

Even before the Romans left, a new and very different kind of

The Anglo-Saxons

11

invader descended on Britain. Like a magnet, the wealthy island drew marauding bands of Jutes, Angles, and Saxons from their homelands in northern Europe. Revelling in battle and joyous on the raging seas, these barbarians won their way across England destroying all signs of Roman civilization and pushing the Celts to the island's fringes. So completely did the Anglo-Saxons displace the earlier inhabitants that they became the dominant element in the island's population and imposed on it their language and institutions.

With the island conquered, these warlike invaders settled down to till the soil. They gradually formed seven small kingdoms, known as the Heptarchy, and satisfied their love of battle by fighting among themselves. Eventually three kingdoms—Northumbria, Mercia, and Wessex—came to overshadow the others in importance. By A.D. 802 King Egbert of Wessex had become the leading ruler and Wessex emerged as the centre of Anglo-Saxon England.

The Danes The consolidation of Anglo-Saxon England under Egbert came just in time, for the country was once again threatened by invaders. For over a hundred years the Danes, also called "Vikings" or "Norsemen", kept Britain and all of western Europe in a state of terror. In their magnificent open ships, whose high prows and sterns were carved into the likeness of dragons or snakes, these daring mariners sailed along the coast of Europe leaving a train of destruction in their wake. The first Viking raiding party attacked Britain in 793. A horrified English monk described the dreadful event:

> The pagans from the northern regions came with a naval force to Britain like stinging hornets and spread on all sides like fearful wolves, robbed, tore and slaughtered not only beasts of burden, sheep and oxen, but even priests and deacons, and companies of monks and nuns. And they came to the church of Lindisfarne, laid everything waste with grievous plundering, trampled the holy places with polluted steps, dug up the altars and seized all the treasures of the holy church. They killed some of the brothers, took some away with them in fetters, many they drove out, naked and loaded with insults, some they drowned in the sea. . . .

After seventy-five years of raiding and plundering, the Danes began a systematic conquest of England in 865. At first they drove all before them. They established small Danish kingdoms in eastern and northern England and even captured London. Meanwhile in Wessex, the great **Alfred, King** hero king, Alfred the Great, was preparing to counter-attack by re-**of the** organizing the local militia and building a navy. In 878 he defeated **West Saxons**

12

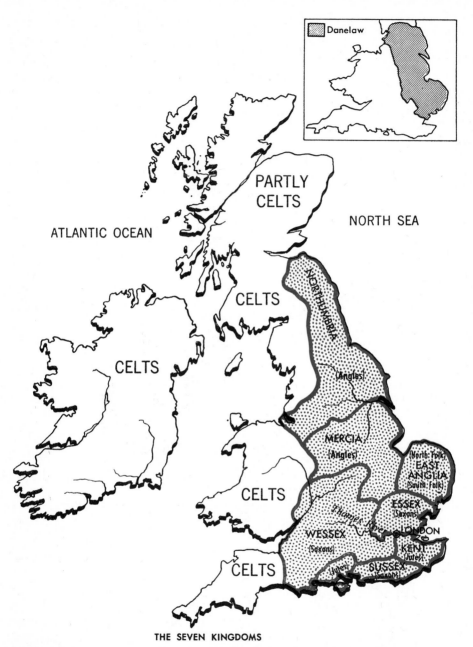

THE SEVEN KINGDOMS

By 600, with the invasions over, these seven kingdoms had been established. Throughout the seventh century a succession of strong kings made Northumbria the most powerful kingdom in the Heptarchy. By 750, however, Mercia had become dominant. After the death of the great Mercian king, Offa, in 796, Wessex achieved a supremacy that she never lost.

the Danes at Salisbury Plain and forced them to withdraw into an area which became known as the Danelaw. Six years later he defended the mouth of the Thames by land and sea and in 886 recaptured London. By the time of his death in 899 Alfred had stemmed the Danish tide. Under his son and grandsons the Danish settlements were forced to accept Saxon rule.

Yet the strength of Saxon England depended on the ability of the king, and when, about 1000, the Danes again attacked in large numbers, the Anglo-Saxons were governed by one of the weakest kings they had ever had. Unable to defeat the invaders, Ethelred the Unready (979-1016) taxed his people to raise money, called the Danegeld, to buy them off. This was like trying to fight off bears with honey. By 1013 the Danes controlled most of England and the country had become part of the Danish Empire. From 1016 to 1035 the country was governed

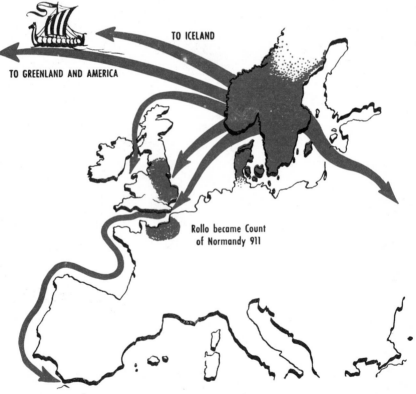

PATH OF THE NORTHMEN

by the Danish king, Canute, but when Canute's son died in 1042 the crown went to an Anglo-Saxon, the son of Ethelred the Unready, known to history as Edward the Confessor because of his deep devotion to religion.

Less than twenty-five years later another successful invader was to reach England's shores. But the foundations of English society were laid in Anglo-Saxon times, to which we must now turn our attention.

SEA RAIDERS

Viking ships were magnificent vessels which threw terror into the hearts of those who saw them approaching. They were built of solid oak planks fastened together with wooden nails and iron bolts and were caulked with cord of animal hair. One, discovered deep in the sand of a Norwegian beach, was 76 feet long and 17 feet wide. They were propelled by a large square sail and a row of oars along each side. The ships carried eighty sailors and warriors, each of whom was carefully selected for the honour. In 1892 a ship patterned on the unearthed Viking ship crossed the stormy Atlantic in four weeks.

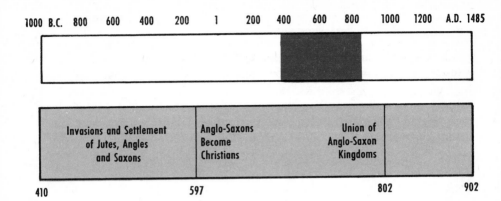

1000 B.C. 800 600 400 200 1 200 400 600 800 1000 1200 A.D. 1485

| Invasions and Settlement of Jutes, Angles and Saxons | Anglo-Saxons Become Christians | Union of Anglo-Saxon Kingdoms | |

410 · 597 · 802 · 902

CHAPTER THREE

ANGLO-SAXON ENGLAND: THE PEOPLE

Social Groups: Aristocracy

Anglo-Saxon society, unlike our own, was divided into distinct classes. Men were born noble, free, or slave. The highest class, the aristocracy or the nobility, was headed by the king and his relations. It was originally made up of tribal chieftains who led the people in time of war. After the Anglo-Saxons had conquered Britain, these military leaders, called *earls,* became large landowners and assisted the king in governing the country. Less prominent than the earls were the *thegns,* the professional warriors of Anglo-Saxon England, many of whom received land from the king or an earl in return for loyal military service. Counted among the aristocracy, too, were such leaders of the Church as bishops and abbots.

Peasants

The great majority of the Anglo-Saxons were farmers. Many were free men called *coerls* who owned their own land and could come and go as they wished. For a number of reasons, these men slowly lost their freedom. In time of war a freeman might ask a thegn to be his lord and protect him, and then the thegn in turn would demand agricultural services from the coerl. Thus the freeman would no longer be free to do as he wished. Other calamities, such as illness and bad harvests, spelled ruin to many who were forced to sell part of their labour to stay alive. Before long most tillers of the soil were driven into the class of serfs or semi-free men. They were not allowed to leave the community without permission and had to work for their lord several days a week, farming their own small share of the village lands the rest of the time.

Slaves

The slaves were the lowest class in Anglo-Saxon society. Some were descendants of the original Britons, while others were captives and

16

convicted criminals. A slave had few legal rights. He was regarded as a piece of property that could be bought and sold. He could be put to death if he stole from his lord or ran away. A considerable trade in slaves developed between Britain and Europe and it was the sight of English slaves in a Roman market that inspired Pope Gregory to send Christian missionaries to the island.

Most of the people of Anglo-Saxon England lived in villages. The **The Village** typical village consisted of from ten to thirty small huts, each with its small garden. Standing among the peasants' homes were the church, the mill, and sometimes the home of the village lord. The village lands usually included woodland where pigs rooted and peasants gathered firewood, the common pasture for grazing sheep and oxen, a meadow

ANGLO-SAXON AGRICULTURAL METHODS

for hay, and other land for the raising of crops. This farm land was often divided into three open fields in which each villager held a number of long narrow strips of about one acre. The crops were rotated among the three fields. The first year one field would be sown with rye or wheat, the second year with barley or oats, and the third year it would lie fallow, for the Anglo-Saxons had no knowledge of fertilizers which are now used to restore food to the soil. Farming techniques were primitive: dull wooden ploughs were laboriously pulled by oxen and seeds were scattered by hand. Since they grew their own food and made their own clothes, the villagers were largely self-sufficient. Most of them were born in the village and died there without having ventured more than a few miles away from it.

Although most people were villagers, a small number lived in towns, **The Borough** or boroughs as they were called. The typical borough was a market or trading place enclosed by walls or earthen ramparts. Like the village, it had open fields and meadows which were used by the inhabitants. Some towns grew quickly either because their trade thrived or because

17

they were centres of Church or government. London, by far the largest and most important borough, carried on a vigorous and regular trade with the rest of England and the cities of north-west Europe, Scandinavia, and even Italy.

The Role of Religion
When the Anglo-Saxons arrived in Britain they were pagans and worshipped many strange gods. Some of the names of these gods are familiar to us because they have been used in the names of days of the week: Thor, the Thunderer; Woden, the god of magic; Tiu, the god of darkness; and Freya, the goddess of plenty. Like most warlike people, the Anglo-Saxons emphasized valour in their religion. Their heaven was Valhalla where courageous warriors feasted and drank with the gods.

In time Christianity came to England. The great Pope Gregory sent Saint Augustine and a band of missionaries from Rome to convert the pagans in 597. Meanwhile, Celtic Christians from Ireland, led by Saint Aidan, had begun a reconversion of the land from which their religion had been driven by the Anglo-Saxon invasions several hundred years before. By the middle of the seventh century Christian influences were felt throughout Britain.

Yet the differences in Roman and Celtic practices caused a good deal of confusion. When King Oswy discovered that his wife, a Roman Christian, would be engaged in her Lenten fast while he, a Celtic Christian, would be celebrating a feast, he decided to end the confusion. In 664, at a Church council, the Synod of Whitby, he persuaded the churchmen to follow Roman rather than Celtic practices. The leader of the Church of Britain was the Archbishop of Canterbury, appointed by the Pope, the head of the Christian Church.

The conversion of the Anglo-Saxons to Christianity was of immense importance. Britain for all time became Christian. Her civilization was tied by Christianity to the civilization of the Continent. Monasteries were built to house groups of monks and here the homeless and starving often found sustenance. Since monks and priests were almost the only people who could read and write, the monasteries became the centres of learning in Anglo-Saxon England and the churchmen, because of their learning, played an important part in the political life of the country.

PLAN OF A VILLAGE

In early Anglo-Saxon times the villages consisted of a few scattered huts in a small clearing in the forest. The buildings were very primitive and were often surrounded by a palisade. By late Anglo-Saxon times the village was taking on an appearance similar to that shown opposite, an appearance it was to retain for centuries, although there was no completely uniform system throughout Britain.

Cattle grazing
in fallow field

Sheep herd

Fish pond

Lord's house

Brushwood
for fuel

Meadow

Blacksmith

Barn

Swineherd

Village

Barley field

Honey bees

Wheat field

geese

Flour mill

Lord's land

Holdings of
one peasant

Typical holdings of other peasants

R. HUNZ

King Alfred
and Education

Most Anglo-Saxons were illiterate and cared little for learning. Alfred, however, had received an education as a boy and was determined to educate his people. He supported the monasteries, opened schools for the sons of nobles, and brought foreign scholars into the country to teach and write. His court became a centre of learning and he insisted that the court officials spend long hours studying.

> I wonder at your assurance, [Alfred said to them] that having taken upon yourselves the rank and office of wise men, you have neglected the studies of the wise. Either abandon at once the exercise of the temporal [political] powers that you possess, or endeavour more zealously to study the lessons of wisdom.

So began the study of history in England, for, according to the monk who wrote a life of Alfred, "wonderful to relate, almost all his ealdormen and officials, though unlearned from childhood, gave themselves up to the study of letters, preferring an unfamiliar discipline to the loss of office." Alfred's love of history also led him to begin the *Anglo-Saxon Chronicle*, the first historical record written in English. We are dependent on this source for much of what we know about Anglo-Saxon government and law, which we must now examine.

A MONASTERY

The first monastery was built at Canterbury by St. Augustine soon after he landed in 597. In time there were many monasteries where dedicated men and women retired to become monks and nuns and lead quiet, saintly lives. The monasteries were usually self-contained, with their own farm lands. Monks performed the work of bakers and butchers, blacksmiths and masons. The monasteries became centres of learning and monks spent years copying precious manuscripts, for there were few books. Since devout Englishmen often left them money and lands, many monasteries became very large and wealthy.

ESTABLISHMENT OF ANGLO-SAXON GOVERNMENT AND LAW

410   902

CHAPTER FOUR

ANGLO-SAXON ENGLAND: GOVERNMENT AND LAW

Today Britain is a monarchy, but Queen Elizabeth II does not really rule. In Anglo-Saxon England the king ruled. To assist him there was the *Witan* or council of wise men in which sat the great nobles, the leading churchmen, and others whom the king especially wished to give him advice. The king did not have to consult the Witan and its sole duty was to give him advice when he asked for it. The Witan met very seldom and the day-to-day work of government was carried on by the king and his personal advisers who made up his Household. *Central Government*

The Anglo-Saxon kingdom was divided into shires or counties. Each shire was under the rule of an earl, a powerful member of the aristocracy. He presided over the shire moot, a combined law-court and council composed of all the freemen of the shire, which met twice a year. The earl also commanded the *fyrd*, or shire militia, which he led into battle in the king's service. *Local Government: The Shire*

Assisting the earl was an official appointed by the king, known as the shire-reeve or sheriff. He maintained law and order and collected the land rents due to the king and the fines levied in the shire court. As time passed, he became more important in local government than the earl and was the real link between the king and local government.

Each shire was divided into smaller units called *hundreds*. The hundred also had a moot which met every month. It was presided over by a reeve who was either the representative of the king or of some great noble in whose lands the hundred lay. Here in the hundred moot most of the legal work was done, for this was the court that looked after the activities and misbehaviors of the ordinary people. *The Hundred*

21

AN ANGLO-SAXON HUNDRED COURT

One man is declaring on oath that another has stolen his pig. Seated in the chair is the hundred reeve who presided over the court. The hundred court met every four weeks and was the place where most legal work was done.

Justice:
Law

Justice in Anglo-Saxon England was much different from the justice we have today.   Originally a crime was not looked upon as a crime against society as a whole or against the state, but was regarded simply as a crime against the injured person.   He, his family or kinsmen sought to punish the offender, on the principle of "an eye for an eye, and a tooth for a tooth".   Slowly, however, the idea grew that the law-breaker was a menace to society and that society and the government should assume some responsibility for justice.   As a result, it came to be a function of the moot to act as a court and impose cash fines in place of the earlier primitive vengeance.

Every crime carried a fine· which varied with the seriousness of the offence.   To cut off an opponent's nose in a brawl might cost fifty shillings, but to sever a big toe might cost only six.   The fine also varied with the class of person against whom the crime was committed, a feature of the law which was clearly set forth in a doom, or law, drawn up by King Ine, who reigned from 688 to 695.

If anyone fights in the king's house he shall forfeit all his inheritance and it shall be in the king's judgement whether or not he shall lose his life.   If anyone fights in a monastery he shall pay 120 shillings' compensation.   If anyone fights in the house of an alderman or of some other distinguished statesman, he shall pay 60 shillings' compensation and another 60 shillings as a fine (to the king).   If, however, he fights in the house of a peasant he shall pay 30 shillings as a fine and 6 shillings to the peasant.

22

Today a man charged with breaking the law comes before a trained **Trial**
judge and a jury. The members of the jury hear the case, listen to the
witnesses, and decide whether the accused is guilty or innocent; the judge
pronounces sentence on the guilty. An Anglo-Saxon trial was very
different. The injured man swore that his complaint was true and
the defendant then swore to his innocence. Then all the freemen who
attended the moot decided not who was right or wrong, but whether
the defendant would have to prove his innocence and, if so, by what
means.

If the crime was not too serious and the accused well known in the
district, he was allowed to try to clear himself by *compurgation,* or oath-
helping. A number of people would be asked to swear on oath that he
was innocent of the charge. If they did, he was freed because he
obviously had a good standing among the members of his own community, from whom little could be kept secret. For more serious
offences, or if he could find no oath-helpers, the accused would be
forced to undergo the *ordeal.* This form of trial was in some respects
a religious ceremony, based on the belief that God would protect the
innocent and punish the guilty.

The accused might be told to carry, for ten yards, a piece of red-
hot iron which had been blessed by a priest, or to pick a stone out of
boiling water. The inflamed hand was then bound up. If, on the
third day, the skin was not infected, he was declared innocent. Or he
might be lowered, bound hand and foot, into cold water in a well,
which like the iron or the boiling water had been blessed by a priest.
If he floated he was guilty, because the water was obviously rejecting
an evil spirit.

One of the dooms of Edward the Elder, about 920, sets out the
procedure for trial by ordeal:

> If anyone is obliged to go to the ordeal, he shall come three
> days in advance to the priest in charge of the consecration
> [of the iron or water]; and before he does he shall feed him-
> self on bread, water, salt and herbs; and on each of the three
> days he shall attend mass; and on the day he undergoes the
> ordeal he shall make an offering and take communion; and
> then, before he goes to the ordeal he shall swear on oath that
> ...he is innocent of the charge made against him. And if
> it is water he must sink an ell and a half [about six feet] to
> clear himself. If it is iron three days must elapse before the
> hand is uncovered.

Anglo-Saxon government and law seem primitive to us, yet in the **Summary** six centuries they had been in England the Anglo-Saxons had moved a long way forward. Government by tribal chieftains had given way to government by a king assisted by a council. Throughout the whole land the authority of the king was felt. The primitive justice of private vengeance carried out by the victim's kin had been replaced by a system of law carried on in organized courts, with the sheriff on hand to see that justice was properly administered.

Out of these shire and hundred moots were to come the system of law and justice that we possess today. Later generations were to build on these foundations. The growth of the legal system and the triumph of the rule of law, which neither king nor subject could escape, was one of the greatest accomplishments of mediæval England and one of the lasting glories of the English-speaking peoples.

TRIAL BY ORDEAL

By late Anglo-Saxon times the ordeal was a common method of trial. In the ordeal of hot water a man was required to pick a stone out of the pot of boiling water. The injured hand was then bound up for three days. If it healed it was a sign the man was innocent; if it infected it was a sign he was guilty. Trial by ordeal was a direct appeal to God; the boiling water was blessed by priests. Most Anglo-Saxons, if they were guilty of a crime, probably preferred to confess their guilt rather than challenge God and so endanger their souls. Priests, officials, and freemen of the court were present to ensure that the correct procedure was followed.

| The Norman Conquest | The Norman Monarchy Established in England |

1066   1072   1135

CHAPTER FIVE

THE NORMAN CONQUEST

In 1066 Edward the Confessor died without an heir. The Witan placed the crown on the head of Harold Godwin, Earl of Wessex, but there were other claimants to the throne. Among them was William, Duke of Normandy, known to history as the Conqueror. William maintained that Edward had promised him the throne and that Harold had once sworn to support him as well. Having failed to get the crown by legitimate means, he was determined to wrest it from Harold by force.

The Normans were Vikings who had swept out of the storm-tossed North Sea about A.D. 900 and turned their dragon-prowed ships southward to the coast of France, where they established a settlement in Normandy. By the year 1000 Normandy was one of the most powerful kingdoms in western Europe and Duke William, its ruler in 1066, **William, Duke of Normandy** was one of the most gifted military leaders of his day. William was short and powerfully built, with broad shoulders and arms well muscled from long training with the lance and heavy battle-axe. His forbidding eye suggested a violent temper; yet behind this rather grim exterior was a man shrewd enough to know "when to smite and when to spare".

When William decided to invade England, soldiers from all over Europe flocked to his side, lured by the love of adventure and the desire for plunder. For weeks William trained his armed host and gathered the ships necessary for the Channel crossing. Soon he was ready to move with the best trained and equipped army in Europe.

King Harold realized that serious danger threatened from Normandy and with his forces he constantly patrolled the southern shore of England, while contrary winds kept William ashore in Normandy. Suddenly the news arrived that another claimant to the throne of

25

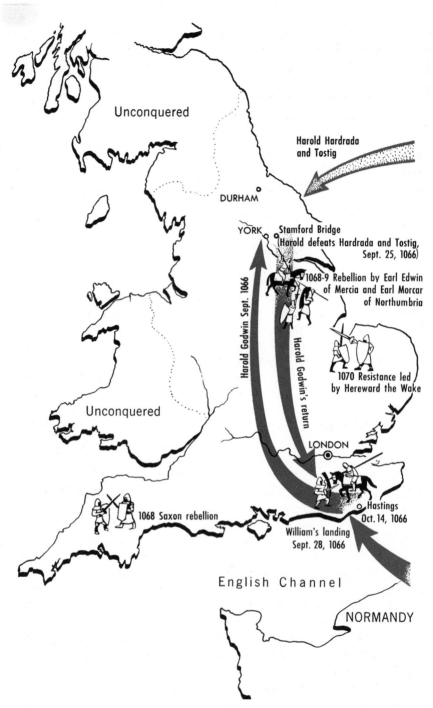

Unconquered

Harold Hardrada
and Tostig

DURHAM

YORK   Stamford Bridge
       (Harold defeats Hardrada and Tostig,
                    Sept. 25, 1066)

1068-9 Rebellion by Earl Edwin
of Mercia and Earl Morcar
of Northumbria

Harold Godwin Sept. 1066

Harold Godwin's return

1070 Resistance led
by Hereward the Wake

Unconquered

LONDON

Hastings
Oct. 14, 1066

1068 Saxon rebellion

William's landing
Sept. 28, 1066

English Channel

NORMANDY

THE NORMAN CONQUEST

THE BATTLE OF HASTINGS

Once the English lines were broken, the English infantry was no match for the heavily armed and mounted Normans. Cavalry charges were almost unknown to the Anglo-Saxons, who were accustomed to fighting on foot.

England, Harold Hardrada of Norway, aided by the King's unscrupulous brother Tostig, had landed in the north. Racing north to meet his new enemy, King Harold defeated him at Stamford Bridge where both Hardrada and Tostig fell in the fray. Three days later favourable winds brought William to the undefended shores of southern England.

Rushing back from the north with unbelievable speed, Harold and his exhausted troops took their stand on a hill near Hastings. Successive attacks by the Norman infantry failed to break the solid English line. The famed Norman cavalry also attacked, only to reel back with men and horses gashed and split by the English battle-axes. Believing that victory was within their grasp, the English *fyrd* disobeyed orders and broke their lines to pursue the enemy. It was a disastrous move, for the Norman horsemen suddenly turned and cut the advancing foot soldiers to pieces. Harold and his household troops (or housecarls) stood firm until William ordered his archers to shoot high in the air. A shower of arrows descended on the English ranks; King Harold received one in the eye. With their leader dead the English were overcome. The field belonged to William, truly the Conqueror.

Many English nobles immediately came to terms with William, hoping thereby to keep their lands and liberty. Southern England soon fell into his grasp. London opened its gates to the conquering army and on Christmas Day, 1066, William was crowned King of England.

The Battle of Hastings 1066

Before his coronation, according to a monk who kept a record of these events, William had—

> . . . sworn at the altar of St. Peter the Apostle, and in the presence of the clergy and people, that he would defend the holy churches of God and their ministers, that he would rule justly and with kingly care the whole people placed under him, that he would make and keep right law, and that he would utterly prohibit all spoliation and unrighteous judgements.

Northern England only gradually and reluctantly acknowledged William as King. There were serious uprisings in 1067 and again in 1069. Determined to become master, William crushed all opposition with shocking ferocity. Between York and Durham not a house was left standing, crops were burnt in the fields and animals killed; for years the region was a desolate wilderness. From wooden fortresses vigilant Norman nobles kept the whole countryside in subjection.

Under William and his two sons, Rufus and Henry I, the Norman influence was extended to Scotland and Wales as well. By the time of Henry's death in 1135 the Normans were the undisputed rulers of England. They had conquered the land by force of arms; but they knew that only through a strong monarchy, respected by the people, could they hope to keep it.

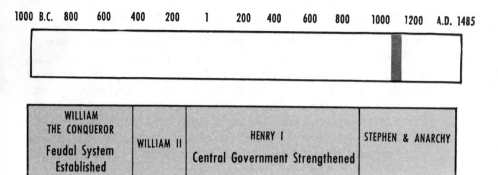

CHAPTER SIX

THE NORMAN MONARCHY

When William the Conqueror became King of England, he was determined, above all, to be a strong monarch. He had no wish to uproot all that had developed in the past, for he knew that such action would bring chaos rather than peace. To secure the support of the inhabitants, he retained Anglo-Saxon laws and institutions, particularly in local government. Yet because he was a conqueror he was able to make changes in the central government which strengthened the position of the king. *William 1066-1087*

William established the only system of government he knew, a system we now call feudalism. Having conquered the country, the King owned all the land. He kept a portion of it for himself as a *royal demesne*, or crown land, and gave the rest to his barons, in return for their promise to supply him with mounted knights in time of war. The barons who held land directly from the king were called the tenants-in-chief. Some of the land was given to the Church, on the same terms. In this way the Church was made part of the Anglo-Norman feudal system. *The Feudal System*

To obtain enough knights for the king's service, the tenant-in-chief sublet his land on similar terms, while keeping part of it for himself. If he owed the king fifty knights, he might let the land out to four lesser barons, each of whom promised ten knights. These men would likewise sublet the land. The man who held land of another was a vassal, the man who owned the land a lord, and the land itself was termed a fief. The king was lord of the tenants-in-chief and overlord of all other vassals. Everyone owed his first allegiance to the king, not to his immediate lord. In this way William hoped to strengthen the

29

king's position and reduce the possibility of serious baronial revolts.

Feudalism was more than a method of land-holding and organizing an army. It involved a strong personal relationship as well. The lord gave protection to his vassal and the vassal owed his lord loyalty as well as service. This relationship was emphasized in the ceremonies for the giving of homage and the swearing of fealty or faithfulness.

Central Government William made few changes in the central government. In his task of government the king was assisted by the officials of his Household, who were much like our higher civil servants. Among these officials were the Chancellor, the king's secretary, the Justiciar, the head of the judicial system, and the Treasurer, who was responsible for managing the royal finances. Three times a year, at Christmas, Easter and Whitsuntide, the king and his Household met with the Great Council. This body, which had replaced the Anglo-Saxon Witan, was composed of the king's tenants-in-chief and its function was to give him advice on great matters when he asked for it. The Household officials, with the

HOMAGE

In the act of homage the vassal knelt and placed his hands between those of his lord and said: "I become your man, from this day forward, of life and limb and of earthly worship, and unto you shall be true and faithful." In the ceremony of fealty the vassal promised that he would be faithful and true for the lands he held of his lord, and swore, "I shall lawfully do you the customs and services which I ought to do, so help me God and his saints."

addition of a few trusted barons, made up a smaller council, the Curia Regis or King's Council, upon which the king relied for day-by-day advice and administration.

Occasionally the king sent out royal commissioners, who were often members of the Curia Regis, into various parts of the kingdom to transact royal business. The earliest important use of such commissioners

GOVERNMENT
1066-1154

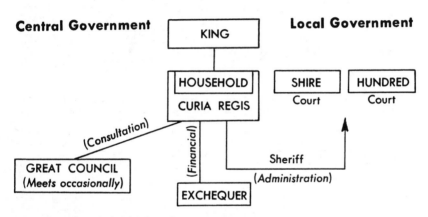

Central Government

KING

Local Government

HOUSEHOLD

CURIA REGIS

SHIRE
Court

HUNDRED
Court

(Consultation)

(Financial)

Sheriff

GREAT COUNCIL
(Meets occasionally)

(Administration)

EXCHEQUER

was to gather information for the *Domesday Book.* William wanted exact information about the country he had conquered and the commissioners visited every shire and hundred to obtain it. "So narrowly did he cause the survey to be made," wrote a monk in the *Anglo-Saxon Chronicle,* "that there was not a single hide or rood of land nor—it is a shameful thing to tell, but he thought it no shame to do—was there an ox or swine that was not set down in the book." Here was proof indeed that no detail was too small to escape the supervision of the Norman king. The Domesday Book 1086

William's second son, Henry I (1100-1135), further strengthened the position of the monarch. Henry knew that strength depended upon wealth and he was determined to make certain that every penny owing to the king came into his treasury. He created a part of the Household known as the Exchequer. Twice a year every sheriff accounted at the Exchequer for the rents he had collected from the royal estates, the fines levied in the courts, and sometimes special levies collected when the king's son was made a knight or his daughter married. To this The Exchequer

31

THE EXCHEQUER

A trembling sheriff looks on as an Exchequer official studies the wooden tally. The sheriff has already turned the money he has collected for the King into the Lower Exchequer where he was given the tallies, notched to show the sums received and where they came from. Here, in the Upper Exchequer, the accounts are balanced. The arithmetic is done by the Treasurer who sits at a table with a checker-board cloth and counters of different value. One official wrote that the proceedings were like a game of chess in which the battle was waged between the Treasurer and the sheriff, "while others sit by like umpires to watch and judge the proceedings".

day in Great Britain the Cabinet Minister in charge of the finances is called the Chancellor of the Exchequer.

Local
Government

William and his successors made little change in local government. The Anglo-Saxon *fyrd* was maintained to reduce the king's dependence on the barons. To limit the power of the barons William abolished the large Anglo-Saxon earldoms, except on the borders of unconquered Wales and Scotland where a strong force was necessary to keep the Welsh and Scots in check. The shires and hundreds were retained as the units of local administration and justice. Sometimes commissioners were sent out for special purposes, such as the Domesday investigation, or to act as judges in the shire courts. However, it was not until the reign of William's great-grandson, Henry II, that the latter practice became common and the shire courts in effect became royal courts. In their concern for sound justice and their respect for existing Anglo-Saxon institutions, William and his sons showed that they realized that good and strong government depended on law and order among a contented people.

When Henry I died in 1135, the government of England seemed to rest on firm foundations. Yet everything hinged on the strength and

32

ability of the monarch. Unless he could control the ambitious and often unruly barons and keep the governmental machine working, the whole system would collapse. And collapse it did on Henry's death.

The choice for the throne lay between Henry's daughter Matilda and his nephew Stephen. The barons quickly took sides and the country was soon embroiled in a civil war. By promising to relieve the barons of many of the restrictions placed upon them by the strong Norman kings, Stephen secured their support and was duly crowned King. **King Stephen and Anarchy 1135-1154**

The new monarch was too weak to control the country. He quarrelled with his Household and angered the Church. The barons enriched themselves at his expense and that of their weaker neighbours, and strengthened themselves by building castles and creating private armies.

For nineteen years Britain writhed in the agony of civil war. Finally, however, the time of troubles drew to an end. Everyone could see that only poverty and destitution would follow a continuation of the war. Stephen grew tired of fighting. His only son had died and he

LAWLESS BARONS

As the power of the kings declined after the reign of Stephen, the barons took the law into their own hands. As one monk wrote: "They oppressed the wretched people of the country severely with castle-building. When the castles were built, they filled them with devils and wicked men. Then, both night and day they took those people they thought had any goods . . . and tortured them with indescribable torture. . . . They levied taxes on the villages every so often and called it 'protection money'. . . . Many thousands they killed by starvation. . . . Christ and his saints were asleep." By this time the wooden fortresses on mounds of earth, built after the Conquest, had been replaced by stone castles surrounded by moats.

33

promised that on his death Matilda's son should become King. In 1154 Stephen died and young Henry of Anjou became King of England.

Although the years of Stephen's reign had been years of turmoil and anarchy, the machinery of government, established by the Norman monarchs on sound Anglo-Saxon foundations, did not completely break down. It needed only the driving power and the lubrication provided by a strong king. Such a king was Henry II, who was able to take up the ruler's task where Henry I had laid it down. He was to be one of the country's greatest monarchs.

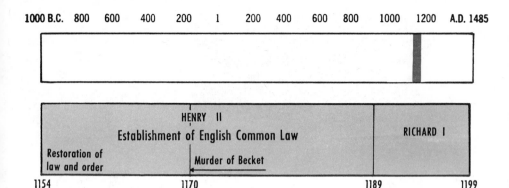

| 1000 B.C. | 800 | 600 | 400 | 200 | 1 | 200 | 400 | 600 | 800 | 1000 | 1200 | A.D. 1485 |

Restoration of law and order
1154

HENRY II
Establishment of English Common Law
Murder of Becket
1170

RICHARD I
1189   1199

HENRY II AND THE COMMON LAW

England's new king, Henry II, was one of the great European princes of his day. He ruled not just England but an empire extending from England to Spain. Short and coarse, he was not at first glance an imposing monarch and his bowed legs did not add to his dignity. Yet his hard grey eyes were those of a shrewd and determined man and he had a superb memory and a first-class mind. Although his ungovernable temper occasionally made him harsh and tyrannical, he was a brilliant king, devoted to the art of government.

Henry II 1154-1189

Henry's immediate problem was to restore law and order after the civil war between Stephen and Matilda. His first task was to make the barons submit to his will, and he set out at once to destroy the castles they had built during the years of anarchy. To reduce his dependence on the barons, he hired mercenary troops and strengthened the Anglo-Saxon *fyrd*. In 1181 his famous law, the Assize of Arms, stated exactly what equipment every man should possess and be prepared to use to support the king. Sometimes the restless nobility complained and on one occasion rebelled, but all such opposition failed and Henry was soon in a very strong position.

Restoration of Law and Order

Meantime, Henry had turned his attention to the legal system in his determination to restore law and order. First he dismissed many sheriffs who had not been enforcing the law. Then by the Assize of Clarendon in 1166 he assumed responsibility for the administration of criminal law. With the Assize of Clarendon came the final victory of the idea that a criminal is the enemy of society and that it is the duty of the community and the government to bring him to justice.

Criminal Law

In the Assize of Clarendon Henry laid down the procedure that

35

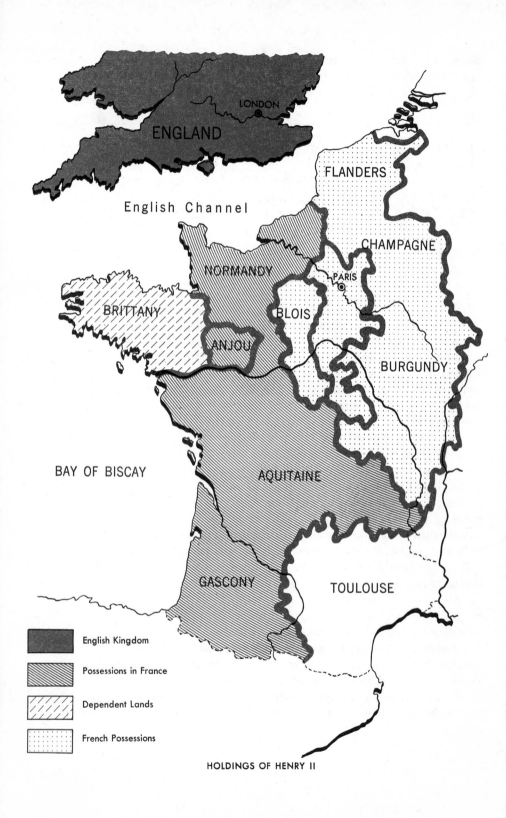

ENGLAND

LONDON

English Channel

FLANDERS

CHAMPAGNE

NORMANDY

PARIS

BRITTANY

BLOIS

ANJOU

BURGUNDY

BAY OF BISCAY

AQUITAINE

GASCONY

TOULOUSE

English Kingdom

Possessions in France

Dependent Lands

French Possessions

HOLDINGS OF HENRY II

was to be followed in criminal trials. In every hundred twelve good men were to state on oath the names of those who were suspected of breaking the law. These twelve men, called the jury of accusation, made their statements before travelling judges sent out regularly to the shire courts by the king. Jails were to be built in every district, where criminals could be held under the sheriff's eye until the judges arrived.

In these turbulent times, however, it was not just criminal cases **Civil Law** that were a source of discontent and restlessness. Before the days when

GOVERNMENT
HENRY II

Central Government KING **Local Government**

HOUSEHOLD   SHIRE   HUNDRED

CURIA REGIS

(Consultation)   (Financial)   Sheriff

GREAT COUNCIL
(Meets occasionally)   Travelling Judges

EXCHEQUER

every man had a title deed to his property, it was common for men to seize the possessions of others and to claim that they were legally theirs. To enable his subjects to bring these civil cases into court, Henry II developed a series of writs or orders from the king. The one most frequently used was the Writ of Right. Suppose a man, N——, complained to the king or his officials that his property in Middleton had been taken away from him by Earl W—— This writ would be sent from the King's Household:

> The King to Earl W——, greeting. I command you without delay to give full right to N—— with regard to the land in Middleton . . . and unless you act in this matter so that I hear no further complaint as to the default of justice the Sheriff of Nottingham will do so.

If the Earl refused to settle the matter, the king would order the sheriff to bring him and N—— before the king's justices, along with two men

37

TRIAL BY BATTLE

Trial by battle, introduced by the Normans, was a common method of determining guilt. The accuser had to be prepared to defend his charge "by his body" unless he was old or crippled. Very often the battle was waged between "champions" selected by both parties. The trial usually ended in death, for if the defeated man lived he was often hanged. Although there was no religious ceremony involved, it was believed that God would aid the innocent. The standard weapons were axes, but if the axes broke the combatants were ordered to fight with hands, teeth and feet. The above illustration is based on a thirteenth-century document depicting a battle between Walter Blowherme and Hamo le Stare. Walter accused Hamo of aiding him in a crime and, according to the record, "Hamo venit et defendit totum; [et decit] quod vult se defendere per corpus suum. . ." Hamo was defeated.

from the district who would swear to the facts of the case. Thus even the most powerful men in the country were made to feel the strong arm of the king and the law.

Trial   Henry also developed a new system of determining guilt in civil cases in his own courts. Up to this time a dispute over land could be settled by compurgation or oath-helping, the ordeal, or trial by battle. Henry substituted a form of trial by jury. Twelve men of the shire were chosen to state whether the Earl of N—— was in the right. This procedure was clearly more reasonable than the older methods.

Neither the jury of accusation in criminal cases nor the jury in civil cases was like a modern jury. Now the jury is composed of people who know nothing about the case beforehand. Henry's juries were the exact opposite. They were supposed to know the facts and state them on oath. In one sense they were almost witnesses, whereas the modern juror is to a certain extent a judge of the evidence presented. Nevertheless, it was out of Henry's system that the modern jury grew.

Common Law   Because of his system of travelling judges, his responsibility for the criminal law, and his improvements in the administration of civil law, Henry II deserves to be known as the father of the modern common law. As a result of his reforms the same legal system existed throughout the country and was common to all Englishmen. In Britain the common

38

law was a great unifying force which paved the way for the change from the feudal to the modern state. In time the common law governed the king as well as his subjects. The idea of the rule of law governing all men was mediæval England's greatest contribution to the achievements of history. The common law which Henry and his judges began to forge was eventually carried to North America, where it became the proud inheritance of two younger branches of the English-speaking peoples.

In his attempt to re-establish law and order Henry came into conflict with the Church. Relations between the king and the Church were always difficult in mediæval times, for there was only one Church in all Christian countries and it possessed a special position within every state. Among its many rights was the privilege of having its own courts to control the spiritual life of all men and to try all cases involving clergy. Early in Henry's reign his judges reported that churchmen arrested on a criminal charge claimed that they could be tried only in Church courts, which were more lenient than those of the king. Henry might have accepted this prerogative, called "benefit of clergy", if it had involved only churchmen, but since the only test as to whether a man was a churchman was his ability to read a few words of Latin, many people escaped punishment in the royal courts by claiming "benefit of clergy".

Henry II and the Church

In a council held at Clarendon in 1164 Henry persuaded the leading churchmen to agree that a priest, once convicted of a crime in a Church court, would be handed over to the king's court for punishment. Victory was not to be this easy, however, for the head of the Church in England, Thomas à Becket, the Archbishop of Canterbury, refused to accept the agreement. His refusal astounded Henry. Becket had been one of his faithful officials and as a reward for his services Henry had secured for him the position of Archbishop. Now he found his one-time servant thwarting his plans.

Thomas à Becket

Both men became increasingly angry and bitter as the controversy went on and neither would give way. At one point, in a fit of rage, Henry burst out in the hearing of some of his attendants that he would be glad to be rid of that priest. Taking the King at his word, some overzealous friends murdered Becket in his own cathedral at Canterbury in 1170. The murder shocked the Christian world. Thomas à Becket became a martyr and later a saint, at whose tomb countless miracles were said to have taken place. Henry realized that he had gone too far and, although it had never been his intention to have

Becket killed, he knew that he had to make a public penance and a partial surrender.

In spite of this defeat Henry II had made a gigantic contribution to the history of England. When he died in 1189, he left the monarchy stronger and the country more peaceful than ever before. So stable was the kingdom and so efficient was the central government that his eldest son, Richard the Lion-heart, could leave the country for years on end. Richard I was not a statesman like his father. His chief interest was in war and he is often regarded as the perfect mediæval knight, brave and reckless, handsome and chivalrous. He spent his time fighting in France, over much of which he was lord, and visited England only

Richard the Lion-heart 1189-1199

THE PENANCE OF HENRY II

Chroniclers describing Henry's penance said that he walked the three miles to Becket's tomb barefoot and clad only in a woollen smock. His feet were gashed by sharp stones and bled fiercely. At the tomb "he lay prostrate for a great while and in devout humility, and of his own free will was scourged by all the bishops and abbots there present and each individual monk of the church of Canterbury." He sat there and prayed all day and night, neither eating, drinking, nor permitting even a rug to be given him.

twice in his ten-year reign. His most famous exploit was the Third Crusade, to wrest the Holy Places from the Moslem Arabs. On his way home from the Holy Land he was captured and had to be ransomed by the English people. Despite his long absences the royal government established by his father continued to function effectively. No better proof of the excellence of Henry II's government could be found.

As always, however, the smooth functioning of the system depended on the king or his ministers. Henry had increased the power of the king for the good of the nation, but that power could also be misused. The barons had submitted to Henry II reluctantly and they continued to obey the just rule of Richard's officials. But would they continue to obey a king who in their opinion misused his power? The reign of King John answered that question.

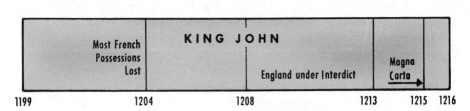

Most French Possessions Lost	KING JOHN England under Interdict	Magna Carta →

1199   1204   1208   1213   1215   1216

CHAPTER EIGHT

KING JOHN AND MAGNA CARTA

In the spring of 1199 King Richard the Lion-Heart was besieging the Castle of Châlus in France. Late in the afternoon he started a tour around the fortress walls. One of the defenders, cross-bow in hand, saw the King and shot at him. The arrow hit Richard and a week later he died. As ruler of England and his possessions on the Continent Richard left his young brother John, perhaps the most famous king in English history because his name is associated with the Magna Carta, the first great charter of English liberties.

King John 1199-1216   A contemporary once said of John's family, "From the Devil they come. To the Devil they go." Perhaps it was true, for, like his father, Henry II, John had a furious temper and a broad streak of cruelty which shocked even the rough age in which he lived. He had none of the handsome dignity of his brother Richard and too little of his father's cool and calculating shrewdness. Yet John was by no means a fool. He was an able man, genuinely interested in government, who showed considerable skill during a crisis.

John's Problems   The difficulties which led up to Magna Carta in 1215 were partly John's fault, yet they were also due to circumstances over which he had little control. John had inherited not only a strong monarchy, but also a discontented baronage. While the barons had accepted the strong rule of Henry II and Richard, they had come increasingly to believe that their traditional rights and powers were being slowly taken away as the king's power increased.

Moreover, John had become king at a time when being king was no easy task. The late twelfth century was a period of great prosperity and rising prices. For example, John had to pay almost four times as

42

RETURN AFTER DEFEAT

Throughout much of his reign King John was at war with King Philip of France, who wanted to annex the King's possessions on the Continent. Philip captured Normandy and in 1214 John crossed the Channel to reconquer it. His army was badly defeated at the Battle of Bouvines and John returned to England to face the discontented barons.

much to hire a soldier as his father had in 1160. Today it would be easy for the government to increase its revenue by raising taxes, but mediæval kings were limited in their ability to raise money. John's income came largely from his own lands, the fines of the royal courts, and his rights as a feudal lord, such as the tax levied when his son was knighted or his daughter married.

In an attempt to increase his income to meet rising costs, John and his officials made the fullest possible use of the royal powers and in so doing they pushed these powers beyond the usual limit. For example, they increased fines and charged high rates for royal writs. The barons complained, but John was too self-centered and domineering to pay any attention. In addition he quarrelled with the Pope over the appointment of the Archbishop of Canterbury. The Pope countered by laying England under an interdict which closed the church doors and stopped all religious services. When further negotiations failed, Pope Innocent III, one of the great mediæval popes, excommunicated the King, thereby denying him the sacraments of the Church. The Pope also relieved John's subjects of their allegiance to their King.

Finally, John was a complete failure as a military leader. By 1204 he had lost most of the English possessions in France. Ten years later, having at last given in to Pope Innocent, John decided to attempt a reconquest of his French possessions. But when he called the feudal

43

host to assemble at Portsmouth, his barons refused to answer his call and John was forced to employ professional soldiers, called mercenaries. His war in France was a disaster, John was hopelessly defeated.

The Barons' Revolt

The barons who had been taxed for what now turned out to be a lost cause refused any further demands by the King for money. Extremists among them wished to fight the King, but the moderates tried to reach some agreement with him on the many troublesome issues that had arisen. This group, led by Stephen Langton, the new Archbishop of Canterbury, agreed to meet John on the marshy meadow at Runnymede near London in June 1215. After five days of heated discussions, the Great Charter—Magna Carta—was finally drawn up and formally sealed. Both barons and King solemnly swore to uphold its provisions.

MAGNA CARTA

King John put his seal on Magna Carta on June 19, 1215, as leading barons watched. In the foreground is Stephen Langton, the Archbishop of Canterbury. Langton was a very intelligent and highly educated man who wished a settlement of the dispute rather than civil war. Both King and barons trusted him and most historians agree that the charter itself was in great part his work. Langton's great achievement was to turn a baronial revolt into a Great Charter.

It is important to understand exactly what Magna Carta was. The **Magna Carta 1215** charter was a document which attempted to set out the accepted terms of the feudal relationship between the king and his barons, so that in

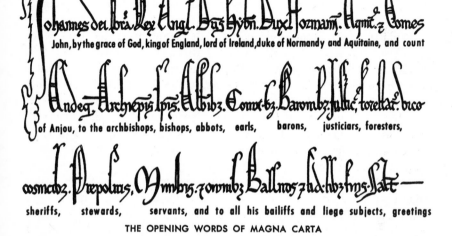

John, by the grace of God, king of England, lord of Ireland, duke of Normandy and Aquitaine, and count of Anjou, to the archbishops, bishops, abbots, earls, barons, justiciars, foresters, sheriffs, stewards, servants, and to all his bailiffs and liege subjects, greetings

THE OPENING WORDS OF MAGNA CARTA

future the king could not ignore them and increase his own power. For example, Clause Twelve, one of the most famous sections, said:

> No aid [tax] shall be imposed in our realm except with the common council of our realm, except be it to ransom our person, to make our eldest son a knight, or for once marrying our eldest daughter; and for these only a reasonable aid shall be levied.

This clause simply restated the traditional customs which John, in his financial distress, had broken. It does not mean, as some enthusiastic historians have said, "no taxation without the consent of the people". That principle was not to be firmly established for another four hundred years.

Moreover, Magna Carta shows that John had not properly fulfilled his role as the fountain of justice. Unless the King had been misusing his power there would have been no need to include the following clauses:

> In future no official shall put anyone to trial merely on his own testimony, without reliable witnesses produced for this purpose.

45

To no one will we sell, to no one will we refuse or delay right or justice.

These last clauses are important because they embodied the idea that the legal rights of the people could not be touched by the king and that the king was responsible for maintaining those rights. In other words, the king as well as his subjects must obey the law. The English common law was supreme.

John had no intention of keeping all the promises he made when he signed Magna Carta. He believed that many of the clauses went too far and his one-time enemy, Pope Innocent III, agreed and released John from his promise to obey the charter. The disillusioned barons asked the French for assistance in the hope that John might be forced to keep his word, and a French army landed in England. The King was able to organize a large army and was preparing to attack his enemies when he died in October 1216, supposedly after over-indulging in peaches and cider.

With his death, the situation changed overnight. His heir was a nine-year-old boy, Henry III, who could not conceivably menace the barons. A group of moderate barons was formed to govern the kingdom until Henry came of age. With its more radical clauses removed, Magna Carta was reissued and peace was restored. England waited for her new King to grow up to see what the future would hold.

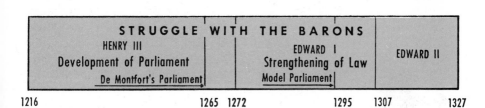

1000 B.C. 800 600 400 200 1 200 400 600 800 1000 1200 A.D. 1485

STRUGGLE WITH THE BARONS

HENRY III		EDWARD I	EDWARD II
Development of Parliament		Strengthening of Law	
De Montfort's Parliament		Model Parliament	

1216   1265 1272   1295 1307   1327

CHAPTER NINE

THE GREAT EXPERIMENT: 1216-1327

Between 1216 and 1327 the English nation tried an experiment in government that was to be of striking importance. In the century before Magna Carta the kings had concentrated so much power in their own hands that the feudal barons felt their traditional share in government was being restricted or ignored. When John was succeeded by his nine-year-old son, Henry III, the government of the country Henry III
1216-1272 passed into the hands of a number of the barons and remained there until the King grew up. For the next century the barons insisted on retaining a greater share in the government of the kingdom. Neither they nor the King had any clear idea of how the powers of government should be shared, but from their insistence and from endless experimentation came the beginning of the body we now call Parliament.

When Henry III took the government into his own hands in 1227 he quickly showed that he was not up to the task of ruling the country. Like his father, King John, he had a strong temper, but his was the temper of a spoiled and wilful child, not that of a strong and determined man. He had no taste for the art of government, and his policies were inconsistent and muddled. The young King was interested in architecture and his remodelling of Westminster Abbey showed that he had excellent taste; but a sense of beauty and form could not make up for lack of political ability.

For thirty years Henry III faced one crisis after another. His wars to maintain his possessions in France were dismal failures. By relying on relatives and foreign friends and giving them the great offices in the country, he aroused the hostility of his English barons. His willing financial support of the Pope further annoyed his subjects, who paid for

47

his extravagance in heavy taxes. Frequent meetings of the Great Council did nothing to remove the hostility or the grounds for disagreement between the King and his barons.

Some of these meetings of the Great Council were now beginning to be called Parliaments. The word "Parliament" comes from the French *parler* which means "to talk". When we speak of Parliament today we think primarily of the House of Commons, made up of the elected representatives of the people. The beginning of this idea of representation can be traced to the reign of Henry III. As early as the reign of John, the King had summoned representatives of the shires to discuss matters with him and his Council. In 1254 an important event occurred when the barons refused to grant the King money without the consent of a group of men, composed of two knights, or commoners, elected by the freemen of every shire. King Henry summoned this body of shire representatives to Parliament to listen to his proposals and consent to

WESTMINSTER ABBEY

Henry III was revered in his own day for his love of fine buildings and particularly for his contribution to Westminster Abbey. In 1250 he relaxed penances for one year to all sinners who would "assist the fabric of the church of wonderful beauty now being built by the king at Westminster." As always, his preference was for French designs and architects. An interesting feature of this view of the south side of the Abbey is the use of French flying buttresses, the arched structures built to support the four-storey walls.

THE PROVISIONS OF OXFORD

Determined barons met King Henry at Oxford in 1258 with the Provisions which they had drawn up for reform of the government. The Provisions called for a committee of fifteen men chosen by the King and barons to advise the King on all aspects of government and be responsible for the reforms. A committee of twelve barons was to meet the fifteen three times a year at Parliament to supervise their work. Henry III was enraged, yet he had no alternative but to agree.

the taxes. It was to be a long time, however, before the commons were present at every Parliament.

In 1258 the differences between the King and the barons came to a head. When Parliament met in that year, Henry was faced with the unanimous opposition of the barons and was forced to accept a committee of them to help him govern the country. In return for this concession, the barons promised to help the King out of the financial difficulties into which his support of the Pope had led him. In a letter circulated throughout the kingdom, Henry promised to obey the Provisions of Oxford, the name given to the list of reforms drawn up by the committee of barons.

Provisions
of Oxford
1258

> The King to all. You are to know that we have granted to the nobles and magnates of our kingdom that the state of our kingdom shall be ordered, rectified, and reformed according to what they shall think best to enact for the honour of God and our faith and the good of our kingdom.

The Provisions, which outlined a detailed scheme for the reform and reorganization of the Royal Household, the civil service, and the courts, showed that the barons had the best interests of the country at heart. One clause struck out at bribery:

49

SIMON DE MONTFORT

A French nobleman whose grandmother was heiress to a large English estate, Simon de Montfort came to England in 1230 and soon became one of Henry III's foreign favourites. He married the King's sister and thereafter held high offices in the government. In 1240 de Montfort went on a Crusade and on his return spent much of his time in France. By 1258 he had become a critic of Henry III and until his death at the battle of Evesham in 1265 was his leading opponent.

And the justices shall accept nothing unless it is a present of bread and wine and like things: namely, such meat and drink as have been customarily brought for the day to the tables of the chief men. And this same regulation shall be understood to hold for all the king's councillors.

Above all, the barons decided that Parliaments were to meet three times a year. Nothing was said in the Provisions of Oxford about the representatives of the commons.

It was impossible for this situation to last very long. What had happened was that the King's power had been taken over by a committee of barons. The King accepted the limitations on his power only because he saw no immediate alternative. When Henry appealed to the Pope, the Pope agreed that the barons had gone too far and he relieved Henry of his promise to obey the Provisions of Oxford. Moreover, the barons soon began to disagree among themselves. An extremist Simon wing, led by Simon de Montfort, Henry's brother-in-law, was anxious de Montfort to reduce the King's power even further. In 1264, when the King of France, who had been asked by both sides to settle some disputed points, decided in Henry's favour, Simon de Montfort sought to secure by force what he and his followers could get in no other way.

50

Although many barons sided with the King, de Montfort easily defeated the over-confident royalist forces at the Battle of Lewes in 1264 and captured the King and his young son, Prince Edward. For fifteen months the harsh and aggressive de Montfort ruled England. In 1265, in an attempt to increase his support, he invited to a Parliament not only representatives of the shires but also men from the towns or boroughs. But the English people were even more opposed to a revolutionary dictatorship, no matter how well intentioned, than they were to monarchical misgovernment and de Montfort's following slowly crumbled away. When Prince Edward escaped in 1265 and quickly formed a large army, de Montfort's dictatorship was at an end. Under low-lying black clouds and in a driving rain de Montfort was defeated and killed—some say stabbed in the back—at the Battle of Evesham.

Although the King had triumphed over the rebellious barons, the young prince, who succeeded his father as Edward I in 1272, had learned much about the art of government from his experiences. Edward I, known as Longshanks because he stood well over six feet in height, was every inch a king. Edward was a model Christian knight, gentlemanly, chivalrous, and a great warrior. To these fine qualities he added a respect for the law unknown in a king since the time of Henry II. So great was his belief in law as the basis of good government, and so important were his reforms, that he became known as the "English Justinian" after the great Roman law-maker. **Edward I 1272-1307**

With the assistance of expert advisers on his Council, Edward began at once to reform the system of law and administration, making use of the Provisions of Oxford. While pleasing the barons in this way, he also limited their authority by strengthening the royal courts. He was careful to make sure that all new laws were passed only with the consent of Parliament, although it was not yet legally necessary to do this.

Edward's passion for order and efficiency led him into campaigns to conquer Wales and Scotland and to regain lost English possessions in France. He invaded Wales twice, finally killing the gallant Welsh prince Llewelyn, and permanently joined Wales to England. In reply to the demands of the Welsh barons for a prince of their own, Edward proclaimed his infant son Prince of Wales. From that time on the King of England's eldest son has borne that proud title. **Annexation of Wales 1284**

Edward next turned his attention to turbulent Scotland. His attempts to unite the two countries roused Scottish national pride to a fever

51

pitch and under their King, John Balliol, the Scots took up arms against the English monarch. Never a man to waste words when the time called for action, Edward moved quickly, and soundly defeated the Scots at Dunbar. To their dismay, he carried the famous Stone of Scone, used in Scottish coronations, back to England and placed it in Westminster Abbey, where it is still in use whenever a British monarch is crowned.

In 1297 a Scottish knight, William Wallace, again roused the Scots against the English. He inflicted a spectacular defeat on the enemy at Stirling Bridge, but in a battle at Falkirk his army was destroyed by Edward. The fiercely independent and patriotic Scots soon found a new leader in Robert Bruce, who became their King. Before Bruce could lead another attack on the English, Edward I had died and his weak son, Edward II, reigned in his place. At Bannockburn, Bruce routed the English army. This battle settled the question of whether Scotland could be united to England. After Bannockburn Scotland remained independent for three centuries, in spite of intermittent war and constant hostility.

Edward I's Welsh and Scottish wars, as well as his costly and unsuccessful expeditions to France, had important political results. The King found the knights owed him by the barons no longer sufficient and had to employ professional soldiers for long periods of time. Since these had to be paid, the expense of conducting a war was much increased. To secure the necessary financial and political support for his wars, Edward turned increasingly to Parliament. Parliament met more often than ever before and the commoners, or representatives of the shires and towns, were summoned more frequently.

Edward wanted the representatives from the shires and towns at Parliament for several reasons. They brought with them, from their own community, petitions for changes in law or policy that they asked the King and his Council to hear and consider. To grant their reasonable requests and pass new laws with their consent immeasurably strengthened the King's position and increased his popularity in the country. Most important, perhaps, was the fact that the King, always in need of money, found that taxes could be granted and collected more easily if the representatives of the wealthy classes of shire and town added their consent to that of the magnates. Since the days of Edward I, the principle that taxes could be granted only by Parliament has been the foundation of parliamentary government, and disaster has awaited any king who refused to abide by it.

Defeat of the Scots at Dunbar 1296

Victory of the Scots at Bannockburn 1314

52

The climax of the experiment with representation came with the calling of the Model Parliament of 1295. The Model Parliament was so termed because it included the Great Council of nobles, the higher clergy and representatives of the lower clergy, and representatives from both shire and borough. It was the largest and most complete assembly of its kind that England had ever seen. King Edward appeared before

The Model
Parliament
1295

GOVERNMENT
EDWARD I

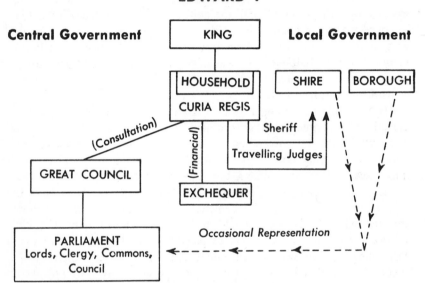

it to discuss the war in France and to appeal for a large grant of money to carry it on. Even after this, however, representatives of the shires and boroughs were not always present at Parliament. Edward I himself, who knew their value, summoned them to only eight of the twenty Parliaments called between 1295 and 1307. Not until after 1327, when his grandson, Edward III, ascended the throne, were the commons invariably present when Parliaments were held. As late as the seventeenth century the king continued to meet occasionally with the nobles in a Great Council. But though the representatives were not yet organized into a Parliament as we know it, all the elements of the modern institution were present in King Edward's Model Parliament.

In spite of his use of Parliament and his attempts to secure the cooperation of the barons and the commons, the last years of Edward I's reign were marked by increasing controversy between the King and his subjects. Edward constantly demanded more men and money than the people wished to give him. Like King John before him, he occasionally overstepped the limits of the law in his attempts to secure revenue and was frequently called to account at Parliament. An increasing number of petitions of protest against his actions were presented in the courts and at Parliament. Only Edward's great ability and his diplomatic skill prevented a serious crisis.

Edward II 1307-1327

When he died in 1307 he left the kingdom to his weak and irresolute son, Edward II. Lacking both the ability and the prestige of his father, the cheerful but temperamental Edward II soon found himself at odds with many of the barons. After twenty years of skirmishing in Parliament and on the battlefield, he was deposed and murdered by a baronial party aided by his wife, the Queen. The crown passed to his fourteen-year-old son, Edward III.

By the time the young Edward III came to the throne in 1327 the period of experiments in government was over. It had now been established that the government of the country was not a matter that concerned the king alone. The king and his Council were still the most important part of government, but they could no longer deny a voice to the king's subjects. Since the baronial revolt of 1215 and the signing of Magna Carta, Parliament had emerged as the instrument through which the nation could have some control over the king. Before Parliament the king had to plead for money and in Parliament his subjects could air their grievances and expect to have them sympathetically considered. It was to be a long time before Parliament controlled the king and governed the country in his name, as it does today, but the faint beginnings of this process had been established by 1327.

EDWARD III	RICHARD II	HENRY IV	HENRY V	HENRY VI	EDWARD IV / RICHARD III

← Hundred Years War → · ← Wars of Roses →

1327	1337	1377	1399	1413	1422	1461	1485

CHAPTER TEN

THE SUNSET OF MEDIÆVAL ENGLAND: 1327-1485

The struggle between king and barons for control of Parliament and government ended soon after the young King, Edward III, came to the throne. There was a new spirit abroad in the land; it was an age when the peoples of England were beginning to think of themselves as English, and like his subjects, the new King was highly nationalistic. These were the years when English replaced Norman French in the schools and

Edward III
1327-1377

GOVERNMENT
EDWARD III

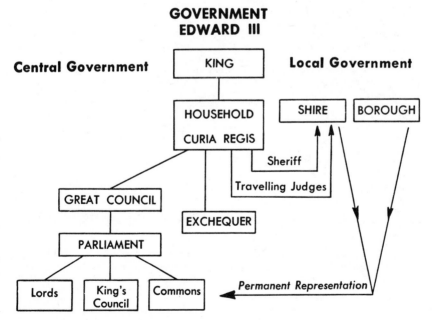

Central Government   KING   Local Government

HOUSEHOLD / CURIA REGIS · SHIRE · BOROUGH

Sheriff

Travelling Judges

GREAT COUNCIL · EXCHEQUER

PARLIAMENT

Lords · King's Council · Commons

Permanent Representation

55

the law-courts. In 1362 the King for the first time addressed Parliament in the English tongue. Handsome and chivalrous, the young monarch revelled in the pomp and pageantry of late mediæval England. He ruled for fifty years and most of his reign was to be spent in wars with France.

The Hundred Years War

The nation was in whole-hearted agreement when King Edward claimed the title of King of France in 1337. This claim started a series of wars that were to last for over a century and have therefore been called the Hundred Years War. Edward's barons and subjects shared his enthusiasm for a triumphant war on the Continent, where both glory

ENGLISH LONGBOWMEN

At Crécy and Agincourt the longbow's worth was proved. The bow was often six feet long and, if properly handled, sent the arrow a great distance, with terrific force. Enemy crossbowmen and mounted knights found it difficult to get within fighting range. If the knights did manage to approach the English lines, they were confronted by sharp stakes which served as protection for the archers. King Edward III realized the importance of the longbow and in a Proclamation of 1363 ordered his subjects to become expert archers.

56

and gold awaited the strong and adventurous. Domestic problems fell into the background for many years, as England echoed with tales of the glories of English arms.

In the great naval battle of Sluys in 1340 the English destroyed a French fleet with 35,000 men-at-arms aboard. In this striking victory English soldiers, armed with the longbow, swept the French decks and cleared the rigging of their enemies, who sought to destroy them by hurling down great stones when the ships were locked together. The victory at Sluys removed any threat of an invasion of England. Six years later at Crécy in France the unprecedented range and power of the

Because of the bowmen, the proclamation said, "it is well known that high honour and advantage comes into our realm, and no mean advantage to ourselves in feats of war." Yet of late, the King felt, archery had fallen into disrepute and people gave "themselves up to the throwing of stones and of wood and of iron; and some to handball and football and hockey. . . ." Thus Edward's Proclamation ordered that "every man . . . if he be able-bodied shall upon holidays make use, in his games, of bows and arrows, or darts, or both, and learn and practise archery."

57

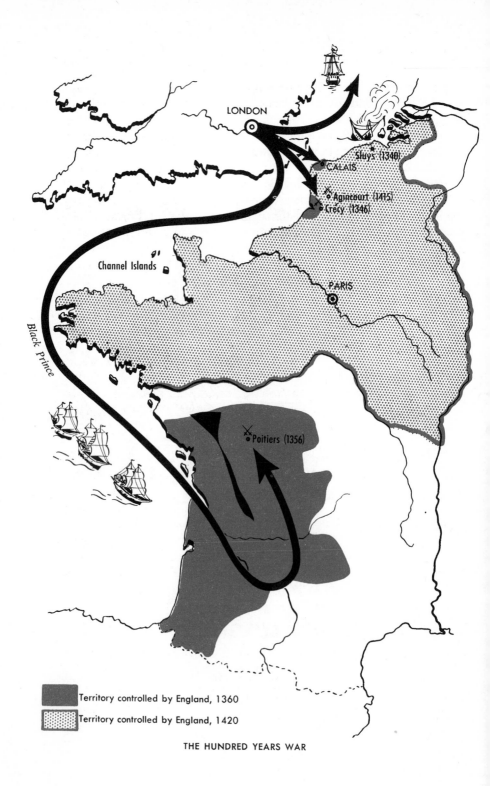

LONDON

Sluys (1340)

CALAIS

Agincourt (1415)
Crécy (1346)

Channel Islands

PARIS

Black Prince

Poitiers (1356)

Territory controlled by England, 1360

Territory controlled by England, 1420

THE HUNDRED YEARS WAR

English longbow was again demonstrated. As Genoese crossbowmen and French knights advanced against the English lines, they were suddenly met by a hail of death-dealing arrows. Charges by the French knights, clad in heavy armour, were suicidal, as the sturdy English yeomen's arrows pierced all but the heaviest plate. By the day's end the field was littered with the cream of the French army—the "flower of French chivalry"—many of them dead or wounded and others, their horses shot out from under them, lying helpless in their heavy armour. Ten years later English archers and the genius of the Black Prince, Edward's eldest son, again cut the French army to ribbons at Poitiers.

In spite of these successes, the tide began to turn against the English. The Black Prince died in 1376 and his father, Edward III, died the next year. Both France and England were exhausted by the constant fighting and, although no peace was declared, the actual fighting stopped. The war did not start again in earnest until 1415 when Henry V, whose exploits in war have since been made famous by Shakespeare, determined to conquer France.

The power of Parliament rapidly increased during Edward III's wars with France. Always in desperate need of money, Edward called Parliament often. The members met together to hear the King's request and then withdrew into groups to consider the matter. At first the representatives of the shires and the towns debated separately, but about 1340 they began to meet together. In time they became known as the House of Commons. The barons, who were not elected representatives but who inherited their place with their title, met by themselves and were eventually called the House of Lords. *The War and Parliament*

Parliament met the King's constant demands for money with demands for reforms of many kinds. It went beyond the principle that the king could not levy taxes without its consent; it tried to secure some control over how the money was spent. Parliament also claimed the right to some supervision of the conduct of the King's ministers and officials. The members often refused to grant taxes until the king had agreed to their requests. At first these requests were in the form of petitions, but as time went on they were drawn up as Bills. When a Bill was passed by Parliament and approved by the king it became a Statute and part of the law of the land. By the time Edward died in 1377 Parliament had become a body of great importance. A united baronage and the people could use it with effect against the king. Yet at the same time Parliament was strong only as long as its members were united.

Richard II
1377-1399
After Edward's death the kingdom was left in the hands of his ten-year-old grandson, Richard II, son of the Black Prince. As so often happened when the monarch was a child, the barons fell to quarrelling among themselves and each party tried to use Parliament for its own ends. The House of Lords became a battlefield where baronial factions struggled for control of the land. At this time the House of Commons was easily intimidated by the magnates and its members usually found it convenient to champion the winning side.

For over a century the struggle for power between the king and the barons and between the rival groups of barons went on. After twenty years of accepting dictation from the powerful nobles, Richard II suddenly hit back at them in 1397. Supported by a timid House of Commons who agreed to whatever the king asked, Richard set out to take revenge on his enemies. The leaders of the barons were executed or banished from the country. The very severity of his vengeance was frightening and people looked on with horror as Richard asserted that there were no limits to his power. In 1399 the standard of revolt was raised by his cousin, Henry of Lancaster, whom Richard had deprived of his lands and banished from the country. Richard's regime collapsed about him like a house of cards and he was forced to surrender to his victorious cousin. Parliament meekly recognized Henry as king.

Henry IV
1399-1413
The accession of Henry IV did not end the struggle for power. Barons who had supported Henry demanded their reward; those who had opposed him and lost sought revenge. In 1403 Henry was forced to fight against a coalition of northern barons which he defeated at the Battle of Shrewsbury. Within his Council his relatives and restless, ambitious magnates intrigued and jockeyed for position and power. Parliament refused to grant the King all the money he wanted and constantly tried to expand its powers at the King's expense. Henry IV was a strong king, as was his son Henry V, and they could keep the barons under control. But the situation was charged with the prospect of trouble if ever a weak king should come to the throne.

Henry V
1413-1422
On his accession in 1413, Henry V at once became master in his own house and won the enthusiastic support of the barons for a renewal of the war against France. At first the war went well and at Agincourt in 1415 English archers once again proved their superiority over the French knights. However, the English triumph was short-lived. After the death of Henry V in 1422 a revived French nation took heart and rallied behind the heroic Maid of Orleans, Joan of Arc, who came forward to lead her people. Although Joan was captured and burned

60

as a heretic by the English, their army was gradually pushed back foot by foot towards the sea. When the war ended in 1453 only the little port of Calais remained in English hands. Britain had lost the Hundred Years War and France had emerged as a strong state.

End of the Hundred Years War

After the disastrous conclusion of the war with France, the full energies of the barons were concentrated on a struggle for power at home.

PARLIAMENT

Henry VI opens Parliament in the presence of the bishops and abbots (left), the clerks and Councillors, and the nobles (right). The Commons crowded into the room, at the lower left to hear the King. At other times during the session they would come to report their decisions through their speaker. The records of Parliament, known as the "Rotuli Parliamentorum," still exist and are used by historians to discover the way in which Parliament developed. The formal opening of Parliament has changed very little; to this day a similar ceremony is observed in Great Britain, in Canada, and in other Commonwealth countries.

61

Henry VI
1422-1461

Henry V's heir was his nine-month old son, Henry VI. The latter's scheming uncles ruled for him and the royal Council and Parliament were soon embroiled in their bitter feuds. As the King grew up it became obvious that he was not capable of restoring order. In 1453 he became insane and in 1455 the conflict moved to the battlefield. The King's supporters took as their badge the red rose of Lancaster, since Henry was of the House of Lancaster, while his opponents wore the white rose of their leader, the Duke of York. The Wars of the Roses, as the ensuing conflict is called, went on for thirty years. Rival groups of barons created their own small armies, every man wearing the crest or livery of the lord he followed. The ordinary people took little part in the conflict. Yet most Englishmen found they needed the protection of a strong lord against the bands of armed men who roamed the

Wars of
the Roses
1455-1485

AN AGE OF LAWLESSNESS

Even before the Wars of the Roses, barons maintained their own body of personal followers and dressed them in the livery of their family. With the decline in the king's power, "livery and maintenance", as it was called, grew out of hand. Often these armed bands were little more than ruffians or desperadoes. The group shown here, threatening a peaceful couple, are abviously of that sort. Their shields carry the crests of the lord they serve; their motley garb suggests they have been engaged in plundering.

country. "Spend somewhat and get yourself a lord, for thereby hang the law and the prophets," was the advice given to one young man. During these troubled times men lost respect for the law, for judges and juries were often intimidated by armed and insolent soldiers. It was a familiar complaint that, "The law serveth for nought else but to do wrong."

The Wars of the Roses demonstrated again that the combination of a weak monarch and unruly barons was the greatest danger of mediæval government. They also heralded the end of mediæval England. As the war dragged on and battle followed battle, the death toll among the aristocracy was high and the baronage almost destroyed itself in suicidal wars among its members.

The machinery of mediæval government had momentarily broken down. Yet the king's Council and Household, the courts and Parliament were suitable instruments to provide good government. They only required the firm hand of a strong king to make them work. That strong king appeared in 1485 when Henry Tudor landed in England from foreign exile and assumed the leadership of the Lancastrian forces. At the Battle of Bosworth he decisively defeated the Yorkist troops led by King Richard III. Although few suspected it at the time—for this battle seemed no different from a dozen others which had taken place in the last thirty years—the Wars of the Roses were over. When Henry picked from a bush at Bosworth the crown fallen from the head of the slain Richard and placed it on his own head, a new age had begun for the people of England.

Battle of Bosworth 1485

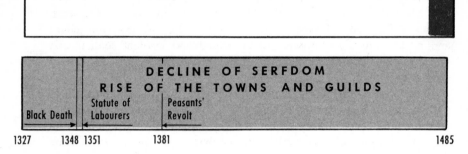

DECLINE OF SERFDOM
RISE OF THE TOWNS AND GUILDS

Black Death | Statute of Labourers | Peasants' Revolt

1327   1348 1351   1381   1485

CHAPTER ELEVEN

COUNTRY AND TOWN IN THE LATE MIDDLE AGES

Social Groups: Aristocracy   The twilight period of mediæval England, the years from 1300 to 1485, was one of great change in English society. The warring nobles of Norman times became less concerned with governing their own estates as though they were small kingdoms and more anxious to establish their power in the national government. Shrewd marriages often consolidated separate estates, while the Hundred Years War and the Wars of the Roses killed off the nobility and decreased their numbers. By the late mediæval period, the knights of Norman England had become country squires more interested in farming and sheep-raising than in war and politics. It was among the English peasants, however, that the most important social changes took place, as they slowly moved from serfdom to freedom.

Peasants   At first glance, rural England seemed to have changed very little from Anglo-Saxon days. Peasants still lived in the country villages and cultivated their scattered strips in the open fields, as their forefathers had done for generations. Yet there had been changes. As early as the twelfth century some lords had agreed to accept cash payments in place of the labour services which the villeins owed them. After 1300 this practice became widespread, as landlords needed money to meet rising costs.

The Black Death 1348   The Black Death hastened the process of freeing the serfs from labour services. This highly infectious and dreaded plague swept over Europe from Asia and reached England in 1348. The disease, whose germs were carried by rats, spread rapidly in the sewage-laden streets of the towns and villages. Within two years it had probably killed about a half of the English population. As one eye-witness reported:

64

THE HORROR OF THE BLACK DEATH

The pestilence seized especially the young and strong, commonly sparing the elderly and feeble. Scarcely any one ventured to touch the sick, and healthy persons shunned the precious possessions of the dead as infectious. People perfectly well one day were found dead on the next. Some were tormented in various parts of their body, and from these many, by means of lancing, or with long suffering recovered. Others had small black postules scattered over the whole body, from which very few, nay scarcely a single person, returned to life and health.

As a result of the high death rate there was more land available than there were peasants to till it. One chronicler wrote that:

After the pestilence many buildings both great and small in all cities, towns and boroughs fell into ruins for want of inhabitants, and in the same way many villages and hamlets were depopulated, and there were no houses left in them, all who had lived therein being dead; and it seemed likely that many such hamlets would never again be inhabited. In the following winter there was such a dearth of servants for all sorts of labour as it was believed had never been before. For the sheep strayed in all directions without herdsmen, and all things were left without none to care for them.

Because of the shortage of labour, wages rose. Many peasants fled from the bondage of their native village to work for money wages in the towns or for other lords, thereby gaining their freedom. To prevent the rise of wages and prices, Parliament passed the Statute of Labourers in 1351, providing heavy penalties for any villein who left his lord or for any landowner who paid higher wages than those usually paid before

Statute of
Labourers
1351

65

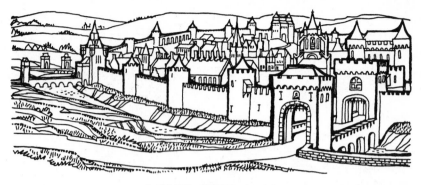

A WALLED MEDIÆVAL CITY

Most towns in the Middle Ages were protected by walls of some kind, for the country was poorly policed. The earthern mounds of early mediæval towns were later replaced by stone walls similar to those seen in the illustration. Carefully chosen men guarded the solid oak gates, which were securely locked from dusk to dawn. Within the walls houses and churches stood amid pleasant gardens and orchards. Many citizens cultivated strips of land which lay in the unenclosed fields outside the towns. By late mediæval times the walls were falling into disrepair and many of them were beginning to disappear.

the plague struck. However, more often than not, both peasants and employers ignored the Statute.

Faced with increasing costs and fewer labourers, many lords leased their land for a cash rent. Some of the wealthier peasants rented the land and farmed it profitably, thereby creating a large class of small but independent farmers. By good management many of them in time became prosperous, bought more land, and merged with the country squires.

On some manors, however, the lords still attempted to force villeins to perform field work while others used the Statute of Labourers to keep down wages. Dissension between lords and villeins increased until in 1377 landlords complained in Parliament that their villeins claimed—

> to be quit and utterly discharged of all manner of serfage, due as well of their body as of their tenures, and will not suffer any distress or other justice to be made upon them; but do menace the ministers of their lords of life and member, and, which more is, gather themselves in great routs and agree by such confederacy that every one shall aid other to resist their lords with strong hand

The Peasants' Revolt 1381 The discontent of the peasants finally erupted into open violence in 1381 when the government imposed a Poll Tax of one shilling to be paid by all persons over fifteen, except beggars. In twenty-eight shires, indignant and enraged peasants and townsfolk stormed the manor houses, demanding their rights and committing violent deeds. Under their peasant leader, Wat Tyler, they marched on London. The terror of the governing class was in marked contrast to the courage of the young King, Richard II, who calmly rode to meet the rebel mob and agreed to their demands. That evening the mob stormed through London, celebrating their apparent victory by murdering the Archbishop of Canterbury and a number of prominent lawyers and clergymen. On the following day, when the King again met the rioters, the insolent Wat Tyler was killed by one of Richard's followers who believed he was threatening the King. The brave young King prevented a massacre by riding fearlessly towards the rebels shouting that he would be their leader. Moved by the King's bravery and by his promise of pardon, the rebels dispersed and the crisis passed. Although Parliament, dominated as it was by landlords, refused to carry out the King's promise and abolish serfdom, the custom gradually disappeared during the next century.

A STREET SCENE IN A LATE MEDIÆVAL TOWN

The usual market-day activities were sometimes enlivened with entertainment by travelling jugglers, clowns, and minstrels. Most towns received charters from the king which allowed them to have a fair once or twice a year. Travelling merchants visited the fairs with goods such as fancy cloths, pottery, jewellery, and spices, which were not available in the town market.

Towns Changes of equal importance were taking place in the towns. Of England's 200 towns in 1300, few contained more than three or four thousand people and London, with 30,000 inhabitants, was the only city of any size. Most of the towns were enclosed by walls and were farming communities as well as centres of trade and commerce. They were far from pleasant places in which to live. The narrow muddy streets were littered with the garbage that citizens tossed through the doors and windows. Yet life could be interesting in the towns. Citizens gossiped in the busy market-place, watched carnivals, pageants, and touring entertainers, or worked off their surplus energy in street brawls. Others chose to admire and worship in the beautiful cathedrals and churches.

Guilds Most townsmen formed guilds or associations to promote their common interests. Each trade—shoemakers, bakers, goldsmiths, or weavers—had its own guild, which set prices and wages and tried to ensure a high standard of workmanship. Usually a boy entered the guild as an unpaid apprentice, bound to a master craftsman for seven

NEW HOMES IN THE FIFTEENTH CENTURY

In spite of the Wars of the Roses, many Englishmen prospered in the late Middle Ages, as the new country and city houses showed. While the very wealthy built new homes, completely of stone, many well-to-do men were content with half-timbered houses like that shown above. Glass windows and brick chimneys for the fireplaces became common fo: the first time, though it was many centuries before the poor people had either. Indeed, for over three hundred years there was a luxury tax on window panes which put them beyond the reach of many people.

A FIFTEENTH-CENTURY INTERIOR

The interiors of the new homes of late mediæval England were beginning to look like the interiors we know today. The great spacious halls of the castles and manor houses were being replaced by smaller, more private rooms such as the dining area shown above. Cooking utensils and dishes were becoming more refined and elaborate.

years while he learned the trade. He then became a journeyman working for a master who paid him wages. His great ambition was to become a master himself. Some masters became very rich, particularly as trade expanded, and formed a class of wealthy merchants.

CHANGING HABITS OF DRESS

By the fifteenth century the simplicity of mediæval dress was giving way to the elaborate and ornate clothes of the late sixteenth and early seventeen centuries.

Trade   Throughout the Middle Ages England's chief article of foreign trade was raw wool, although wheat, tin, lead, and fish were of considerable importance. Towards the end of the Middle Ages trade in woollen cloth began to replace the export of raw wool. Until the industrial changes of the eighteenth century, cloth-making was England's greatest industry and cloth export was its most important commercial enterprise.

The centre of English trade and commerce was London, whose leading citizens were becoming wealthy and influential. Kings often turned to the merchants for loans and, even if they did not always repay them, they sometimes rewarded the merchants with titles and commercial privileges. Many merchants bought country estates and in time mingled with the aristocracy, who in turn sometimes invested the surplus capital derived from their land holdings in trade.

England in the late Middle Ages was in the midst of an immense social ferment. The old class structure was breaking down in the face of new economic and social forces. The process was slow and the results were not obvious for another century. It is not surprising that the period was also one of ferment in the minds of men.

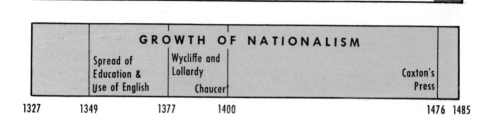

1000 B.C. 800 600 400 200 1 200 400 600 800 1000 1200 A.D. 1485

GROWTH OF NATIONALISM

Spread of Education & Use of English

Wycliffe and Lollardy

Chaucer

Caxton's Press

1327 1349 1377 1400 1476 1485

CHAPTER TWELVE

THE SPIRIT OF THE LATE MIDDLE AGES

The most remarkable change in the spirit and outlook of late mediæval England was the growth of English nationalism. Conquests had made England the home not of one people but of many: Celts, Anglo-Saxons, Danes, and Normans. The structure of feudalism imposed on England by the Normans, by dividing the country among the great nobles, was in some ways an obstacle to national unity and a national outlook. By the end of the thirteenth century, however, conquered and conquerors were slowly merging into one people. The feudal system was being changed by the centralized national government, a national common law, and a national Parliament. Throughout the country all men began to regard themselves as Englishmen.

The Growth of Nationalism

This growing national spirit can best be seen in the development of the English language. After the Norman Conquest French became the language of the ruling class. The affairs of Church and State were carried on in Latin or French, although priest and judge had to know Anglo-Saxon to deal with the people. Written Anglo-Saxon English did not completely die out, however, and with the emergence of a nationalistic feeling, during the Hundred Years War, it was revived. Edward III frequently spoke in English and contemporary poets imitated him. In 1349, three years after the battle of Crécy, one schoolmaster led the way by making his students learn English instead of French. By 1362 English had been made the language of the law-courts and a poet soon could write:

Language

Learned, unlearned, old and younge.
All understand the English tongue.

71

So it must have been, for in 1399 Henry IV made his claim to the throne in English, though an English strange to us:

> In the name of Fadir, Son, and Holy Ghost, I Henry of Lancastre chalenge yis Rewme of Yngland and the Corone with all ye membres and ye appurtenances, als I yt am difendit be right lyne of the Blode comyng fro the gude lorde Kyng Henry therde, and thorghe yat ryght yat God of his grace hath sent me, with helpe of my Kyn and of my Frendes to recover it: the whiche Rewme was in poynt to be undone for defaut of the Governance and undoying of the gode Lawes.

One obstacle to the development of a uniform English language was the existence of several quite distinct dialects in different parts of the country. The dialect from which modern English stems was that used around London, for London was the centre of fashion and economic life and the home of Parliament and the courts. Moreover, Geoffrey Chaucer, who was a man of genius and prestige, wrote in that dialect and proved that it was a language of great beauty and precision.

Chaucer   Chaucer, the son of a rich wine merchant, was born about 1340. In his famous *Canterbury Tales* Chaucer describes a company of people on a pilgrimage to Canterbury to the tomb of the murdered Thomas à Becket. To pass the time each pilgrim tells a story and these, taken together, provide us with a rich pageant of mediæval life. The monk was described by Chaucer as follows:

> Full many a deyntee hors hadde he in stable
> And whan he rood, men might his brydel her
> Ginglen in a whistling wynd as clear.

The poor parson stood higher than the monk in Chaucer's estimation:

> But Cristes lore, and his apostles twelve
> He taught, but first he folwed it himselve.

Education   The spread of English was hastened by the growth in the number of schools. In the days of Henry III very few people were educated and even literate knights were the exception. Yet by the end of the Middle Ages not only the squire and the merchant, but also their wives and daughters could usually read and write. The elementary schools were attached to nunneries, monasteries, or churches, and gave young people some training in reading, singing, and theology. More advanced were the grammar schools where the main subjects were Latin grammar and composition. Girls were admitted to the elementary but not the grammar schools. After 1350 more and more schools were endowed with funds which came from gifts and bequests and English became a subject of study. At the same time new colleges were established at the Universities of Oxford and Cambridge which had been in existence since the twelfth century.

Life in school and college was a combination of serious study and boisterous play. One very early textbook begins with the teacher asking, "Are you ready to be flogged while you learn?" and the pupils' answer, "We would rather be flogged for learning's sake than be ignorant." If the teachers tended to use a strong hand, the pupils sometimes answered in kind. One famous philosopher is said to have been slain by his pupils with their pens. At Oxford the undergraduates were said to "sleep all day and roam about all night" and one law made the penalty for night-walking twice that for shooting an arrow at a teacher with the intent to wound him. In 1314 two large bands of students met on Oxford's High Street "with swords, bucklers, bows, arrows and other arms, and there they fought together" leaving many dead and wounded when they dispersed.

At the same time the universities were a fertile seed-bed of new ideas and had won an international reputation for good scholarship. Although at that time all university teachers were clergymen, it was in Oxford that criticism of the Church began. The Church had always exercised a great and beneficial effect on the minds and spirit of the people and for the most part still did. Yet there were too many churchmen like Chaucer's monk, who were more concerned about their stable and fine dress than about religion. Ambitious churchmen often spent more time in politics than in the pulpit. Few nobles could match the wealth and splendour of the bishops and leading abbots. As generations of devout Englishmen had left property to it in their wills, the Church soon controlled much of the best land in the country. Nationalistic Englishmen increasingly began to resent the payment of money for the maintenance of the popes who lived for a long time in France, under the control of England's traditional enemy.

The leading critic of these abuses was John Wycliffe, an Oxford scholar and priest who was born about 1320. Wycliffe attacked the worldliness of the higher clergy and demanded a genuine spiritual revival. His followers, known as Lollards, or poor priests, moved about the country preaching to the people. Since Wycliffe felt that the people should come close to God through the Bible, he had translations of it made in English. At this point, however, the Church authorities, who had always resented his criticism, stepped in to stop the movement.

Wycliffe and Lollardy

73

EDWARD IV VISITS CAXTON'S PRESS

William Caxton, a successful London merchant, studied the art of printing in Germany where it had been discovered about 1450. In 1476 he established the first printing press in England. With the encouragement of Edward IV he translated and printed almost one hundred books in England. His best-known book was "The Golden Legend" which dealt with the lives of the saints. Caxton also printed some of Chaucer's works, thereby spreading the use of the dialect used by Chaucer and contributing to its adoption as the language in general use.

In seeking to base religion solely on the Bible, as well as in other ways, Wycliffe had questioned some of the basic articles of Church teaching. He and his followers were denounced as heretics, and Lollardy was stamped out or driven underground, where it remained for a century and a half, until England broke with Rome and became a Protestant nation.

Printing The speed of new ideas in the English language and the growth of English nationalism were stimulated by the invention of the printing press. Developed in Germany about 1450, the first press was established in England by William Caxton in 1476. The widespread use of books in English hastened the process of national growth and unification in every way. By the end of the Middle Ages a nationalistic England had found an English tongue. A century later the great Elizabethans were to use the language as it had never been used before.

TIME CHART

IN THE BRITISH ISLES		ELSEWHERE
POLITICAL	**OTHER**	
55-54 B.C. Caesar's first landings	Celts inhabit Britain	
A.D. 43 Permanent occupation by Claudius	43-410 Roman civilization in Britain	c. 6 B.C. Birth of Christ c. A.D. 27 Death of Christ
122-27 Construction of Hadrian's Wall		
410-42 Romans leave Britain		410 Barbarians sack Rome
449-615 Barbarian invasions	449-615 Barbarian invasions	
664 Synod of Whitby	597 Augustine lands	
793 Beginning of Danish invasions		790 Irish monks reach Iceland
871-99 Alfred the Great	Anglo-Saxon England	800 Charlemagne crowned Holy Roman Emperor
886 The Danelaw established		874 Danes settle Iceland
958-1016 Ethelred the Unready		
		980 Danes explore Greenland
		1000 Leif Ericsson blown to coast of North America (Vineland)
		1003-6 Danes from Greenland live three winters in North America
1016-35 King Canute		
1042-66 Edward the Confessor		
	1055-65 Edward rebuilds Westminster Abbey	
1066 Norman Conquest	Norman Feudalism	
1085 Domesday survey		
1135-54 Civil War		1095 First Crusade
1166 Assize of Clarendon		1147 Second Crusade
1170 Murder of Becket		
		1189 Saladin takes Jerusalem
		Third Crusade (Richard I)
1215 Magna Carta		1193 Richard captured
	1221-24 Begging Friars settle in England	

75

TIME CHART

IN THE BRITISH ISLES		ELSEWHERE
POLITICAL	**OTHER**	
1258 Provisions of Oxford 1265 Simon de Montfort's Parliament 1275 First Parliament of Edward I		1270-95 Marco Polo in Asia
	1282-84 Conquest of Wales 1291-1314 Wars with Scotland	
1295 Model Parliament 1297 Edward forced to confirm charters such as Magna Carta 1327 Beginning of permanent representation of commons		
1340 Parliament asserts control over taxation	1337 Hundred Years War begins	
	1348-49 Black Death 1362 Use of English in Parliament and courts 1370-1400 Chaucer's literary activity	
1376 "Good" Parliament impeaches King's ministers		
	1381 Peasants' Revolt 1382 Wycliffe's doctrines condemned	
1399 Parliament accepts Henry IV 1430 Vote restricted to those holding land worth 40 s.		1400-85 Steady westward expansion across Atlantic
	1430-31 Capture and death of Joan of Arc	
	1453 End of Hundred Years War	1451 Columbus born 1453 Fall of Constantinople 1454 Invention of printing in Germany
1455-85 Wars of the Roses	1476 Caxton's printing press	
		1483 Columbus appeals to Portugal to finance a trip across Atlantic to reach India
1485 Battle of Bosworth Beginning of Tudor dynasty		1486 Columbus interests Queen Isabella of Spain in his plan 1492 Columbus discovers America

BOOK II

THE TRIUMPH OF PARLIAMENT

1400

1450

1485
1500

1550

1600

1650

1700
1714

1750

1800

1850

1900

1950

2000

RULERS OF ENGLAND FROM 1485-1714

1485-1509	Henry VII	
1509-1547	Henry VIII	
1547-1553	Edward VI	Tudor
1553-1558	Mary I	
1558-1603	Elizabeth I	

1603-1625	James I	
1625-1649	Charles I	
1660-1685	Charles II	
1685-1688	James II	Stuart
1689-1702	William and Mary	
1702-1714	Anne	

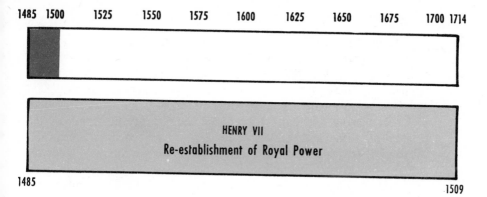

CHAPTER THIRTEEN

HENRY VII AND A STRONG MONARCHY: 1485-1509

England in 1485 was a country sick in body and spirit. For a generation it had suffered the raging fever of a civil war. The disease might have proved fatal had a remedy for its ills not soon been found. Few realized it at the time, but the nation could not have found a better doctor than the lean and unattractive Welshman, Henry Tudor, Earl of Richmond, who had won the battered crown at Bosworth. If Henry did not have a pleasant bedside manner, he at least understood the cause of his patient's illness and was much concerned for her welfare.

Though he was only twenty-eight years old, Henry had seen much of life. He was not only intelligent and industrious; he was also shrewd and calculating. Of all English kings, he was the supreme politician, the one monarch who never made a serious political blunder. He had a genius for organization and the priceless gift of being able to select the right man for every job. All of these great abilities were needed to rule England in 1485. Henry had staked his life on winning the English throne and he meant to keep it. He knew that if he won, he won everything; and if he lost, he lost all.

Henry VII
1485-1509

Behind the stern and unbending mask of the politician who trusted no one and had no close friends, glimpses of a warmer person may sometimes be caught. He loved music and his account books record payments to a wide variety of musicians including "a woman that singeth with the fiddle", "the child that playeth on the recorders", and "Watt the luter that played the fool". He enjoyed hunting and jousting and all the pomp of the mediæval aristocracy of which he was a member. Henry played tennis too and his game was either very hard or very bad, for on one occasion he lost a dozen balls.

79

The King had little time for such amusements, however, for governing England after the Wars of the Roses was a business demanding all **Dangers to** his time and energy. His first task was to secure a firm grip on the **the throne** throne. A willing Parliament accepted the verdict of the battlefield and formally recognized him as King. Then Henry married Elizabeth of York, daughter of King Edward IV, hoping by this union of the Houses of York and Lancaster to appease his enemies somewhat. There were ten men with better claims to the throne than his, however, and for fifteen years after the Battle of Bosworth his rivals eagerly supported anyone with the slightest chance of driving Henry from the throne.

Simnel   In 1487 a young man named Lambert Simnel was put forward by the Yorkists as the Earl of Warwick, one of the ten claimants. Simnel looked a little like the Earl but was in fact the son of an Oxford baker. Though everyone knew Warwick was locked in the Tower of London, the Yorkists crowned Simnel King in Dublin and sent him off to England with an army to try to unseat Henry. Henry defeated the invaders with little difficulty and offered the troublesome Simnel more permanent employment, appropriately enough in the royal kitchen.

Warbeck   Still undeterred by this miscarriage of their plans, the Yorkists next persuaded Perkin Warbeck, the son of a boatman, to pose as one of the sons of Edward IV who had disappeared mysteriously while living in the tower of London. Warbeck's coronation in Dublin led Henry

HENRY VII AND THE "ROYAL" PRETENDER

80

THE COURT OF STAR CHAMBER

The elaborate design on the ceiling of the room where the Court met gave it its name. The officers of the Court were members of the King's Council. The Court was used primarily to curb the activities of the great nobles, against whom the ordinary courts were powerless. It was extremely powerful, often working in secret and empowered to use torture to secure information. One mighty earl was once fined £15,000 for keeping armed retainers contrary to the King's orders. In time, even the threat of a trial in the Star Chamber was enough to bring over-mighty subjects into line.

to remark that "I think ye will crown apes in Ireland at the last." After Warbeck had led three expeditions against him, Henry's patience and sense of humour were exhausted. With the royal kitchens full, Warbeck was thrown into the Tower with Warwick and both were later executed. Only then was Henry's position reasonably secure.

Meanwhile, to strengthen the monarchy Henry took steps to restrain the overpowerful barons by passing Acts designed to break up their private armies. There had been such laws before, but it was difficult to get them enforced in the ordinary courts, where witnesses and juries could be intimidated by the great men who broke the laws. Henry had the cases tried before a committee of his own Council which came to be called the Court of Star Chamber. Even the greatest of his subjects

The Re-establishment of Royal Power

HENRY VII'S MINISTERS "BALANCE THE BUDGET"

Toward the end of Henry VII's reign two of his agents, Richard Empson and Edmund Dudley, known as "the two ravening wolves", raised money by methods that bordered on sheer extortion. On the flimsiest pretext these two fined the King's subjects and confiscated their property in the King's interest. Few with wealth escaped. As Francis Bacon put it, "The sparing were to be pressed for money because they saved, the lavish because they spent."

soon learned to tremble in the shadow of the royal power.

The whole power of Henry's government was centred in his Council. He chose its members carefully, leaving out the great nobles and appointing instead churchmen, lawyers, and commoners—men who would serve him loyally and never question his power or demand to share it. Parliament, in his time, seemed to be declining in importance. Henry called it only occasionally to vote taxes, but he preferred to get along without having to ask the Commons for money. He was shrewd enough to know that "he who pays the piper" may try to "call the tune".

By careful management and strict economy and by avoiding the expensive foreign wars that had ruined many a mediæval king, Henry succeeded in doing what no monarch after him was able to do: he made his traditional income from Crown lands, court fines, customs duties and so on more than meet the expenses of government. Henry has often been called stingy and certainly he was not a reckless spender. When the explorer John Cabot laid claim to a great part of North America for England in 1497, his reward from Henry was £10 and a pension of £20 a year. Many of Henry's subjects believed that his courts fined people excessively and that his officials secured money by means that verged on extortion. Indeed, Henry was not above stretching the law when it suited him. Whatever his methods, the important fact remains that when Henry became King the treasury was

82

empty and the monarchy weak; when he died the treasury contained one of the largest fortunes in Christendom and the Tudors were firmly established on the throne.

When he died in 1509 Henry left his son a strong central government, strong not because he had created any new institutions but rather because he had injected new life and vigour into the machinery of government built up in the Middle Ages. For this reason he is often known as the last mediæval king. He had given England internal peace which in turn brought growing prosperity. Many foreigners thought that England was the richest country in the world and one wrote home that in one single London street— **Summary** ✓

> . . . there are fifty-two goldsmiths' shops, so rich and full of silver vessels, great and small, that in all the shops of Milan, Rome, Venice and Florence together I do not think there would be found so many of the magnificence that is to be seen in London.

Stability and prosperity made the English proud of themselves and their country. Foreigners sometimes found them conceited and one reported that the English were—

> . . . great lovers of themselves. They think there are no other men than themselves and no other world but England; and whenever they see a handsome foreigner they say that "he looks like an Englishman."

The Italian visitor who wrote these words could not know that there were rough storms ahead for England and that the English would need all the self-confidence and courage they could muster.

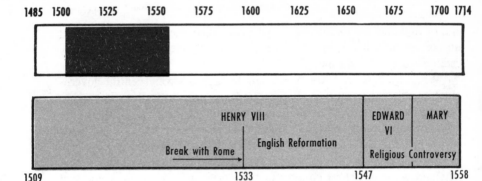

| 1485 | 1500 | 1525 | 1550 | 1575 | 1600 | 1625 | 1650 | 1675 | 1700 1714 |

HENRY VIII	EDWARD VI	MARY
English Reformation		
Break with Rome	Religious Controversy	

1509   1533   1547   1558

CHAPTER FOURTEEN

HENRY VIII AND A NATIONAL CHURCH: 1509-1547

Henry VIII
1509-1547

Henry VIII was an exciting and dynamic king. His subjects regarded him as the ideal man of his time and felt that with his accession to the throne in 1509 they had entered "a golden world". The Venetian Ambassador declared that Henry was—

HENRY VIII
"BLUFF KING HAL"

the handsomest potentate I have ever set eyes on. He speaks French, English, Latin and a little Italian, plays well on the lute and harpsichord, draws the bow with greater strength than any man in England and jousts marvellously. He is fond of hunting and never takes his diversion without tiring eight or ten horses.

In the ballroom the young monarch performed wonders, "leaping like a stag", and his mighty figure brought gasps of admiration from the ladies of the court.

To the casual observer Henry seemed to be friendly, open and good natured, but his close associates knew that beneath the bluff exterior there was another Henry, a violent and forbidding man. The French Ambassador admitted that he was afraid of the King. Writing in our own day, the great Sir Winston Churchill, himself a keen judge of men and statecraft, sees two Henrys,

one the merry monarch of the hunt and banquet and procession, the friend of children, the patron of every kind of sport, the other the cold acute observer

84

of the audience chamber or the Council, watching vigilantly, weighing arguments, refusing except under the stress of great events to speak his own mind.

No more determined monarch ever sat upon the English throne: "I will not allow anyone to have it in his power to govern me," the young King declared emphatically. Such was the man who mounted the throne at eighteen amidst the wild cheers of his subjects. Not even the King himself foresaw that his reign would bring about a revolutionary break with the Roman Catholic Church and a great increase in the power and prestige of Parliament.

Henry had never expected to be King of England, but his elder brother Arthur died before their father. To fulfill Henry VII's dying wish and to maintain friendship with the powerful Empire of Spain, Henry married Arthur's widow, Catherine of Aragon, a Spanish princess. Since the law of the Church forbade a man to marry his brother's widow, Henry had to obtain special permission from the Pope to do so. Of the six children born to Henry and Catherine, however, only one daughter, Mary, survived. Henry wanted a son very badly, for no woman had ever governed England successfully. When Catherine failed to give him a male heir he became convinced that, in spite of the Pope's permission, he had broken God's law in marrying her. Moreover, he had long since ceased to love Catherine and had fallen in love with Anne Boleyn, ones of the ladies of the court. Thus in 1527 Henry sought to have his marriage annulled or dissolved by the Pope, on the ground that permission should never have been given and that the marriage had been illegal all along.

The King's ministers, led by Cardinal Wolsey, could not persuade the Pope to grant Henry's request, partly, they felt, because the Pope was then almost a captive of Catherine's nephew, the King of Spain. Henry then tried to coerce the Pope, by securing parliamentary authority to stop the payment of money to Rome, but without success. Determined to have his own way, Henry decided to have the annulment granted in England. The Archbishop of Canterbury, Thomas Cranmer, was more than willing to do this; he believed that Henry was right and as a result had been raised to the second highest office in the land by the King. The marriage to Catherine was declared null and void, and on June 1, 1533, Anne, whom Henry had married secretly, was crowned Queen. This defiance of the Pope's authority was extremely serious and meant, in effect, that Henry had removed the English Church from its age-old obedience to papal authority.

Henry's Break With Rome

85

In 1534 Parliament passed a number of Acts that completely destroyed the Pope's power in England. The most important was the Act of Supremacy, which stated:

> Be it enacted by authority of this present Parliament that the King our Sovereign Lord, his heirs and successors Kings of this realm, shall be taken, accepted, and reputed the only Supreme Head in earth of the Church of England called *Anglicana Ecclesia* . . . .

Thus the Church in England was made a national Church with the king at its head and is therefore often called the "Established" Church. With the passage of this Act the king was supreme in all matters concerning both Church and State.

Doctrine   This did not mean, however, that religious doctrines were changed. Changes in doctrine were taking place in some European countries under the leadership of men like Martin Luther, a German monk, whose protests against certain abuses in the Church led to the name of Protestant being given to the new movement. Henry himself was a fervent defender of the Roman Catholic doctrines and gloried in his title "Defender of the Faith", which had been bestowed on him years before by the Pope for his vigorous opposition to the Protestant doctrines of Martin Luther. His subjects were equally devout and so seldom were the church bells silent that foreigners called England "the ringing isle".

Parliamentary Support   Nevertheless, Parliament and the bulk of the people were prepared to follow the King's lead in breaking the connection with Rome. While few complained of religious doctrine, many criticized the organization of the Church and others, including leading churchmen, were distressed at the shortcomings of the clergy. Of 250 clergy in one diocese 171 could not say the Ten Commandments and 10 did not even know the Lord's Prayer. Tco many of the clergy were worldly and extravagant and paid only lip service to their priestly vows. While the monasteries accumulated great wealth in land and treasure, they decayed from within and the Pope himself was considering dissolving some of them. Good land was in great demand and many Englishmen looked enviously on the estates of the monasteries. With the Church controlled by the King it would be much easier to have the monasteries dissolved and the land sold. The separate system of Church courts had become increasingly unpopular since the days when Henry II fought with Thomas à Becket. Finally, nationalistic Englishmen resented the Pope's interference in their domestic affairs, particularly when he was himself ruler over territories in Italy and was allied to a foreign country, and they

MONASTERIES

When Henry VIII came to the throne there were eight hundred monasteries in England. By 1540 all of them had been dissolved and their lands and buildings sold. Some monastic buildings were used by their new owners as mills or farm buildings. Others were dismantled in whole or part and the materials used to construct other buildings. One eyewitness wrote: "It would have made an heart of flint to have melted and wept to have seen the breaking up of the house and the sorrowful departing. . . . Some persons . . . went in and took what they found, filched it away. . . . It would have pitied any heart to see what tearing up of the lead there was and plucking up of boards and throwing down of the spars."

objected strongly to the constant flow of English money into the papal treasury.

For these reasons most Englishmen supported Henry in his break **Opposition** with Rome, an event which is commonly, if somewhat inaccurately, called the English Reformation. There were those who did not, however, and Henry's onslaught upon them was savage and showed once more that he would tolerate no opposition. Sir Thomas More, a brilliant scholar, and Bishop Fisher were beheaded because they refused to accept Henry as head of the Church. Some courageous monks suffered torture and execution for their loyalty to the Pope. A large revolt in the North, known as the Pilgrimage of Grace, was put down, with difficulty, and the leaders were punished with ferocious cruelty. By 1537 Henry had triumphed over all opposition and although excommunicated by the Pope still retained the loyalty of his subjects. A year earlier he had tired of Anne Boleyn, whom he had executed, and when in 1537 his third wife gave birth to a son, Henry believed that God had approved all that he had done.

From the beginning to the end of his dispute with the Pope, Henry **Role of** had acted through Parliament, for he wanted the support of the nation **Parliament** in his actions. He had encouraged the members to think of themselves

THE EXECUTION OF SIR THOMAS MORE

Sir Thomas More was one of the noblest and most learned men in sixteenth-century England. His famous book "Utopia" (1516) criticizes political and social evils in England and paints a glowing picture of an imaginary kingdom, Utopia, in which these evils do not exist. His wit, learning, and personality so attracted Henry VIII that he showered many honours upon More and eventually made him Lord Chancellor of England. When Henry VIII launched his attack upon the Pope, More resigned his high post. In 1535 he was executed for his refusal to recognize Henry as head of the Church. More remained cheerfully courageous to the end. As he ascended the rickety scaffold he said to his attendant, "I pray you, Mr. Lieutenant, see me safe up, and for my coming down let me shift for himself." After praying, he spoke to his executioner, "Pluck up thy spirits, man, and be not afraid to do thine office. My neck is very short; take heed, therefore, thou shoot not awry."

as important people and of Parliament as a partner in government. From 1529 to 1536 Parliament had remained in session for many months at a time. The Commons, particularly, gained from this experience and for the first time became more important than the House of Lords. Above all, Henry had asked Parliament to participate in carrying out a religious and political revolution. Henceforth it would be difficult for any king to deny Parliament some real share in the government of the country. Parliament was no longer just the king's servant and it had some ambitions to be his partner. Within a century it was determined to be his master.

Throughout his reign Henry provided the nation with a succession of queens (in all he had six wives) and an inexhaustible source of gossip. As he grew older the handsome monarch of 1509 became bloated and ugly. So fat was he that a special carriage had to be built to move him upstairs and he could barely squeeze through an ordinary doorway. As his body was increasingly tormented with disease, he became more cruel and ferocious. An invasion from Scotland enraged him and he instructed the commander of the army to sack and burn, "putting man, woman and child to fire and sword without exception", until "not one stick stand by another, sparing no creature alive".

Yet, as he lay on his deathbed, both King and subjects looked back on a reign full of great accomplishments. The country was peaceful and prosperous. Wars with France, though they had drained the treasury so carefully built up by his father, had stimulated national pride, and Wales had been incorporated into England. The Scots had been defeated at Flodden in 1513, although Henry's attempts to force them into an alliance were unsuccessful. Above all, he had begun the revolution in religion that we call the Reformation by establishing a national Church, Catholic in doctrine but under the headship of the nation's king.

However, the Reformation was not yet over. Changes in the government of the Church paved the way for changes in doctrine as well. Even during Henry's reign there was a strong and growing sentiment in favour of Protestantism. Moreover, there were still many Englishmen who wished to see the Pope's power restored in England. For eleven years after Henry's death the English nation underwent the greatest crisis of the Tudor period. Controversy over religion threatened to destroy the unity of the nation and the stability of the government.

Religious Controversy 1547-1558

During the short reign of Henry's son, Edward VI, from 1547 to 1553, the government-controlled Church moved rapidly towards Protestantism. In these years, the scholarly Thomas Cranmer, Archbishop of Canterbury, inspired and fashioned the superb prose of the Book of Common Prayer which became, and still remains, the basis of the Anglican ritual.

Edward VI 1547-1553

In 1553 Edward was succeeded by his Roman Catholic half-sister Mary, the daughter of Catherine of Aragon. With the enthusiastic support of her husband, King Philip of Spain, Mary attempted to restore Roman Catholicism in England. The use of the Book of Common Prayer was abolished and most of Henry's Acts were repealed. Those who opposed these actions were savagely repressed. A statute passed in 1401 titled *De Heretico Comburendo (Concerning the Burning of Heretics)* ordered that:

Mary I 1553-1558

89

No one either openly or secretly shall preach, teach, or impart anything, or compose or write any book, contrary to the Catholic faith or the decisions of Holy Church . . . or the sheriff shall have them burned before the people in some prominent place, so that such punishment shall inspire fear in the minds of others and prevent such nefarious doctrines and heretical and erroneous opinions . . . from being supported or in any way tolerated.

Mary revived and made effective use of this Act. During her five-year reign some three hundred Protestant heretics were burned at the stake, among them Archbishop Cranmer and Bishops Ridley and Latimer. Had Mary lived longer she might have succeeded in her plans to restore the old religious order, although the revulsion that followed the burning of the old and frail Archbishop did not speak well for her success. As one contemporary said, "The burning of the Archbishop hath harried the Pope out of the land."

By the time Mary died in 1558 the fierce fires of religious conflict threatened to engulf the nation. It remained to be seen whether her successor, Henry VIII's last heir, could extinguish them.

LATIMER AND RIDLEY

The most notable victims of Mary's crusade to stamp out Protestantism were Bishops Latimer and Ridley and Archbishop Cranmer. Latimer and Ridley were burned together at the stake at Oxford. As the fire was being kindled, Latimer cried out, "Be of good comfort, Master Ridley, and play the man. We shall this day light such a candle, by God's grace, in England, as I trust shall never be put out." The frail old Archbishop Cranmer recanted his Protestantism seven times before his death. Finally his courage returned and proclaiming his real faith, he put into the flames first the unworthy hand that had signed his recantation.

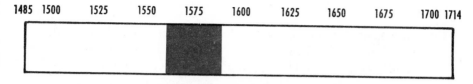

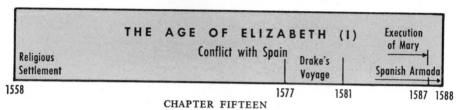

THE AGE OF ELIZABETH (I)

Conflict with Spain

Religious Settlement

Drake's Voyage

Execution of Mary

Spanish Armada

1558   1577   1581   1587 1588

CHAPTER FIFTEEN

THE ELIZABETHAN EPIC

As Elizabeth's coronation procession moved slowly towards West- *Elizabeth I* minster, the spectators who had feared the accession of another woman *1558-1603* must have been reassured. The proud, erect figure and the keen, flashing eyes proclaimed that here, indeed, was the daughter of Henry VIII. Like her father, Elizabeth was equally at home in the saddle, the ball-room, the library, and the Council chamber. The new Queen was intelligent, shrewd and tactful. Few women have known how to choose and handle men better than the daughter of Anne Boleyn. But as there had been two Henrys, so there were two Elizabeths—the gay, witty flirt who enjoyed the attentions of an army of suitors, and the some-times violent and angry shrew who boxed the ears of her advisers when she was displeased with them. Yet the Queen had an instinctive under-standing of her people, to whom she gave her chief love. Her subjects responded with a devotion that came to be close to worship.

Many dangers beset Elizabeth on her accession but she feared nothing *The Religious* more than division among her people. Her first concern was to quiet *Settlement* the religious conflict she had inherited from Mary, and her plan for the English Church was designed to appeal to as many of her people as possible. Her first Parliament in 1559 passed a new Act of Supremacy which again repudiated the power of the Pope and made Elizabeth the supreme ruler in Church and State. The Act of Uniformity required all Englishmen to adopt one form of worship which was to be based on Cranmer's Prayer Book revised to please those who preferred the accustomed form of worship. The basic beliefs of the Church of England were summed up and established in the Thirty-nine Articles.

To the many men of the time who were more concerned with national unity and political stability than with matters of religious

91

faith, these measures seemed to offer an acceptable compromise—a Church still largely Catholic in organization and ritual but partly Protestant in doctrine. But, like all compromises, the Elizabethan Church won

ENGLISH REFORMATION 1529-1603

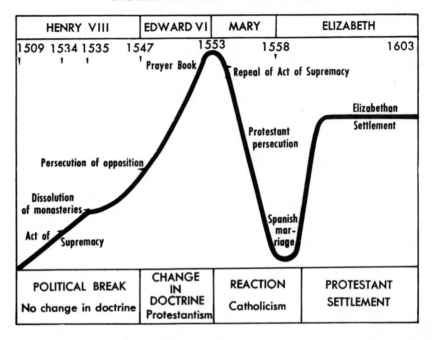

HENRY VIII	EDWARD VI	MARY	ELIZABETH
POLITICAL BREAK No change in doctrine	CHANGE IN DOCTRINE Protestantism	REACTION Catholicism	PROTESTANT SETTLEMENT

firm friends very slowly. Many devout Roman Catholics refused to give up their faith. Another group wanted to eliminate everything in the Church that was associated in their minds with Roman Catholicism. Since these people wanted a "purer" form of worship, they soon came to be called Puritans.

The Puritans believed that no priest was needed to interpret God's word as revealed in the Bible. They objected, therefore, to everything in the Prayer Book, like the use of the Cross in baptism, which could suggest that the priest had special power to transmit God's grace to men. To them, the robes traditionally worn by the clergy were "the livery of the Pope" and the use of music in the service sheer paganism. "The service of God," they argued, "is grievously abused by piping with organs, singing, ringing and trawling songs from one side to another;

92

with the squeaking of chanting choristers disguised in white surplices."

The Puritans also argued against government of the Church by bishops. In their eyes, bishops were no better than "petty popes". Here

QUEEN ELIZABETH—"GOOD QUEEN BESS"

the Puritans ran foul of Elizabeth, for the appointment of bishops, and therefore, to a considerable extent, the control of the Church, was in her hands. Elizabeth naturally took their demand that bishops be abolished as a challenge to her supremacy and even as an attack on

93

the Crown. She saw them as "criminals whose desire it is to destroy allegiance to princes". In those days no one believed that a state could tolerate differences of faith among its subjects. So, in weakening loyalty to the Established Church, the Puritans seemed to Elizabeth to be fomenting division within the nation and undermining loyalty to the State. To preserve her own authority and to keep the country united she set about to stamp out organized Puritanism. The movement went underground where it grew in strength to become one of the most difficult problems facing Elizabeth's successors.

The Roman Catholics The Roman Catholics posed an even more dangerous threat to the unity of the country and the authority of the Queen. In Catholic eyes Elizabeth, as the daughter of Henry and Anne Boleyn, was illegitimate and so had a doubtful right to the throne. Moreover, she was a heretic whom the Pope had excommunicated and declared deposed, thus releasing her subjects from their duty of obedience to her. The Pope and the Catholic powers of Europe were working to restore Catholicism in England and for most of the reign the country lay under the threat of invasion. In these circumstances English Catholics found themselves painfully divided between their loyalty to their faith and to their country. The question each had to face was: "If a Catholic invasion comes, which side will you take, the Queen's or the Pope's?" A few went further and asked themselves: "Should I help restore true religion by contriving the Queen's death?"

Mary Queen of Scots Danger first threatened Elizabeth from the north where the great-granddaughter of Henry VII, Mary Stuart, Roman Catholic Queen of Scotland, claimed to be the legitimate ruler of England. There were many people in England and abroad who supported the claims of the beautiful and impulsive Mary. But Mary's private life proved to be her undoing. There had been many strange rumours about the Scottish Queen and when the mysterious death of her second husband was followed, three months later, by her marriage to the man suspected of murdering him, the Scots had had enough of her. In 1568 Mary fled to England and threw herself on Elizabeth's mercy.

Elizabeth might well have had Mary put to death and so rid herself of a rival to the throne. Her generosity in not doing so was met by Mary's persistent plotting to secure the throne of England and restore Roman Catholicism. In this Mary had the support of King Philip of Spain, the champion of Catholicism in Europe. Finally, in 1587, her patience exhausted by these constant intrigues against her, Elizabeth had Mary beheaded. Meanwhile, Philip, tired of waiting for Elizabeth's overthrow from within the country, had decided to conquer England himself.

More than religion lay behind Philip's decision to attack England. **The Elizabethan Sea-Dogs** Since the days of Columbus, Spain had built up a vast empire in America. From Mexico and Peru, Spanish galleons sailed home with fabulous treasures from the gold and silver mines there. They were like a magnet which attracted daring English sailors thirsting for glory and gold.

One such freebooter, or sea-dog, was John Hawkins, a native of **John Hawkins** Plymouth. He had engaged in the profitable business of stealing Negroes

MARY QUEEN OF SCOTS

While in semi-captivity, Mary was a constant source of worry to Elizabeth and her subjects. Elizabeth's councillors pleaded with her time and time again to execute Mary, but the Queen refused. In 1583 a "Bond of Association" was drawn up which pledged the thousands who signed it to kill Mary if ever a plot should lead to Elizabeth's death. By 1585 the evidence of Mary's intrigues was too obvious to be ignored and she was tried and found guilty of treason. Parliament demanded that the death sentence be carried out, but Elizabeth continued to oppose her execution. Finally she reluctantly signed the death warrant in 1587. No sooner was Mary executed, however, than Elizabeth claimed it was all a mistake and that she had really not wanted her killed.

SLAVE-CATCHING ON THE AFRICAN COAST

Slave-catching was no easy business, as Hawkins found out on his second voyage to the African coast. After purchasing a number of slaves from Portuguese slavers, Hawkins and forty of his men landed at a Negro town, hoping to capture some slaves on their own. The Negroes fled at the approach of the Englishmen who broke up into small groups to search for gold in the native huts. The Negroes returned and, attacking fiercely, killed six members of the landing party and wounded many others. Hawkins returned to his ship with only ten Negroes. In time the coastal Negroes became the chief middlemen in the slave trade and sold great numbers of unfortunate Negroes into captivity.

from Portuguese slave-catchers off the coast of Africa and selling them to the Spanish colonists. It did not trouble him that Spain forbade foreigners to trade with her colonies. He was quite prepared to use force to open up markets, though once in the country he prided himself that he always made an honest bargain. Philip was infuriated by such "honest traders" and on his third expedition Hawkins found himself trapped in the Mexican port of Vera Cruz, where his vessels were battered by thirteen Spanish warships. Only two English ships returned from that expedition.

One of the ships that escaped was commanded by a brown-bearded mariner with steel-blue eyes, the prince of the courageous and gallant Elizabethan sea-dogs. Bold, daring and resolute, Francis Drake did **Francis Drake** not pretend that he carried on an honest business. He was out for loot, adventure, and a fight with the Spaniards. For twenty years he was the scourge of Spain and his name alone, *El Draco,* "the Dragon", inspired terror in the hearts of his enemies.

In 1577 Drake set out on his most famous voyage. Five years earlier he had looked out on the Pacific from a tree top in Panama and ever since his imagination had been fired by dreams of conquest in that

96

DRAKE'S REWARD

Drake returned from his fantastic exploits around the world in the autumn of 1580. As he anchored in Plymouth harbour the news that he had returned spread quickly and everyone hastened to the docks, much to the dismay of a preacher who looked down on rows of hastily emptied pews. Queen Elizabeth could not be too open in her approval, however, for the Spanish loot bulging in the holds of the "Golden Hind" would hardly please Philip of Spain. Drake was told to make himself scarce and went quietly away to serve his Queen.

ocean. Through the treacherous Magellan Strait, whose rocky coasts were littered with wrecks, he sailed in the teeth of a Pacific gale into a pirate's paradise. From Santiago to Valparaiso to Lima, along the west coast of South America, he sacked and plundered and sank unsuspecting Spanish ships until his *Golden Hind* could hold no more of the treasure of Spain. Knowing that a mighty Spanish squadron would be awaiting him if he returned by the way he had come, Drake sailed north, hoping to find a passage that would lead him safely back to the Atlantic. His quest was fruitless and he set his course westward across the Pacific, returning to England by way of the Cape of Good Hope, the first Englishman to have sailed around the world. At Deptford, near London, Queen Elizabeth knighted him, Sir Francis Drake, on the deck of his own ship.

The sea-dogs usually sailed with the Queen's blessing and sometimes with money of her own invested in their enterprises. In public, however, it was good policy for her to deplore their activities. She explained to the outraged Spanish ambassador, her face a picture of innocence, that their actions were beyond her control. Well might the Spanish

97

King rage as ship after ship entered Plymouth harbour, their holds laden with "pieces of eight" plundered from Spanish ships.

War in the Netherlands

Other events closer to home further damaged relations between England and Spain. In the Netherlands, then a part of the Spanish Empire, the Protestant Dutch revolted against Spanish rule. Philip was determined to crush their revolt and to re-establish Spanish power even more firmly in those lands. Elizabeth well knew that if Philip mastered the Netherlands he would have a convenient base from which to invade England. At first she gave the Dutch as much indirect and unofficial aid as she could without provoking war with Spain; but in 1585, with the Dutch tottering before the combined forces of Spain and France, she could hesitate no longer in coming openly to their aid. A small English army under the Earl of Leicester moved across the English Channel to support the rebels.

The Spanish Armada 1588

This meant war. The execution of Mary Queen of Scots in 1587 spurred Philip on and he began to assemble a vast invasion fleet. All Europe was convinced that England's days were numbered. Even the boldest English sailors felt that the odds against them were overwhelming. Believing that the best defence was to attack, the courageous Drake led a raid into the harbour of Cadiz in Spain, where the great Armada was being prepared, and sent thousands of tons of shipping to the bottom. In spite of such hampering tactics, however, the "Invincible Armada" was at last ready to sail in 1588. One hundred and thirty ships, carrying 27,000 men and 2400 guns, moved majestically towards the coast of England. Across the Channel in the Netherlands a great Spanish general, the Duke of Parma, waited with 30,000 men for the ships to secure control of the Channel and then ferry his troops across.

The English also waited. As a chain of flaming beacons signalled the Spaniards' approach, Queen Elizabeth went to the coast to give heart to her troops as they prepared for battle.

> Let tyrants fear . . . [she said] . . . I am come . . . at this time, not for my recreation and disport, but being resolved in the midst and heat of the battle to live or die amongst you all, to lay down for my God, and for my Kingdoms, and for my people, my honour and my blood, even in the dust. I know I have the body of a weak and feeble woman, but I have the heart and stomach of a King, and of a King of England too; and think foul scorn that Parma or Spain or any Prince of Europe should dare to invade the borders of my realm; to which rather than any dishonour shall grow by me, I myself will take up arms; I myself will be your general, judge, and rewarder of every one of your virtues in the field.

DEFEAT OF THE ARMADA, 1588

The smaller, faster English ships stayed to the windward of the giant Spanish fleet and poured a devastating fire upon it, rather than move in and board, as was customary in naval battles. As the galleons heaved over to manoeuvre into firing position, they were exposed below the water line, a vulnerable position of which the English gunners took full advantage. Many galleons began to leak so badly that they had to leave the battle. The middle decks of the Spanish ships were turned into slaughter houses as the cannon-balls rained down furiously on the masses of soldiers. The decks ran red with blood and English sailors reported having seen blood flow from the gunports as the ships tilted.

While the army waited, the navy, under Lord Howard, with Drake as second in command, put out to sea. Against the slow, awkward, and cumbersome floating fortresses of the Spaniards which were designed to enable armies to fight at sea, the English used light, fast and manageable vessels, little more than gun-platforms manned by sailors. For a week the English fleet harassed the Armada as it attempted to fight its way up the Channel. Then one night the English sent fireboats into the midst of the Spanish host in Calais harbour, forcing many galleons to slip anchor and move off in disorder. On the following day the English fleet attacked in full force, moving quickly among their slow-moving opponents and inflicting serious damage on them. Violent gales also came to the aid of the English as the Spaniards attempted their escape around Scotland and many a galleon ended as a battered wreck along the rugged coast. Less than half the Spanish fleet and one-third of the men who had manned it ever saw Spain again. English seamanship and courage, English gunnery, and English gales had triumphed over the galleons of Spain.

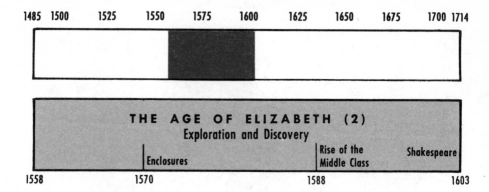

1485 1500 1525 1550 1575 1600 1625 1650 1675 1700 1714

THE AGE OF ELIZABETH (2)
Exploration and Discovery

Enclosures

Rise of the Middle Class

Shakespeare

1558 1570 1588 1603

CHAPTER SIXTEEN

ELIZABETHAN ENGLAND

Compared with the turbulent years before the Armada, the last fifteen years of Elizabeth's reign were relatively quiet. With the Catholic powers of Europe momentarily subdued, the threat of invasion no longer hung over the land. The danger of a Catholic uprising in England had been removed. However, Elizabeth's last years were not unimportant. Profound social and economic forces were changing the structure of Tudor society, stimulating voyages of trade and discovery, and creating new problems with which the Queen and her successors would have to deal.

The Growth of the Middle Class

The middle ranks of Englishmen—the merchants, the lawyers, the landowners who were neither nobles nor yeomen working their own land —were growing so rapidly in numbers, wealth, and unity of outlook as to become a new class and a new centre of power in English society.

The Boom

One reason for their rise was a more plentiful supply of money. After Spain's conquest of Mexico and Peru, a steady stream of silver from the mines there flowed from the New World to Spain and from Spain to the rest of Europe. It caused what we would call a boom. On the one hand, since people had more money to spend, trade and manufacturing grew apace to supply the new demand. On the other hand, because so much more money was in circulation, the price of goods kept going up. Merchants and manufacturers flourished and so did some landowners, since the growing towns needed more and more of the produce of the countryside. However, landlords often found that they could not make the most of these new opportunities without drastic changes in the way they managed their estates. The demand for wool was particularly strong, and landlords were tempted to evict their

100

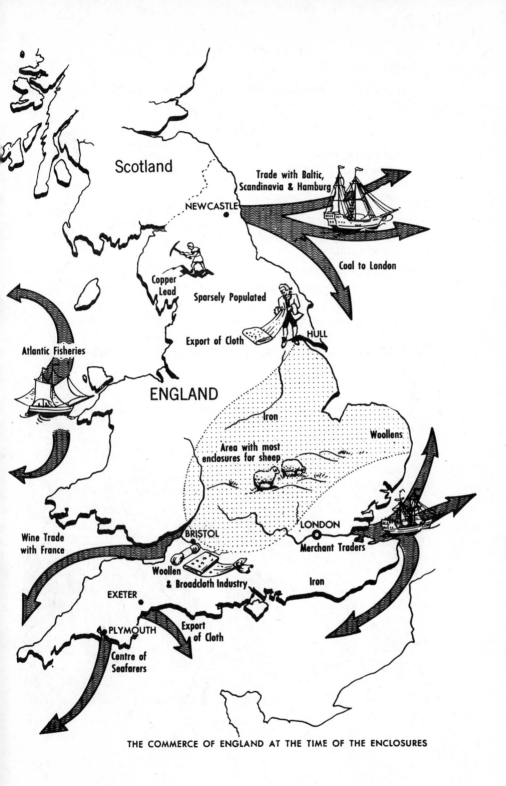

THE COMMERCE OF ENGLAND AT THE TIME OF THE ENCLOSURES

tenants and turn farm land into fenced sheep pastures. Many public-spirited Englishmen deplored such developments:

> I will tell you in one country where I came I saw a strange wonder; for, whereas in many other countries men did use to eat the sheep, in that country sheep had eaten up both the men and their houses. For in the pastures, where I saw great flocks of sheep feeding, I might, near unto certain footpaths, behold here and there a piece of an old stone causeway which had been in times past some street or by-lane in some town or village, but now there was neither house nor town nor man left more than the shepherd and his sheepish master to look upon them.

The Enclosures Less destructive of the peasants' old way of life was the plan of improving crop yields by consolidating the scattered strips of the old open fields into compact hedged "enclosures", so that each man could use his own land as he thought best. Yet enclosures of either of these kinds affected a relatively small part of the countryside. Not until well after Wolfe took Quebec did the old mediæval open fields disappear

TENANT EVICTION

TUDOR POVERTY AND PROSPERITY

The economic changes in Tudor England had good and bad results. The landlords who evicted their tenants in order to enclose large areas for pasture became wealthy themselves and could afford to build mansions. The evicted tenants, on the other hand, drifted to the cities or became beggars and vagrants. One beggar lamented: "Vorsooth, I am as honest a man's son as the best of them were, but vortune (Call you her a saint? Rather a devil) hath left me a beggar; and yet my vather a good yeoman, and lived many a winter's season in good repentation [reputation], and kept a homely house among his neighbours, and brought up his children cleanly so long as our old lease and landlord dured."

completely. Many landlords "improved" their estates simply by raising their tenants' rents! But it is only fair to say that landlords who did not do so had a hard time making ends meet in face of rising prices.

The innovations of improving landlords had important social and political consequences. The middling landowners, or gentry, grew in wealth and importance and took the place of the old nobility as the dominant group in the countryside. The tenants turned off the land to **Social** make way for sheep often found it hard to get work. Some went to the **Distress** towns but others became beggars and vagabonds. The problem they posed was so serious that Parliament tried again and again to devise a ways of getting them back to work and at the same time of relieving the suffering of those truly unable to work. One of these attempts, the Poor **The Elizabethan** Law of 1572, began: **Poor law**

> Where all the parts of this Realm of England and Wales be
> presently with Rogues, Vagabonds, and Sturdy Beggars exceed-
> ingly pestered, by means whereof daily happeneth in the
> same Realm horrible murders, thefts, and other great out-

103

rages, to the high displeasure of Almighty God, and to the great annoy of the Common Weal. . . .

The Expansion of Trade   The expansion of trade and commerce was even more important than the changes in land-holding practices. More money, a plentiful supply of labour, and larger markets acted together to bring about changes that foreshadowed the Industrial Revolution of the eighteenth century. Great advances were made in coal and iron mining, ship-building, and the manufacture of a wide range of goods. The chief industry, however, remained the making of cloth. Always famous for her wool, England now began to replace exports of raw wool by exports of finished cloth. Merchants purchased the raw wool and distributed it to spinners, mainly agricultural labourers and their wives, who worked on it in their homes. An agent picked it up and took it to the weaver who performed the next operation, and so on until the cloth was finished and ready to be shipped and sold. This system, known as the "putting-out system", enabled many ambitious men with little money to get started on the road to fortune.

Overseas Trade and Exploration   Other Englishmen found that wealth and glory could be gained in the expansion of England's overseas trade. The penetration of English traders into remote parts of the world was less spectacular than the defeat of the Spanish Armada but of no less importance in the history of Britain. Enterprising merchants formed companies to trade wherever trade could be found. The Muscovy Company brought back goods from Russia and the Baltic. The Levant Company carried the treasures of Baghdad and Damascus to England where they stirred the imaginations, clothed the bodies, and stimulated the appetites of the Elizabethans. English merchants sailed to India and the fabled Spice Islands of the South Seas. When Elizabeth signed a charter to create the East India Company in 1600, she had set England on the road to empire in Asia.

The Search for the North-West Passage   Other daring Elizabethan seamen, like Martin Frobisher and John Davis, lured on by the prospect of wealth to be gained, sought the elusive North-West Passage around America to China. Their expeditions into the ice-packed Arctic Ocean greatly increased geographical knowledge but they discovered neither wealth nor a passageway. A search for a North-East Passage was no more successful.

In 1583 English expansion took another important step when Humphrey Gilbert attempted to establish a settlement in Newfoundland, off whose banks the English had fished since Cabot's voyage in 1497. **Sir Walter Raleigh**   Two years later, in 1585, the dashing courtier, poet, and explorer, Sir Walter Raleigh, tried to plant a colony in America, naming it Virginia

104

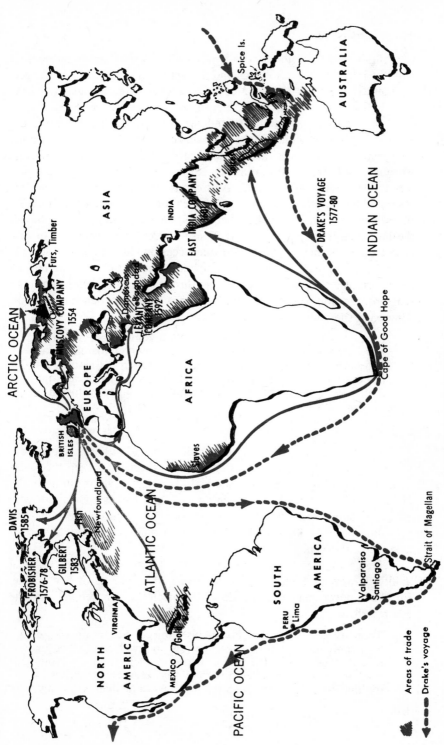

THE EXPANSION OF ELIZABETHAN ENGLAND

ARCTIC OCEAN

Furs, Timber

MUSCOVY COMPANY
1554

EUROPE

ASIA

AUSTRALIA

Spice Is.

INDIA

EAST INDIA COMPANY

DRAKE'S VOYAGE
1577-80

Damascus
LEVANT Baghdad
COMPANY
1592

Cape of Good Hope

INDIAN OCEAN

AFRICA

Slaves

BRITISH
ISLES

DAVIS
1585

FROBISHER
1576-78

GILBERT
1583

Fish

Newfoundland

VIRGINIA

ATLANTIC OCEAN

NORTH
AMERICA

MEXICO

Gold

SOUTH
AMERICA

PERU
Lima

Valparaiso
Santiago

Strait of Magellan

PACIFIC OCEAN

Areas of trade

Drake's voyage

after his Queen. Both these attempts failed, but Raleigh is credited with the introduction of tobacco and the potato into Europe. Moreover, he pointed the way for other colonizers who were to make the next half-century a great period of English colonization in America.

The Middle-Class Puritans, and Parliament

The middle-class merchants and the wealthy landlords were often Puritan in their religion. From the benches of the House of Commons they were soon to make their voices heard. Like her father, however, Elizabeth believed that Parliament existed to serve her and that she was the real ruler of England. As long as the members of Parliament restricted themselves to discussions of such matters as wages, enclosures, the poor laws, and trade, Elizabeth was content. At times, however, the increasingly strong and vocal House of Commons ventured to discuss matters of high policy. On one occasion, like an angry schoolmistress, the Queen informed Parliament bluntly that such matters as her marriage, the succession to the throne, foreign policy, and the religious question were her business and not theirs. When the occasion demanded she could speak very sharply:

> I have in this assembly found much dissimulation, where I have always professed plainness, that I marvel thereat; yea, two faces under one hood, and the body rotten. ! . . . And . . . beware however you prove your Prince's patience as you have now mine. And now to conclude, all this notwithstanding (not meaning to make a Lent of Christmas) the most part of you may assure yourselves that you depart in your Prince's grace.

Elizabeth was an extremely able politician and although Parliament was growing in strength she was able to control it. To keep the Commons from getting out of hand, she had her ablest advisers sitting in the House, ready to defend the Queen's policy and frown upon those who were too outspoken against it. She took an interest in elections and sometimes let it be known that "the Queen would be pleased" if certain men were returned.

Elizabeth and Her Subjects

There was more to her management of Parliament than political ability, however. She had won the love and reverence of her people. Elizabeth never married; she devoted herself to her people and she assured them:

> There is no prince that loveth his subjects better, or whose love can countervail our love; there is no jewel, be it of never so rich a prize, which I prefer before this jewel; I mean your love, for I do more esteem it than any treasures or riches— for that we know how to prize, but love and thanks I count

ELIZABETHAN THEATRE

London's first permanent theatre was built in 1576. By the end of the century there were eight theatres built along both banks of the Thames. Most of them were simple circular structures enclosing an open-air courtyard and surrounded by tiers of covered galleries. The stage, supported by trestles, projected from one side of the courtyard. Over the stage was a ceiling supported by two pillars on each side. At the back was a second, or rear stage, which actors entered and left by two doors on either side. Overlooking this rear stage was a balcony with windows. Most of the action took place on the front stage, while the rear stage was used to indicate some definite interior. Little scenery was used and locality was indicated by a placard. There were no actresses in Shakespeare's time, and the parts of women were played by boys.

inestimable. And though God hath raised me high, yet this I count the glory of my crown—that I have reigned with your loves.

Her subjects responded with enthusiasm. One playwright wrote:

Are you then travelling to the temple of Eliza?
Even to her temple are my feeble limbs travelling. Some call her Pandora, some Gloriana, some Cynthia, some Belphoebe, some Astrea—all by several names to express several loves. Yet all these names make but one celestial body, as all those loves meet to create but one soul.
I am one of her country, and we adore her by the name Eliza.

Elizabeth's reign was a great and glorious age, perhaps the greatest England has ever known; the Queen embodied its greatness and its glory and gave to it her name.

Perhaps the most glorious pages in the history of Elizabethan England were written by Elizabethan poets and playwrights. Challenged

107

by great issues and inspired by national pride and confidence, they produced some of the greatest imaginative literature in the history of the
world. Running through all of their writings was a profound love of
England and her monarch. Towering above the rest was William
Shakespeare, the embodiment of the brilliance of Elizabethan England.
In his hands English achieved a force and perfection seldom equalled
in any language. Like his contemporaries, Shakespeare reflected the
intense nationalism and patriotism of Elizabethan England. Few men
have not been moved by his tribute to his country:

> This royal throne of kings, this scepter'd isle,
> This earth of majesty, this seat of Mars,
> This other Eden, demi-Paradise,
> This fortress built by Nature for herself
> Against infection and the hand of war,
> This happy breed of men, this little world,
> This precious stone set in the silver sea,
> Which serves it in the office of a wall,
> Or as a moat defensive to a house,
> Against the envy of less happier lands,
> This blessed plot, this earth, this realm, this England.

Before many years had passed "this royal throne of kings" was to be
ravaged by civil war. When the great Queen died in 1603 old problems
were still demanding settlement and new problems were arising. For
forty-five years she had succeeded in ruling England where many another
might have failed. It remained to be seen whether her Scottish successor could follow her example and somehow reconcile royal authority
with the aspirations of his subjects.

Literature

William Shakespeare 1564-1616

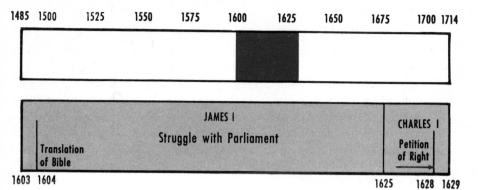

CHAPTER SEVENTEEN

THE STUART FAILURE: 1603-1629

"James I, King of England."   To James Stuart, son of Mary Queen of Scots, and ruler of Scotland, the words had a pleasant ring.   He was Elizabeth's closest male relative and he had been waiting impatiently for her death.   For though the Queen had been hesitant about naming her successor, it seemed likely that James would be her heir.   At last in March 1603, a weary horseman clattered into the courtyard of Holyrood Palace in Edinburgh bearing the news that Elizabeth was dead and that James was to succeed her.   The new King of England was eager to be off, for England, he felt, was a stage worthy of his great talents.

James I
1603-1625

His new subjects hailed their foreign King with enthusiasm. "The people of all sorts rode and ran, nay rather flew, to meet him, their eyes flaming nothing but sparkles of affection, their mouths and tongues uttering nothing but sounds of joy."   The conceited James did not realize that the peaceful succession of any king would have been welcomed with equal warmth by a people long troubled by Elizabeth's refusal to marry and the fear that her death might cause a struggle for the succession.

No one was impressed with the King's appearance.   Large goggling eyes stared vacantly from an over-large head.   A thin beard straggled aimlessly over his chin.   A tongue too large for his mouth blurred his speech and "made him drink very uncomely, as if eating his drink, which came out into the cup of each side of his mouth."   Broomstick legs barely supported the awkward body, made even more undignified by the padded clothes designed to protect him against the knives of assassins whom the King imagined lay perpetually in wait for him.

109

Yet James I had many qualities desirable in a king. He had a keen mind and a "sense of the dignity of kingship". He was clever and learned, skilful and witty in debate. In his desire that Roman Catholics should be allowed to follow their faith, his views were more advanced than those of his subjects. At another time in England's history he might have been a successful ruler. England in 1603, however, would have taxed the ingenuity and ability of any monarch. The Puritans and the middle class were becoming increasingly difficult to control. An ambitious and determined House of Commons was but a reflection of their growing strength.

— James vs. Parliament

The Scottish James did not understand the new forces in English society, nor did he know how Elizabeth had been able both to dominate and to co-operate with Parliament to make her system of government work. James was not a tyrant who wished to destroy the liberties of the people and the power of Parliament, as some historians have said. He wanted only to rule as his Tudor predecessors had done. It was the representatives of the new classes in the House of Commons who wanted to make changes and who demanded more power for Parliament. We can see now that the changes they demanded were essential for the development of parliamentary government. In 1603, however,

WHO SHALL RULE?

110

they were radicals, people who wished to upset the constitution. In opposing them, James I and his son, Charles, had both law and tradition on their side. Basically, the struggle of the seventeenth century between king and Parliament was to see which would be supreme. For that reason the seventeenth century is, perhaps, the most important period in English history.

Throughout the reigns of James I and Charles I the struggle for political power centered mainly on questions of religion and finance. To understand what happened, it is necessary to remember that the Stuart kings were poor. The king's need for money and Parliament's insistence on its historic right to control taxation were at the root of most of the disputes. They also gave Parliament a way of forcing concessions from the king.

No sooner had James arrived in England than he was made aware **The Puritan** of the religious problem. Representatives of eight hundred clergymen **Problem** of Puritan sympathies met him at Hampton Court in 1604 and requested moderate changes in religious ceremony and doctrine. Enraged by some of the discussion, the King accused the Puritan clergymen of challenging his authority over the Church. He dismissed them, saying, "If this be all they have to say, I shall make them conform themselves or I will harry them out of the land or do worse." James was as good as his word and his actions against them drove the Puritans into active opposition to the monarchy. They were more than ever determined to use Parliament, in which many of their party sat, to carry out reforms the Crown was blocking. Before their dismissal, however, the clergy had agreed to publish a new edition of the Bible, which has come to be known as the King James version.

James' first meeting with Parliament in 1604 marked the beginning **The Financial** of an eighty-four-year struggle between king and Parliament. A miserly **Issue** House of Commons refused to grant him enough money to carry on the government of the country and James soon dismissed the members. Ten years later, still hopeful, he summoned his second Parliament, only to find that the Commons ignored his request for taxes and turned their attention to their grievances against him. After two stormy months of bitter but fruitless discussion, James dismissed Parliament again and sent four outspoken and offensive members to prison in the Tower of London.

To raise money James was forced to adopt measures which broke the spirit, if not the letter, of the law. The customs duties were increased on goods coming into the country. Wealthy subjects were

111

THE KING JAMES VERSION OF THE BIBLE
One permanent result of the Hampton Court Conference of 1604 was the decision to produce a new, uniform version of the Bible. Prior to this time Englishmen used several translations which contained variations in text and interpretation. James believed that a standard version, used by all preachers, would lead to uniformity of worship. Under his energetic direction, a group of fifty scholars and churchmen completed the difficult task of translation and the Authorized Version of the Bible was published in 1611. For more than three hundred years it remained the standard translation of the Bible in English and it is still the most popular version in England, Canada, and the United States. It is estimated that ninety million copies have been published in England alone. No other book has done more to mould the character, thoughts, language, and literature of the English people and to unite the English-speaking people throughout the world.

"urged" to make "voluntary" gifts to the King. Titles of nobility were sold, as were monopolies, which gave the purchaser the sole right to trade in or manufacture certain articles. Proclamations by the King and Council, rather than statutes passed by the King and Parliament, became the normal means of carrying on the government. An alert and jealous middle class soon regarded the King's devices as a deliberate attempt to escape dependence on Parliament for money. Common-law lawyers saw in the use of Proclamations a means whereby the King might make himself superior to the established law of the land. Parliamentarians, Puritans, and lawyers were soon united in opposition to the King.

The Catholic Question — Meanwhile, anti-Catholic feeling, born of the persecutions of Mary's reign and nurtured by the long war with Spain, was given fresh life by the attempt of a misguided Catholic, Guy Fawkes, to blow up the Parliament buildings in 1605. James' toleration of Roman Catholics

112

THE GUNPOWDER PLOT DISCOVERED

Roman Catholics in England hoped that James I, son of the Catholic Mary Queen of Scots, would remove the Elizabethan laws against their religion. Disappointed by the King's refusal, a small body of desperate and resolute Catholics planned to blow up the King, Lords, and Commons when they gathered for the opening of Parliament on November 5, 1605. The conspirators rented a cellar under the Houses of Parliament, stocked it with barrels of gunpowder, and arranged for a former soldier, Guy Fawkes, to light the torch. However, one of the plotters betrayed the conspirators and the unfortunate Fawkes was discovered before any damage was done. As a result of the plot, feeling against the Catholics increased and laws against them were made more severe.

became increasingly suspect. By 1621, when James again summoned a Parliament, the religious issue had come to the front to make the problem of governing England more difficult for him than ever.

An obstinate and surly House of Commons gave the King only a fraction of the money he requested and proceeded immediately to criticize his peaceful foreign policy and the proposed marriage of his son, Charles, to a Spanish princess who was a Roman Catholic. Such matters had always been the exclusive concern or *prerogative* of the king and James bluntly told the Commons to mind their own business and not meddle in affairs "whereof they were ignorant". He wrote to the Speaker of the House of Commons:

The Parliament of 1621

> We have heard . . . to our great sorrow that our distance from the Houses of Parliament hath emboldened some fiery and popular spirits of some of the House of Commons to argue and debate publicly matters far above their reach and capacity . . . These are therefore to command you to make known in our

113

name unto the House that none therein shall presume henceforth to meddle with anything concerning our Government or deep matters of State, and namely, not to deal with our dearest son's match with the daughter of Spain.

In the past the Commons had often trembled before Elizabeth's wrath, but now they defiantly answered James' outburst with a "Protestation" stating that "the arduous and urgent affairs concerning the King, the State, and defence of the realm and the Church of England . . . are proper subjects of counsel and debate in Parliament." Such a claim had never been made before and the furious King tore the protest from the journals of the House and dissolved Parliament.

The King, however, could not govern without Parliament. When, in spite of his policy of peace, war with Spain broke out in 1624, James was forced to come before a new Parliament and plead for money. Again the Commons granted a sum insufficient to carry on the government and seized the opportunity to appoint a commission to watch over its spending. Then they proceeded to impeach Bacon and Cranfield, two of the King's leading ministers. They accused them of high treason and brought them to trial before the House of Lords. To remedy one abuse, as well as to weaken the King's power and to strike at his methods of raising money, they passed an act prohibiting him from selling monopolies. Shortly after his humiliating surrender to an ambitious and truculent House of Commons, James I died and left the throne and his difficulties to his son Charles.

Charles I vs. Parliament On his accession in 1625 King Charles found that Parliament not only refused to grant enough money to allow him to fight an effective war against Spain, but also blamed him for the military failures that followed. Moreover, the Commons began a furious attack on the Duke of Buckingham, the King's favourite minister. Outraged, Charles dissolved Parliament and resorted to extreme measures to obtain money. He demanded loans from the people and imprisoned those who refused to make them. Attempts were made to draft people without money into the army. Lack of funds made it necessary for the King to billet troops in private homes. The wild conduct of the soldiers and unrest among the people forced him to place sections of the country under martial law, which meant that army officers acted as judges over civilians. In spite of these desperate measures, by 1628 the government was bankrupt and Charles was forced to call Parliament. It was to be a crucial session.

SOLDIERS BILLETED IN A PRIVATE HOME

Charles pleaded with Parliament for co-operation. Parliament's Petition of Right 1628 answer was the Petition of Right, a document which, with Magna Carta, is a milestone along the road to parliamentary government. The Petition declared that there should be no taxation without the consent of Parliament, that no man could be imprisoned without a lawful reason being given, and that the use of martial law and the billeting of troops in private homes were illegal. After lengthy delay a reluctant Charles gave his consent and the Petition of Right became law. In return the Commons voted him the money he wanted. Elated with success, the Commons went on to demand even more concessions from the King. Realizing that there would be no end to Parliament's demands which were aimed at wearing away his own power, Charles dismissed it.

Some Englishmen sympathized with Charles, for in their minds Parliament was going too far. It was one thing to restrain the power of a king who sometimes misused it; it was another to upset the system of government by increasing the power of Parliament at the king's expense. One such man was Thomas Wentworth a leading member of the Commons, who switched sides and eventually became Charles I's principal adviser.

The Parliament of 1629

In 1629 Parliament met again. The members were concerned over the apparent revival of Roman Catholic practices within the Church of England, a revival which they knew was encouraged by the King and his ministers. Charles realized at once that nothing could be secured from this excited House of Commons and ordered Parliament to adjourn. But the House was in the hands of men who wanted to carry the struggle with the King to its bitter conclusion. Before the King's servants arrived to end the session, the doors of the Commons were locked. Several members held the Speaker in his chair. Amidst wild shouting and tumult, the members passed three momentous resolutions drawn up by John Eliot, the Puritan leader of the opposition to the King:

The Three Resolutions 1629

> Whosoever shall bring in innovation of religion, or . . . seek to extend or introduce popery . . . shall be reputed a capital enemy to this kingdom and commonwealth.

AN UNPOPULAR SPEAKER OF THE COMMONS

When Charles I ordered the Speaker to adjourn the unruly Commons in 1629, a contemporary wrote that ". . . as soone as praiers were ended, the Speaker went into the chaire, and delivered the Kinges command for the adjournment of the Howse until Tewsday sevenight following. . . . The Howse made him answere, that it was not the office of a Speaker to deliver any such command unto them, but for the adjournment of the Howse it did properly belong unto themselves, and after they had uttered some thinges they thought fitt to be spoken of, they would sattisfie the king." When Speaker Finch attempted to leave his chair, two young members held him down while others denounced him so violently that he shed an "abundance of tears . . . yet, notwithstanding the Speaker's extremitie of weeping . . . Sir Peter Hayman (a gentleman of his own county) bitterly inveighed against him, and tould him, he was sorrie he was a Kentish man, and that he was a disgrace to his country, and a blot to a noble familie. . . ."

116

Whosoever shall counsel or advise the taking and levying of the subsidies of tunnage and poundage, not being granted by Parliament . . . shall be likewise reputed an innovator in the government, and a capital enemy to the kingdom and the commonwealth.

If any merchant or person whatsoever shall voluntarily yield or pay the said subsidies . . . not being granted by Parliament, he shall likewise be reputed a betrayer of the liberties of England, and an enemy to the same.

After this forthright attack on the royal power, the Commons voted their own adjournment.

A crisis had been reached. The traditional form of government based on the supremacy of the Crown and co-operation between king and Parliament had broken down. Charles knew that government was impossible unless he or Parliament gave way. For twenty-six years he and his father had attempted to work the system of government they had inherited. They had failed. Unwilling to accept the supremacy of Parliament and unable to work with a Parliament which challenged his supremacy, Charles now embarked on an experiment of governing without it.

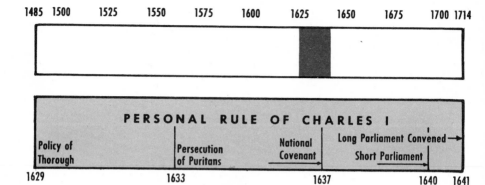

PERSONAL RULE OF CHARLES I

Policy of Thorough	Persecution of Puritans	National Covenant	Long Parliament Convened →
			Short Parliament

1629 — 1633 — 1637 — 1640 — 1641

CHAPTER EIGHTEEN

THE APPROACH TO WAR: 1629-1641

**Charles I
1628-1649**

The man who now undertook to rule England without Parliament was in some ways one of her most admirable kings. Charles I could not speak until he was five or walk until he was seven. Throughout his life he spoke hesitantly and with obvious difficulty. Yet the handsome Charles had the bearing and dignity of a king. Studious and cultured, he surrounded himself with painters, poets, and men of learning. He was courageous, kind and loyal. One who admired him said that those who knew Charles best loved him most and one who knew him very well wrote that "he was the worthiest gentleman, the best master, the best friend, the best husband, the best father and the best Christian that the age in which he lived produced." Like his father, Charles was a stubborn man with high principles. Always convinced that his position was correct, he was completely unwilling to compromise or sacrifice his principles and at times he was slippery and deceitful. All these qualities of character contributed to Charles' ultimate fate which was to die on the scaffold at the hands of an executioner.

Government Without Parliament

From the beginning of his experiment in personal rule, Charles realized that without parliamentary grants he could not afford the luxury of war. For this reason he concluded peace with France and Spain but, although this move cut down his expenses, it put no money in his treasury. Royal officials pored over ancient records to discover every possible means by which the King might increase his income. The search was fruitful, and soon a steady stream of money began to swell the royal exchequer. The government increased the customs duties, sold trade monopolies, Crown lands, titles of nobility, and even the stumps in the royal forests. The King's advisers discovered that by a law passed in

118

the reign of Edward I, every landowner with an income of £40 was required to become a knight. Each new knight had, of course, to pay a high fee for the honour. These fees added no less than £150,000 to the King's income within two years.

One device used by the King to raise money became notorious and caused a great deal of opposition. This was the collection of ship-money, an ancient tax usually imposed on seaports to provide ships for the navy in time of war. Now Charles demanded that the inland counties should pay it as well, even in time of peace. John Hampden, a wealthy Puritan and a prominent Parliamentarian, led the determined resistance to the payment of ship-money.

John Hampden and Ship-Money

By such methods Charles raised just enough money to carry on the government without Parliament. Although the King's measures fell within the letter of the law they offended its spirit and they aroused

CUSTOMS DUTIES—TUNNAGE AND POUNDAGE

One of the most important sources of permanent revenue for the Crown was the customs duties or "tunnage and poundage" levied on the value of some exported and all imported goods. "Tunnage" was a duty on each tun or cask of wine imported into England; "poundage" was a duty of so much per pound sterling on all imports and exports. From 1275 until the reign of Charles I, Parliament had granted these duties to the Crown for life, on the accession of every new monarch.

119

JOHN HAMPDEN AND SHIP-MONEY

When Charles I attempted to increase his revenue by levying a ship-money tax, John Hampden, a leading Puritan and wealthy Buckinghamshire squire, refused to pay the 20 shillings demanded from him. In a famous test case heard before the full bench of twelve judges he protested vigorously that the tax was illegal. The verdict went against Hampden by the narrow margin of seven votes to five, but many Englishmen considered that he had won a moral victory. While most Englishmen in 1638 accepted the verdict peacefully, it increased the discontent that was soon to express itself in civil war.

the opposition of all classes in the country. Those who objected too strenuously were thrown into the Tower of London.

Strafford and Laud

Charles' policy was known as "Thorough" and in carrying it out the King relied heavily on two advisers, Thomas Wentworth, now made Earl of Strafford by the King, and William Laud, the Archbishop of Canterbury. Strafford, who had been a Parliamentary leader, changed sides in 1629, believing that it was "far safer that the King should increase in power than that the people should gain an advantage over the King". He wished to see a vigorous, unified, efficient administration acting in the interests of the whole country. Like the King and Laud, he felt that Parliament acted only in the interests of the classes represented there and by so doing tended to break up society rather than bind it together.

Religious Policy

Under the able, zealous, and quick-tempered Archbishop Laud the policy of "Thorough" was applied to the field of religion as well. Laud felt that Puritanism undermined the unity and authority of the Church of England. He believed that religion was the cement that bound society together, and without it, society would crumble and fall apart. The most important thing was to recover the moral authority of the Church in society. He was less concerned with what men believed than with how they worshipped. As he said, "All that I laboured for in this particular was that the external worship of God in this Church might be kept up in uniformity and decency and some beauty of holiness."

Laud relentlessly crushed those who would not conform to the practices of the Church of England. One preacher was fined £10,000, flogged, placed in the pillory where his ears were cut off, his nose slit, and his cheeks branded "S.S." (Sower of Sedition). Some Puritan clergymen lost their positions and many were fined, while hundreds of ordinary folk sailed from England to found colonies in the New World where they might be able to worship as they pleased. In time the policy of "Thorough" in religion failed miserably. By 1640 all classes in the nation looked to Parliament as the only body that could restrain the King and remedy their grievances.

It was Laud who gave Parliament its chance. Not content with forcing his religious policy upon England, he attempted to make the

PURITANS LEAVING FOR AMERICA

It is not difficult to understand why many Puritans preferred to risk the dangers of a sea voyage to the New World rather than remain in England. One Puritan has left this description of his persecution: "The people fell upon me . . . and knocked me down, and kicked me, and trampled upon me . . . and put me into the hands of the constables . . . and bid them whip me and put me out of town. . . . And when they had led me to the common . . . there they fell upon me with their staffs and hedgestaves, and the constables and officers gave me some blows over my back with their willow rods and so thrust me amongst the rude multitude." On the whole, however, it was the desire for freedom to worship in their own way, rather than fear of violence or persecution that prompted many Puritans to emigrate.

121

THE NATIONAL COVENANT

Charles I's attempt to enforce Anglicanism throughout his entire kingdom angered Scottish Presbyterians of all classes. In 1638, the determined Scots swore to resist to the death the new religious changes and pledged themselves to "adhere to and defend the . . . true religion, and forbear practice of all novations in the matter of the worship of God till they be tried and allowed in free Assemblies and in Parliaments." Many Covenanters opened their veins and signed the document with their blood.

Presbyterian Scots adopt it as well. In 1637 he ordered that a new Prayer Book modelled after the English Book be used in Scottish churches. The Scots were furious. An angry woman gave the signal for revolt when she hurled a stool at the Bishop of Edinburgh as he read the new service. Within a few months thousands of Scots had signed a document known as the National Covenant in which they pledged never to rest until they had restored "the purity and liberty of the Gospel as it was established and professed".

Charles, who was King of Scotland as well as of England, proposed to punish his rebellious northern subjects. But the years of personal rule had left the government in a desperately weak condition. One of the King's advisers told him:

In the Exchequer there is found but £200. . . . The King's magazines are totally unfurnished of arms and sorts of ammunitions and commanders we have none, either for advice or execution. The people through all England are generally so discontented . . . as I think there is reason to fear that a greater part of them will be readier to join with the Scots than to draw their swords in the King's service.

122

The King refused to listen to his advisers and sent a ragged, poorly trained, and unenthusiastic army to the north against the Scots. Fortunately for Charles, a truce was arranged before any fighting began and his army disbanded with the enthusiasm of schoolboys at the end of term. At least one Anglican officer, however, was disappointed that he had seen no action. Writing to his father he expressed his hopes of—

> . . . rubbing, fubbing and scrubbing those scurvy, filthy, dirty, nasty, lousy . . . slovenly . . . loggerheaded, foolish, insolent, proud, beggarly, impertinent, absurd, grand-headed, villainous, barbarous, bestial, false, lying, roguish, devilish, long-eared, short-haired, atheistical, Puritanical crew of the Scotch Covenant.

Charles knew that sooner or later he would have to fight the Scots and he realized as well that only through Parliament could he obtain sufficient money to equip an army and keep it in the field. Thus in 1640 he summoned his first Parliament in eleven years. The members were not prepared to be conciliatory towards Charles. Not a shilling would they grant the King until he had heard their long list of complaints against his advisers and his rule without Parliament. Disappointed and enraged, Charles dissolved this "Short Parliament" within three weeks.

The Short Parliament 1640

Now the Scots forced the King's hand. Pouring across the border, they occupied the northern counties and announced that they would remain there until the King paid them £850 for every day they had been in England. With no money in the treasury, Charles had no alternative but to call Parliament again. His experiment in personal government had failed. He could only meet the Scottish menace by coming to terms with Parliament. Parliament knew this too and, backed by the whole nation, its members were determined to make such personal rule impossible in the future.

Within a six-month period in 1641 this Parliament, which was to become famous in history as the "Long Parliament", completely destroyed the old Tudor system of government. Parliament was henceforth to be called at least every three years and no king could in the future dissolve it before it had sat for fifty days. Taxes, including customs duties, could be levied only with the consent of Parliament. Special courts used by Charles to obtain money, such as Star Chamber, were abolished. To point up the lesson that Parliament was now master, the King's advisers, Laud and Strafford, were arrested and later executed.

The Long Parliament 1641

Up to this point Parliament and the great mass of the people were in complete agreement. They now had what they wanted, a king who could make laws or raise money only through Parliament. Government was to be a partnership, with one partner unable to act without the consent of the other. The way seemed paved for a new form of constitutional government.

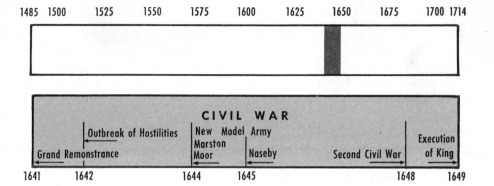

1485 1500   1525   1550   1575   1600   1625   1650   1675   1700 1714

CIVIL WAR

Outbreak of Hostilities	New Model Army			Execution
Grand Remonstrance	Marston Moor	Naseby	Second Civil War	of King

1641   1642   1644   1645   1648   1649

CHAPTER NINETEEN

THE CIVIL WAR: 1641-1649

Parliament did not long remain united in its opposition to Charles. **Divisions Within the Long Parliament** Within a year of the Long Parliament's first meeting the members had split into two groups whose differences were too great to be reconciled. All members had agreed at the start that the King's power must be limited and that Parliament should play a greater part in government. Beyond this point there was no agreement. Some members wanted to abolish virtually all royal power. Others, known as the root and branch group, wished only to make the Church of England Presbyterian, expel the bishops, abandon the Prayer Book, and introduce Presbyterian forms of worship and organization. No amount of discussion could resolve the many differences of opinion, and in time open disagreements led to civil war.

The immediate cause of the division within Parliament was a national rising of the Irish in October 1641 against English domination. All Englishmen were agreed that the rebellion must be put down, but many people asked if it were safe to put an army and money into the hands of the King. Might he not use it against Parliament and the Puritans, rather than against the Irish rebels? The radicals, led by John Pym— King Pym, some people called him—proposed to raise an army but to place control of it in Parliament's hands. This meant taking from the King one of his most important powers and many members of Parliament refused to agree to such a plan. The division of opinion was clearly revealed when Pym introduced into the Commons a docu- **The Grand Remonstrance 1641** ment known as the Grand Remonstrance. It contained proposals which, if adopted, would reduce the King's power over Church and State to almost nothing.

125

So heated was the debate on the Grand Remonstrance that some members "waved their hats wildly in the air" and others "took their swords in the scabbards out of their belts and held them by their pommels in their hands, setting the lower part on the ground." One eye-witness wrote:

> It passed so tumultuously two or three nights . . . that at three of the clock in the morning, when they voted it, I thought we had all sat in the valley of the shadow of death; for we, like Joab's and Abner's young men. had catched at each other's locks and sheathed our swords in each other's bowels, had not the great calmness of Mr. Hampden . . . led us to defer our angry debate until the next morning.

---

1. **Church doctrine and affairs to be regulated by Parliament.**

2. **Bishops to be relieved of all political power.**

3. **Purification of religious ceremony through the abolition of "superstitious ceremonies" and the "monuments of idolatry".**

4. **Royal ministers such as "Parliament may have cause to confide in".**

THE GRAND REMONSTRANCE, 1641

The Remonstrance passed the House of Commons by only eleven votes. The unanimity of a year before was gone.

Charles no longer stood alone in opposition to Parliament. The radicals had divided Parliament and had given the King a party. If he had been content to stand on his rights and to point out the illegality of what the radicals were asking, the King might easily have attracted enough support to discredit the radicals. But Charles blundered. Hearing a rumour that Parliament planned to arrest the Queen, he decided to imprison five leading members of the House of Commons. At the head of an armed force he invaded the House, only to find that the five members had been forewarned and had fled. A few days later, on January 10, 1642, the King left London and later he set up his standard at Nottingham, where he invited loyal followers to rally around him. The dispute was to be decided on the battlefield. By September 1642 the Civil War had begun.

The Civil War — 1642-1648   The Civil War was not fought between Parliament and the King, even though the Roundheads, as the radicals were called by the King's followers, professed to fight on behalf of Parliament, as did their opponents, the Cavaliers, on the side of the King. Parliament itself had split between the contending parties. While 302 members of the House of Commons and 40 members of the Lords supported Parliament, 236 Commoners and 80 Lords followed the King.

The country, too, was divided in its loyalties. Generally speaking,

CHARLES I ATTEMPTS TO ARREST THE FIVE MEMBERS

When Charles discovered that the five members had fled he seated himself in the Speaker's chair and addressed the House: " 'I am sorry for this occasion of coming unto you. Yesterday I sent a Sergeant at Arms . . . to apprehend some that by my command were accused of High Treason; where unto I did expect obedience and not a message . . . . You must know that in cases of treason no person hath a privilege. . . . Well, since I see all the birds are flown, I do expect . . . that you shall send them unto me as soon as they return hither . . . otherwise I must take my own course to find them.' The King, having concluded his speech, went out of the House again, which was in great disorder, and many members cried out aloud, so as he might hear them, 'Privilege! Privilege!' and forthwith adjourned until the next day."

the north and west were Royalist, while the south and east supported the Parliamentary radicals, but there were followers of both sides within each district and even within many families. Father fought against son, brother against brother, nephew against uncle. It was not a class war of rich against poor, but most of the great landlords became Cavaliers, for they feared that the lower classes might join the Roundheads and attempt to overthrow their masters. A popular ballad of the day was supposed to express the Roundheads' ambitions:

> Since then the anti-Christian crew
> Be prest and over-throwne,
> We'll teach the nobles how to crouch,
> And keep the gentry downe;
>
> Good manners hath an ill report,
> And turnes to pride we see;
> We'll therefore cry all manners downe,
> And hey then up go we.

127

CAVALIER AND ROUNDHEAD

For a long war the Parliamentary party had most of the advantages. The territory it controlled was more compact. It had the support of the large cities, particularly London, of the cloth towns and the ports, and it collected revenue from the customs. With few exceptions it controlled the merchant marine and the navy. Above all, the Parliamentary side found a military genius in a country gentleman, Oliver Cromwell.

Charles' hope was to win an early victory and at first it seemed that he might do so. The dashing Cavaliers were so successful that by the summer of 1643 Charles held sway over two-thirds of the country. But his enemies slowly gained strength. In September 1643 the Parliamentary party made an alliance with the Scots in return for a promise that if the war went in its favour, England would become Presbyterian. Meanwhile, in the eastern counties, Oliver Cromwell was forging one of the most amazing armies in England's history. The New Model Army was a dedicated fighting force, formed by iron discipline, tireless drill, and endless prayer. Known as Ironsides because of the armoured coats they wore, Cromwell's soldiers soon showed themselves superior to any opponent. At Marston Moor in 1644 Cromwell led them in a triumphant victory over the Cavaliers. In a letter written soon after the battle, Cromwell claimed no credit for the victory:

The New Model Army

> Truly England and the Church of God hath had a great favour from the Lord in this great victorie given unto us, such as the like never was since the War begunn. It had all the evidences

128

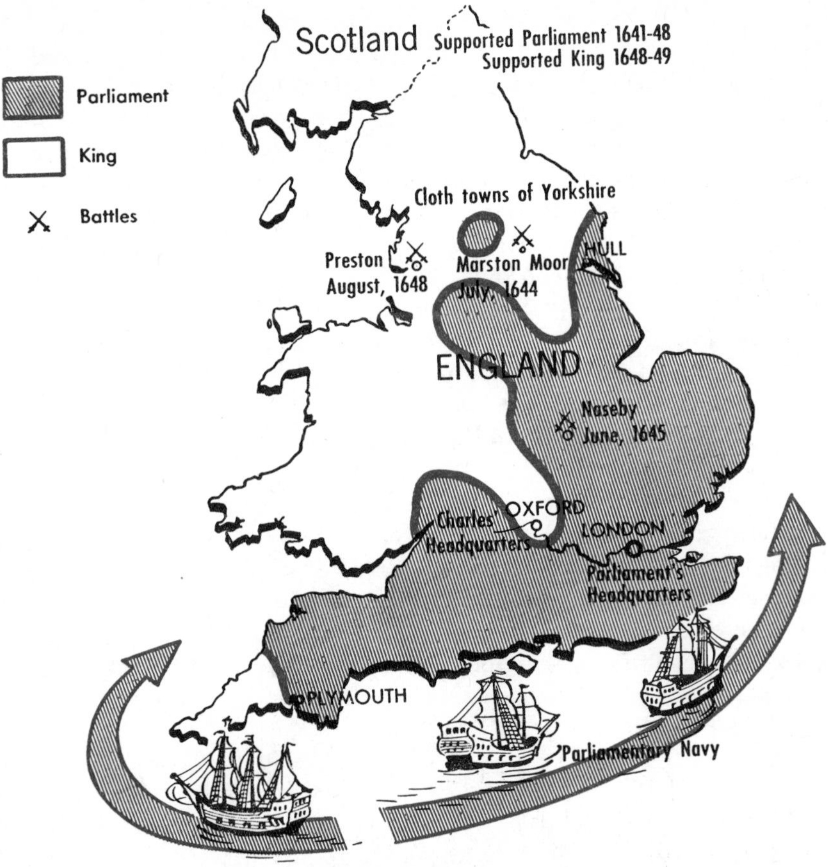
Scotland
Supported Parliament 1641-48
Supported King 1648-49
Parliament
King
Battles
Cloth towns of Yorkshire
Preston
August, 1648
Marston Moor
July, 1644
HULL
ENGLAND
Naseby
June, 1645
Charles' Headquarters
OXFORD
LONDON
Parliament's Headquarters
PLYMOUTH
Parliamentary Navy

THE CIVIL WAR, 1641-1649

> of an absolute Victorie obtained by the Lord's blessing upon the godly partye principally. Wee never charged but wee routed the enimie . . . God made them as stubble to our swords . . . I believe of twenty thousand, the Prince hath not four thousand left. Give glory, all the glory, to God.

From this time on the royalist forces "mouldered away by degrees". In June 1645 the New Model Army led by Cromwell and Sir Thomas Fairfax discovered the King's forces at Naseby and won another decisive victory. The next year was spent in actions against the scattered sections of the King's troops. His army defeated, Charles surrendered in 1646 to the Scots, who had invaded England to aid the Roundheads.

Naseby 1645

However, the victors soon discovered that there were many serious divisions among themselves on religious questions. The English Presbyterians, who had most of the seats in the House of Commons and were backed by the Scots, wanted a Presbyterian England. Another large group, the Independents, which found its greatest support in the Parliamentary army, believed that there should not be any state-controlled Church and demanded religious toleration for all except Roman Catholics and Anglicans. There were many other groups or sects representing every shade of religious opinion. Seeing these divisions among his opponents, Charles hoped to play one off against the other. He told the Scots he would accept Presbyterianism if they would help him reconquer England. When, in 1648, the Scottish Presbyterians moved south, the second Civil War had begun. It lasted only a few months. Oliver Cromwell hurried north to meet the invaders. Although outnumbered three to one, he won a brilliant and conclusive victory over the Scots at Preston.

The Second Civil War 1648

By persuading the Scots to invade England, Charles had sealed his own fate. Nothing could save him now. Disgusted with his double-dealing, the radical army leaders decided that the King must die. Because they knew that the predominantly Presbyterian Parliament would never consent to his execution, they sent a group of musketeers under Colonel Pride to the House of Commons to keep out or arrest

THE EXECUTION OF CHARLES I, 1649

An undergraduate of Christ Church, Oxford, described the execution of the King in his diary: "On the day of his execution, which was Tuesday, Jan. 30, I stood amongst the crowd in the street before Whitehalgate, where the scaffold was erected, and saw what was done, but was not so near as to hear any thing. The Blow I saw given and I can truly say with a sad heart; at the instant whereof, I remember well, there was such a Grone by the Thousands then present, as I never heard before and desire I may never hear again."

about 140 Presbyterian members. This action came to be known as Pride's Purge. The 90 members who were left after the Purge, and who made up what was called the Rump Parliament, immediately set up a commission to try the King for treason.

Pride's Purge 1648

The week-long trial which followed was a gross miscarriage of justice. The King had committed no crime known to English law. The body which tried him had no legal authority. Yet the verdict was "guilty", and the King was sentenced to death. On the 30th of January, 1649, calm and dignified, Charles faced his executioners before the palace at Whitehall as crowds in the gallery shouted "God Save the King." When his severed head was raised for all to see, a deep groan from the people drowned out the cheers of the soldiers.

The Trial and Execution of Charles I 1649

The Civil War was over. By 1649 the extremists had gained complete control of England. They had begun by trying to limit the power of the King; they had ended by killing him. They had once spoken for a united Parliament and people; in the end they helped to bring on a bloody civil war. Their problem now was to establish a government for the country, without a king and by means of a Parliament which by this time represented only a minority of Englishmen.

End of the Civil War 1649

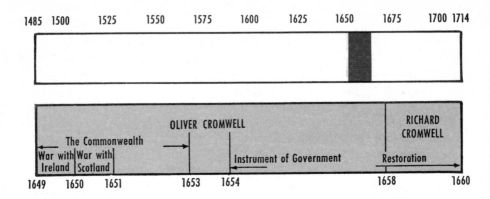

CHAPTER TWENTY

THE FAILURE OF OLIVER CROMWELL: 1649-1660

Oliver Cromwell
1649-1658

The eleven years after the execution of Charles I were dominated by Oliver Cromwell, one of the most interesting and puzzling figures in English history. Cromwell's determination and strength were obvious to all and they are apparent even today in his portraits. One man wrote:

> His body was well compact and strong, his stature [just] under six foot, his head so shaped as you might see it a storehouse and shop both of a vast treasury of natural parts. His temper was exceedingly fiery, as I have known, for the most part. . . . He was naturally compassionate towards objects in distress even to effeminate measure: though God made him a heart wherein was left little room for any fear but what was due to himself. . . . A larger soul, I think, hath seldom dwelt in a house of clay.

In every way Cromwell was a remarkable man. His deep personal religion was the dominant force in his life and he believed that he and his followers were chosen by God to rule on behalf of the "godly" people of England. Both as soldier and statesman he was convinced that he acted only as God's instrument. Moreover, his judgment, his courage, his fantastic energy marked him out as a leader of men.

The Irish Problem

After the execution of Charles, Cromwell's first task was to re-establish order in Ireland where a combination of Royalist and Irish forces threatened the new government. With an army of fifteen thousand men, he savagely stamped out Irish resistance in about ten months. Shortly after landing in Ireland he ordered the massacre of the garrison at Drogheda. Hundreds of people, including priests and monks, were

132

OLIVER CROMWELL

Cromwell was born in 1599, the son of a country squire. He was a descendant of Thomas Cromwell, the man who carried out Henry VIII's break with Rome, and the family estate was at one time monastery land. As a boy he was not particularly devout; in fact he was "notorious for robbing Orchards". Many of his contemporaries say that at an early age he had strange dreams of future greatness and that in one dream a man came to him and told him he would be king. East Anglia, where he lived, was a strong centre of Puritanism and Cromwell became an Independent who believed in freedom of worship. In 1628 he was first elected to Parliament and sided against Charles I, although it was not until 1640, when he supported the Root and Branch party, that he became prominent. It was his success as a military leader, however, that catapulted him into political leadership.

butchered in the streets. Eighty people who had taken refuge in a church steeple were deliberately burned there. The Governor was battered to death with his own wooden leg. The massacre at Drogheda left a tradition of hatred that has poisoned the relations between England and Ireland to this day, but to Cromwell this barbarous act was merely carrying out the will of God. As he wrote:

> It hath pleased God to bless our endeavors. . . . This hath been a marvellous great mercy. . . . Truly I believe this bitterness will save much effusion of blood, through the goodness of God. I wish that all honest hearts may give the glory of this to God alone, to whom indeed the praise of this mercy belongs. I am persuaded that it is a righteous judgement of God upon these barbarous wretches. . . .

133

Scotland

Danger next threatened from Scotland where Charles I's son had been proclaimed King as Charles II. In 1650 Cromwell marched into Scotland and smashed his enemies at Dunbar, a victory which he interpreted as another sign of God's favour. With Ireland and Scotland subdued and under firm control, he was now free to turn his attention to the problem of government.

The Common-wealth 1649-1653

Shortly after the execution of Charles I the House of Lords was abolished and England named a Commonwealth. Government was in the hands of the remaining members of the Long Parliament, contemptuously termed "the Rump" after Pride's Purge. Real power, however, rested with the army. As time passed the Rump Parliament became increasingly unpopular. Cromwell was convinced that it was not providing good government and decided to take drastic action. "These men," he said, "will never leave till the army pull them down by the ears." On April 20, 1653 he went to the Commons with a company of troops and concluded an angry speech by shouting, "Come, come, I will put an end to your prating. You are no Parliament." The soldiers hurried the indignant but powerless members from the chamber. Next day a sign appeared outside: "This House to let—unfurnished". Cromwell had made himself dictator of England.

Yet Oliver Cromwell was not a dictator at heart and had no desire to be one. He desperately wanted to establish his government on a legal basis and to rule through an elected body that expressed the will

Religious Problems

of the people. At the same time he belonged to the Independents or Congregationalists, who opposed the establishment of a state Church or a uniform national religion imposed by the government. They believed that "all species of Protestants" should be able "to worship God according to their own lights and consciences" in their own independent congregations. Cromwell believed that a freely elected Parliament would not agree to such a solution of the religious problem. To safeguard the religious freedom he cherished, Cromwell was driven to adopt policies that seemed to threaten all other freedoms.

To secure a Parliament sympathetic to his plans, Cromwell had the Independent preachers compile lists of suitable God-fearing men from their congregations. From this select group he chose the mem-

The Parliament of Saints 1653

bers of a Parliament which came to be called the Parliament of Saints or the Barebones Parliament because it included one doughty Puritan with the name Praise God Barebones. The Parliament of Saints may have agreed with Cromwell on the religious question, but it did not represent the nation. Within a few months it was universally hated for

CROMWELL'S DISSOLUTION OF THE LONG PARLIAMENT

The Earl of Leicester described this memorable scene which took place in the Commons in 1653: "The Lord General Cromwell came into the House, clad in plain black clothes . . . and sat down as he used to do in an ordinary place. After a while he rose up, put off his hat and spoke at the first . . . to the commendation of the Parliament. . . . Then he put on his hat, went out of his place, and walked up and down the stage or floor in the midst of the House . . . and chid them soundly . . . pointing particularly to some persons. . . . Then the General went to the table where the mace lay, which used to be carried before the Speaker, and said [to his soldiers]: 'Take away these baubles.' "

its attempt to enforce radical Puritan measures. Late in 1653 the army leaders persuaded the Barebones Parliament to dissolve itself.

In the next year Cromwell attempted to rule England under a new constitution, known as The Instrument of Government, prepared by a group of senior army officers. This constitution made Cromwell Lord Protector for life and created a Council of State with twenty-one members. A Parliament was to meet every three years and to sit for at least five months. Religious freedom was guaranteed to all but Catholics, Anglicans, and such as "hold forth and practise licentiousness".

This Parliament proved to be as difficult to work with as its pre-

The Instrument of Government 1654

decessors, and Cromwell established what was in fact a thinly disguised military dictatorship. England and Wales were divided into eleven districts, each under a Major-General whose task it was to maintain public order and the strict observance of the Puritan moral code. Rule through the army proved to be immensely unpopular and his chief supporters in Parliament asked Cromwell to throw over the Major-Generals and become King. The idea of accepting the crown and re-establishing the old form of government appealed to Cromwell, for in his heart he knew that his efforts to find a satisfactory substitute had failed. However, the opposition of his army colleagues and the Independent congregations decided him against it.

Army Rule

Instead, Cromwell accepted yet another constitution under which he had the power to name his successor, who everyone felt would be his eldest son, and to nominate members of a new "other House" to replace the abolished House of Lords. In fact, after so many experiments England had returned to something very like the old trinity of king, Lords, and Commons. It is one of the ironies of history that at the end of his attempts to establish a government for England, Cromwell found himself in much the same position and facing many of the same problems as the King whom he had replaced.

Richard Cromwell 1658-1659

In 1658 Cromwell died and was succeeded by his son Richard, popularly known as "Tumbledown Dick". Richard was a simple country gentleman rather than a soldier or a statesman and the army leaders soon cast him aside. However, the army had no solution either to the problems which faced them. The government of the country had stopped working.

General Monk 1660

At this point a saviour appeared in the person of General Monk, a former supporter of Oliver Cromwell and Commander of the army in Scotland. By 1660, like almost everyone else, Monk had lost his enthusiasm for the great experiment begun in 1641. He was sick of the "intolerable slavery of a sword government" controlled by a small group of army officers who could neither govern nor permit anyone else to. Monk believed in authority, order, and obedience and he marched south from Scotland to secure them. The members of the Long Parliament, including those expelled by Colonel Pride, were called back to London. Arrangements were made to call a new election

The Restoration 1660

and negotiations begun to bring Prince Charles Stuart back from exile. The Puritan revolt was over. All England joyously awaited the arrival of King Charles II whose father had been executed just eleven years before.

136

The excited throngs that greeted the young King were not only tired of well-meaning but futile constitutional experiments; they were also tired of Puritan domination. The English were no more sinful than any other people, but they enjoyed the simple pleasures of the theatre, the cock-fight, and dancing around the Maypole. To the Puritan such frivolities were sinful, for they distracted man from the worship of God. Even walking on a Sunday, unless it were to church and at a slow pace, was to the Puritans an unholy pleasure. The sombre and plainly-cut Puritan dress reflected their view of life as but a sober preparation for the life hereafter. Gone were the rich colours and fabrics, the fancy embroidery and lavish ornamentation, the swirls and ruffles, that had distinguished the garb of the Elizabethans.

Puritan England 1649-1660

Yet if Puritan England was gloomy and quiet, it also throbbed with intense intellectual activity. From all sides came theories about the perfect government, the perfect society, and the perfect religion. A host of pamphlet writers flooded the country with thousands of tracts and a multitude of causes were advanced from the pulpits of churches and from tubs on the city streets.

THE END OF THE MAYPOLES

Earnest Puritans tore down the Maypoles, for fear that the old village dances would lead to immorality or frivolity. But even so, the English continued to celebrate May Day as they had in the past. One Puritan reported that May Day, 1654 "was more observed by people going a-maying than for years past; and, indeed, much sin committed by wicked meetings with fiddlers, drunkenness, ribaldry and the like; great resort came to Hyde Park, many hundreds of coaches, and gallants in attire, but most shameful powdered-hair men, and painted and spotted women. . . . But his highness the lord protector went not thither, nor any of the lords of the Commonwealth, but were busy about the great affairs of the Commonwealth."

137

JOHN BUNYAN

John Bunyan was born in 1628, the son of a tinsmith. He learned to read and write in the small village school. In 1644 he took up arms in the Civil War and soon afterwards became very devout, giving up dancing, bell-ringing, and the playing of games. By 1660 he was a well-known preacher and was put in jail after the Restoration, where he stayed until 1672 because he refused to promise to stop preaching. His jailers were not strict and he had plenty of time to read and write. It may have been during a later short imprisonment in 1675 that he wrote "Pilgrim's Progress", a romantic adventure depicting a Christian's progress towards salvation.

The Levellers, for instance, proposed a democratic system that sounds very familiar to modern ears. They believed that every man should have "a choice of those who are to make the laws for them to live under". As Colonel Rainborough, one of their spokesmen, said, "The poorest he that is in England hath a life to live as the greatest he." The Diggers went further and argued that the business of government was to improve the welfare of the common people. Shovels in hand, they led the way by bringing waste land into cultivation. The Fifth Monarchy men quietly prepared for the rule of Christ on earth and the reign of the Saints. No hope was too high, no dream too weird to find expression. The climax was reached when a dedicated Puritan set out with his wife in a rowboat to convert the Pope. They were never heard of again.

John Milton   Cromwell's Puritan England also produced one of England's greatest writers, John Milton. A poet of note before the Civil War, Milton joined the ranks of the pamphleteers and for twenty years defended Puritan policy. In his most famous prose work, the *Areopagitica,* Milton made a stirring plea for freedom of speech. "Give me the liberty to

138

know, to utter, and to argue freely according to conscience, above all other liberties," he wrote. After the Restoration of Charles II, blind and disillusioned, he wrote the great epic poem, *Paradise Lost.* If the title reveals his sense of failure, the poem also depicts the unshaken will and deep spiritual feeling that made the Puritan experiment both so glorious and so tragic.

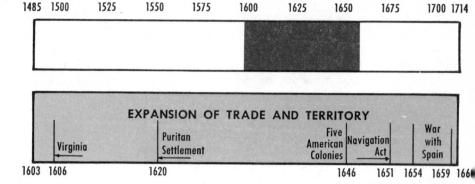

CHAPTER TWENTY-ONE

THE EXPANSION OF ENGLAND: 1603-1660

The Beginning of the British Empire Stuart England saw an expansion of trade and colonization which, though less spectacular than the exploits of the Elizabethan sea-dogs, established the beginnings of the world's greatest empire. While the crippling of Spanish sea power by the defeat of the Great Armada in 1588 paved the way for this expansion, economic ideas of the time provided a further stimulus. People believed that to be strong a nation had to have a "favourable balance of trade" which meant that it must sell to other nations more than it bought from them. The difference would be paid in coin and the country would accumulate gold and silver. It was also argued that a nation should be self-sufficient, that it should not have to rely on other countries which might at some time become enemies. This economic theory and the measures taken to carry it out are known as _mercantilism_. /

"Mercantilism"
Colonies Colonies played an important role in the mercantilist system. Tropical colonies could produce the spices—pepper, cloves, and cinnamon—so necessary to make unrefrigerated and spoiling meat palatable. American colonies could remove Britain's dependence on Baltic countries for vital naval supplies, such as timber, tar, and hemp. As colonial settlements grew, they provided ready-made markets for English manufactured goods. In time a nation which followed a mercantilist policy might become the centre of a self-sufficient empire.

Many of the lower classes in Stuart England heard with envy of the abundant and rich land in the New World where a man might, with **Emigration** hard work, improve his lot. During the reign of Charles I over 55,000 Englishmen swarmed overseas, many of them to escape political and

140

PERSECUTION OF THE PURITANS

It was the lack of religious freedom at home that caused many Englishmen to establish new homes in North America. Puritans, in particular, found the religious policy of the Stuart kings oppressive and many preferred a life on the unknown shores of North America to a life of persecution at home. Historians now agree, however, that many people emigrated because of the desire for land and economic advancement rather than because of religious restrictions. At any rate, the combination of political discontent, economic hardship, and religious persecution resulted in a large-scale English emigration to America.

religious persecution. Writing in 1630, one Englishman expressed the uneasiness of the times:

> I am verily persuaded God will bring some heavy affliction upon this land, and that speedily; but be of good comfort. . . . If the Lord seeth it will be good for us, He will provide a shelter and a hiding place for us and others. . . . Evil times are coming when the Church must fly into the wilderness.

Archbishop Laud's religious policy drove many Englishmen to risk the perils of a long sea voyage to an unsettled and wild country rather than suffer persecution at home.

Most of the people who left England went to North America. In 1606 a group of 105 adventurers obtained a royal charter creating the Virginia Company and in the following year established England's first permanent settlement in North America. From the beginning the settlers in Virginia had a difficult time. One of the members of the expedition wrote that on the first night:

The North American Colonies

Virginia

141

> When wee were going aboard there came the Savages creeping upon all fours, from the Hills, like Bears, with their bowes in their mouths, charged us very desperately in the faces, hurt Captaine Gabrille Archer in both his hands and a sayler in two places of the body very dangerous. After they had spent their arrowes, and felt the sharpnesse of our shot, they retired in to the woods with great noise, and so left us.

By the next spring half of the settlers had died of malaria, cold, and famine. The survivors struggled on and other settlers arrived from England. Eventually they discovered that the soil was well suited to growing tobacco. Although James I denounced smoking as making a "kitchen in the inward parts of man" and as a "custom loathsome to the eye, hateful to the nose, harmful to the brain, and dangerous to the lungs", the habit grew. Virginia prospered from the cultivation and export of tobacco.

The Pilgrims in New England   Farther north thousands of Englishmen, many fleeing from religious persecution, established colonies in New England. Most famous of these bands of settlers were the valiant Pilgrims. In September 1620, 102 Pilgrims sailed from Plymouth in the *Mayflower*. While the ship threatened to disintegrate, so fierce were the Atlantic gales, the Pilgrims drew up the *Mayflower Compact* to provide for the future government of the colony they hoped to found. The Compact began:

> In the Name of God. Amen. We whose names are underwritten, the loyal subjects of our dread sovereign lord, King James . . . have undertaken for the glory of God and the advancement of the Christian faith, and honour of our King and country, a voyage to plant the first colony in the northern parts of Virginia do by these presents solemnly and mutually in the presence of God, and one another, covenant and combine ourselves together into a civil body-politic for our better ordering and preservation.

Blown away from their destination in sunny Virginia they landed on the inhospitable shores of bleak Cape Cod.

The Middle Colonies   In New England, as in Virginia, courage and industry overcame natural obstacles and hostile Indians. By 1640 there were five English settlements between Virginia and New England with a population of 38,000 people. Less than a century later thirteen colonies stretched along the seaboard from Maine to South Carolina, some founded by individuals and others by trading companies.

Although the colonists differed greatly from one another they all regarded themselves as English citizens entitled to all the rights and

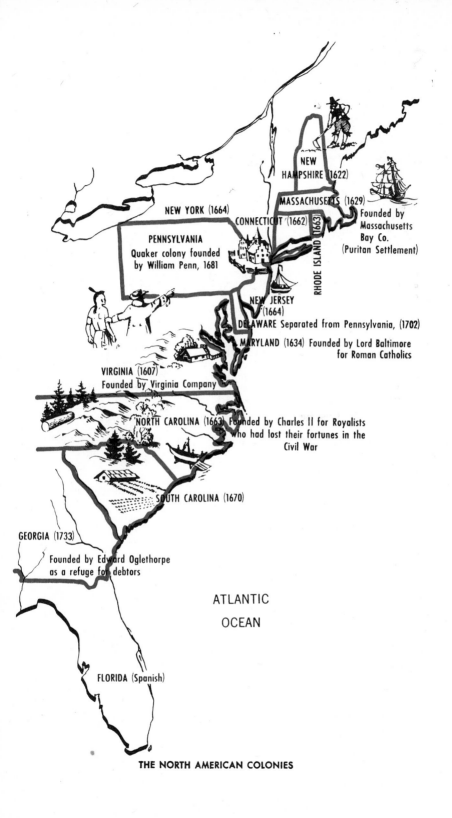

NEW HAMPSHIRE (1622)

MASSACHUSETTS (1629)
Founded by
Massachusetts
Bay Co.
(Puritan Settlement)

NEW YORK (1664)

CONNECTICUT (1662)

RHODE ISLAND (1663)

PENNSYLVANIA
Quaker colony founded
by William Penn, 1681

NEW JERSEY
(1664)

DELAWARE Separated from Pennsylvania, (1702)

MARYLAND (1634) Founded by Lord Baltimore
for Roman Catholics

VIRGINIA (1607)
Founded by Virginia Company

NORTH CAROLINA (1663) Founded by Charles II for Royalists
who had lost their fortunes in the
Civil War

SOUTH CAROLINA (1670)

GEORGIA (1733)

Founded by Edward Oglethorpe
as a refuge for debtors

ATLANTIC
OCEAN

FLORIDA (Spanish)

THE NORTH AMERICAN COLONIES

THE PILGRIMS LAND AT PLYMOUTH, 1620

The Pilgrim Fathers have become the best known group of emigrants to America. Although half the group died during the first winter, the re.t soon established a self-supporting community at Plymouth, where the spot at which they landed is now a national American historical site. More important in the settlement of New England, however, were those colonists who arrived under the auspices of the Massachusetts Bay Company in 1629. By the summer of 1630 nearly a thousand had settled in and around Boston, thirty-five miles north of Plymouth. By 1640 Massachusetts had about 14,000 inhabitants and offshoots of the colony had created Rhode Island and Connecticut. The Puritans dominated the life of New England and the first Governor of Massachusetts wrote proudly that God had "sifted a whole nation that he might send the choicest grain into the wilderness".

Colonial Government liberties of Englishmen. Usually the colonial governments consisted of a governor appointed by the king, a council to advise him, and a legislative assembly elected by the people. There was endless conflict between the governor and assembly just as there was in England between king and Parliament. While England wrestled with her problems at home, the American colonies grew into flourishing and self-reliant communities. These local conflicts were to become more intense as the years passed and were to result in the American Revolution.

The West Indies Other Englishmen sailed farther south to exploit the riches of the West Indies and the Spanish Main. Some became pirates and for the next two centuries the peaceful commerce of the West Indies waters was seldom free from the danger of pirate attacks. The majority swarmed over the islands and established prosperous settlements. The little island of Barbados was among the first to be settled and soon many Englishmen were making fortunes out of tobacco, cotton and

144

particularly, sugar. For many years the West Indian islands were more valuable to England than either the North American colonies or India. England's empire in the West Indies profited by Cromwell's war against Spain in 1654. For some time Cromwell had wanted to form a Protestant Crusade against Catholic Spain. As he told Parliament, "Truly your great enemy is the Spaniard . . . by reason of the enmity that is in him against whatsoever is of God." Cromwell was well aware that Spain was rich and weak; he also knew that a foreign war might distract Englishmen from embarrassing political problems at home.

Employing the tactics which the Elizabethans had found so successful in the past, he launched a surprise attack on Spain's American possessions. Although it failed to achieve its major objects, an English fleet under Admiral Penn captured Jamaica and two Spanish fleets were sunk. These victories were followed by the defeat of the Spaniards at the Battle of the Dunes in Holland. While these triumphs raised England's prestige among European nations, there was grumbling at home. Pirates harassed English merchant ships in the English Channel and the enterprising Dutch were taking over much of England's trade. Many Englishmen were becoming convinced that England's real enemy was not Catholic Spain but Protestant Holland, a religious ally but a commercial rival.

In the seventeenth century Holland was the greatest commercial power in the world. She had the largest fleets of merchantmen and warships and the Dutch merchants threatened to control the sea-lanes. Amsterdam, the capital, was the financial centre of the world. In the Far East the Dutch had easily triumphed over the English early in the century. Both had established trading posts in the rich Spice Islands but by 1623 the Dutch had forced the English out. India alone remained as a field for British trade. While Charles I argued with his Parliaments, the great Mogul Emperor of India, Shah Jehan, was building the magnificent Taj Mahal and permitting English merchants to establish small trading posts on the coast. To have suggested that these humble merchants were laying the foundations for a British empire in India would have brought roars of derisive laughter from the Indians.

Even in North America and the West Indies, where the English were firmly established, the Dutch threatened their trade. English settlers in America preferred to trade with them, despite the opposition of the home government, because Dutch ships were faster, their prices lower, and their credit more liberal. By 1635 they controlled much of the West Indies trade and from their colony of New Amsterdam

The War Against Spain 1654-1659

Rivalry with Holland

145

(renamed New York after its capture by England in 1664), made serious inroads upon the American commerce.

Supported by the Puritan middle class, which was heavily involved in commerce, Cromwell built up the navy. Under such sea-going generals as Robert Blake, the British navy regained the reputation it had established in Elizabeth's day. In 1651 Parliament passed the first Navigation Act designed to strike a blow at the Dutch. The Act required that all trade carried to and from English colonies should be carried in English ships manned by English crews. It also stated that all goods coming to England from foreign countries had to be carried in English ships or ships of the producing nation. This last provision was openly directed at the Dutch who had become the great carriers for other nations.

The Navigation Act of 1651

The Anglo-Dutch Wars

Between 1652 and 1674 England and Holland fought three great naval and commercial wars. Although the battle honours were almost evenly divided, England succeeded in wresting control of her own trade from the Dutch. By the end of the century England had replaced Holland as the leading commercial power. Before that, however, the two nations were forced to forget their rivalry and unite in the face of a common peril, for King Louis XIV of France, determined to master all of Europe, threatened them both.

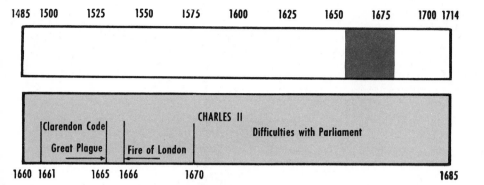

1485 1500 1525 1550 1575 1600 1625 1650 1675 1700 1714

Clarendon Code
Great Plague
Fire of London
CHARLES II
Difficulties with Parliament

1660 1661 1665 1666 1670 1685

CHAPTER TWENTY-TWO

CHARLES II AND RESTORATION ENGLAND: 1660-1685

On May 29, 1660 Charles II of England was thirty years old. He celebrated his birthday by a triumphant return to the London he had left as a young boy many years before. Twenty thousand soldiers, shouting wildly and waving their swords, paraded through streets strewn with flowers and lined by milling crowds of rejoicing people. Women fainted in the crush, bells rang, and fountains ran with wine. Bending over his Bible, an old Puritan shook his head sadly. The reign of the Saints was over. To all appearances the ungodly were triumphant.

The Restoration of Charles II 1660

Well might the Puritan brood. From the new King's court came stories of unrestrained gaiety which shocked even a people sick of an overdose of Puritan morality. As often as not the central figure of the scandals was the Merry Monarch himself. The poetry of the wits who surrounded the court and the plays of the Restoration theatre suggested that even the most unbelievable scandals had not been exaggerated. Horrified Puritans saw in the disasters that overtook London between 1665 and 1667 sure signs of God's displeasure.

In 1665 the last great plague swept across England, leaving a path of terror and death in its wake. Tales of the Black Death of 1348 were overshadowed by the grim realities of an epidemic which killed 7,000 Londoners in one week. In his diary Daniel Defoe wrote:

The Great Plague 1665

> The face of London was now indeed strangely alter'd. . . .
> Sorrow and Sadness sat upon every Face. . . . London might
> be said to be all tears. . . . The shrieks of Women and Children
> at the Windows and Doors of their Houses, when their Nearest
> Relations were perhaps dying, or just dead, were so frequent
> to be heard, as we passed the Streets, that it was enough to
> pierce the stoutest Heart in the World, to hear them.

147

The second disaster, a year later, was almost a blessing in disguise, for the remnants of the plague were driven out before the Great London

THE RETURN OF CHARLES II

A few days after the execution of Charles I, Scotland proclaimed his son, "Charles II, King of Great Britain, France and Ireland", and crowned him at Scone. In 1651, while attempting to invade England, Charles was decisively defeated by Cromwell at Worcester. After many hairbreadth escapes, he sailed to France and eventually established his court at Brussels, now the capital of Belgium. It was from there that he issued the famous Declaration of Breda in which he promised to pardon all those who had fought against his father unless Parliament should decide otherwise, to permit freedom of worship as decided upon in Parliament, to restore property to those from whom it had been unlawfully taken, and to give the army its back pay. So warmly was Charles greeted upon his arrival that he is supposed to have made the sardonic comment that it must have been his own fault that he had been absent so long, for all that he saw indicated that the people ever wished for his return.

148

Fire of September 1666. For three days the fire raged and before it burnt itself out had destroyed half the city. John Evelyn wrote in his diary:

> All the sky was of a fiery aspect, like the top of a burning oven, and the light seen above 40 miles round about for many nights, God grant mine eyes may never behold the like, who now saw above 10,000 houses all in one flame! The noise and cracking and thunder of the impetuous flames, the shrieking of women and children, the hurry of people, the fall of towers, houses, and churches, was like a hideous storm, and the air all about so hot and inflamed, that at the last one was not able to approach it, so that they were forced to stand still, and let the flames burn on. . . . Nothing but the Almighty power of God was able to stop them, for vain was the help of man.

Such disasters were not a promising beginning for a new reign.

The boisterous conduct of the handsome monarch has often hidden **Charles II 1660-1685** the fact that Charles II was one of the most astute of all English kings. His political ability was remarkable. Yet he was also one of England's laziest kings and preferred to secure his own comfort rather than to carry out his royal duties. It has been said that the only principle to which he adhered throughout his life was a determination to live and die in England and not go on his "travels" again. To do even this, however, demanded considerable political agility.

Although the Parliament which recalled Charles II from France **The Restored Monarchy** stated that he had been King by "inherent birthright and lawful and undoubted succession" since his father's death in 1649, Charles was well aware that the restored monarchy was far different from that of Elizabeth or James. No one could forget that a king had been executed and that the nation had managed to get along for eleven years without one. More important, the laws which had been passed by the Long Parliament in 1641 to restrict the power of the Crown were still in effect. Despotic rule was impossible for a king who could not make laws or raise money without Parliament or do justice except in the courts of common law.

The Restoration of 1660 was as much a restoration of parliamentary **The Restoration of Parliament** government as it was of the monarchy. Parliament was in a much stronger position in relation to the king than it had ever been before. From 1642 to 1648 Parliament had governed England. During those years, no monarch warned it away from the "deep mysteries of State", as James I had once done. No monarch would ever do so again. Within

Parliament, the House of Commons, controlling finance and representing the nation, became supreme. The House of Lords had been abolished during the Commonwealth and although it was re-established, it never regained its old importance. Its history henceforth was one of slow but steady decline.

King and Parliament Despite the enthusiasm for his return in 1660, Parliament soon showed that it was not going to let the King have his own way. Parliament granted Charles a fixed income which was considerably less than he needed. The Cavalier Parliament of 1661, so called because it was composed of members devoted to the king, denied him a standing army, in spite of internal unrest and the danger of attack from Scotland. Furthermore, Parliament forced Charles to accept a religious settlement that was just the opposite of his own policy of religious toleration.

The Clarendon Code

This settlement, dictated by the Anglican Cavaliers, was called the Clarendon Code after the King's chief minister, the Earl of Clarendon. Ironically, Clarendon opposed the measure which bore his name; he considered it a stupid blunder. The Code was designed to suppress the political activities of the Puritans, or Dissenters as they were now called, and to prevent any but Anglicans from holding office. When Charles attempted to relax the restrictions against Dissenters, Parliament denied

---

No person to be elected to town government who is not a member of the Church of England.
(Corporation Act, 1661)

All ministers must use the Book of Common Prayer.
(Act of Uniformity, 1662)

Religious meetings of more than five non-Anglicans illegal.
(Conventicle Act, 1664)

Ministers who do not obey the Act of Uniformity forbidden to come within five miles of any city or town.
(Five-Mile Act, 1665)

THE CLARENDON CODE

---

him money, thus showing that it was determined to establish parliamentary control of the Church for ever.

Charles II and Parliament The outbreak of a war with Holland in 1665 showed that it might not be an easy task to maintain harmony between King and Parliament. Although the Commons were eager to fight England's great commercial rival, they were unwilling to grant the King sufficient money to conduct the war effectively. When the war went badly, their enthusiasm for it evaporated and the members demanded the right to control the King's expenditure. At the same time they attempted to bring Clarendon, the King's chief minister, to trial for treason, as an earlier Parliament had done with Strafford.

150

DUTCH FLEET FIRING ENGLISH SHIPS AT MEDWAY

In 1665 the second in the series of Anglo-Dutch naval and commercial wars broke out. This war lasted until the summer of 1667 and on the whole the English had the better of the fighting. However, one of the most humiliating episodes in the annals of the British navy occurred during this period. After the ravages of the Plague and the Great Fire, the British government attempted to economize by not sending a battle fleet to sea. In June 1667, the Dutch, taking advantage of this situation, launched a carefully planned raid up the estuary of the Thames. Three English ships of the line were burnt, and the "Royal Charles", largest vessel of the fleet, was towed away undamaged by the resourceful Dutch.

Faced with increasing opposition from a Commons determined to keep the upper hand, Charles began to build up a group of his own supporters in the House. He granted profitable positions in the government to his friends, appointed Councillors who could win support for his policy in the Commons, and attempted to relax the restrictions against the Dissenters and Roman Catholics. By these means he sought to win wider support in the country as well as in Parliament.

By the late 1670's, however, Charles was having increasing difficulty and Parliament and the Crown were again in open disagreement. In 1670 Charles had negotiated the secret Treaty of Dover with the powerful French King, Louis XIV. Charles promised to support Louis in a war against Holland in return for large cash payments that would make him less dependent on Parliament. The war broke out in 1672 but by 1673 Parliament pressed Charles to make peace with Holland. In the same year it passed the Test Act which tightened the political restrictions against Dissenters and Catholics. A radical group in Parliament also began to demand that the King's Roman Catholic brother, James, should be excluded from the succession to the throne. The question of the

151

succession was an important one, for Charles' Queen had no children.

Charles countered this growing opposition by dissolving the Cavalier Parliament in 1679 and calling a new election. No amount of bribery could overcome the popular dislike and distrust of the King's apparently pro-French and pro-Catholic policy. Talk was in the air of another civil war if James should succeed to the throne. But such talk alarmed many moderate Englishmen who feared a return of civil war; thus when Charles dissolved his last Parliament in 1681 there had begun to be widespread feeling throughout the country in favour of the Crown.

Whigs and Tories

The political and religious controversies of these years had tended to drive people into two fairly distinct groups or parties. Those who supported the King became known as Tories; those who opposed him were called Whigs. The Tories generally supported the Church of England, opposed religious toleration, and preferred to see the balance of power between King and Parliament remain as it was. The Whigs stood for religious toleration, except for Roman Catholics, and the unquestioned supremacy of Parliament over the King. Both names were originally used as terms of abuse: the Tories were named after Irish bandits and the Whigs after Scottish Covenanters who were popularly supposed to be sour-faced and joyless.

The Situation in 1685

Before calling another Parliament Charles was determined to do everything in his power to ensure that his Tory supporters would be in a majority. The clergy and gentry were already solidly behind the party of Church and King. Skilful use of bribery and astute appointments in central and local government offices brought in more supporters. By 1685 Charles felt that an election would have the desired results. Before the election, however, Charles died and his brother James succeeded to the throne. With the throne James inherited the political machine so carefully built up by his brother, but he was not wise enough to use it and by his stupidity he drove even the Crown's most ardent supporters into the arms of the opposition.

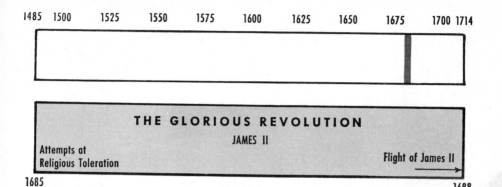

THE GLORIOUS REVOLUTION
JAMES II

Attempts at
Religious Toleration

Flight of James II

1685

1688

CHAPTER TWENTY-THREE

THE GLORIOUS REVOLUTION OF 1688

"When I am dead and gone, I know not what my brother will do," Charles II once lamented. "I am much afraid that when he comes to wear the crown he will be obliged to travel again." In three years Charles' prophecy came true. James, driven from England, was on his way to France, an exile from his own land. James II
1685-1688

James II, King of England from 1685 to 1688, was tactless and stubborn. His main aims were to restore the Roman Catholic faith in England and to revive the king's power. The Whigs were bitterly opposed to both policies. Not even the predominantly Tory Parliament of 1685 would agree to his proposal that the Test Act should be repealed, thus enabling Roman Catholics to hold public office. When the outraged James dismissed Parliament, never to call it again, he had taken the first step towards exile. James' Policies

Determined to have his own way, James forced the judges to rule that he had the right to set aside the laws passed by Parliament. Those judges who opposed his view of the constitution were dismissed from the Bench. James then set aside the Test Act and appointed Roman Catholics to important public offices. Even more alarming was his replacement of Protestant army officers by Roman Catholics. His large army of 16,000 men, camped just outside London, did nothing to relieve the suspicion that he planned a restoration of Catholicism and personal rule.

In May 1688 the King drove away his last Tory supporters. He ordered all clergymen to read from the pulpits the Declaration of Indulgence, which removed all restrictions on Catholics and Dissenters. When seven bishops boldly refused to permit the Declaration to be

THE ACQUITTAL OF THE SEVEN BISHOPS

The acquittal of the seven bishops was greeted with almost universal joy. James' Declaration of Indulgence had aroused resentment and opposition. When the day came for reading the Declaration, there was scarcely a clergyman who obeyed the King's order. When one bishop began to read it, the whole congregation left the church. An observer wrote that when the jury returned their verdict of acquittal, "There was a most wonderful shout, that one would have thought the Hall had cracked. People asked [the bishops'] blessing on their knees. There was continued shoutings for half an hour, so that no business could be done; and they hissed the Solicitor. And at night was mighty rejoicing, in ringing of bells, discharging of guns, lighting of candles and bonfires."

read in their dioceses, James had them arrested. With this act, the traditional loyalty of the Anglican clergy to the monarch vanished. When the bishops were brought to trial, they were acquitted and the cheers which greeted the acquittal clearly revealed the temper of the people.

The Succession Question Nevertheless, James might have remained on the throne until his death, for he was an old man and had no male heir. On his death his Protestant daughter Mary, married to William of Orange, the ruler of Holland, would succeed him. Most Englishmen preferred to ride out the storm rather than provoke a civil war, secure in the knowledge that the next ruler would be a Protestant. But early in the summer of 1688 James' Queen gave birth to a son. Despite rumours that he had been smuggled into the palace in a warming pan and exchanged for the daughter actually born to the Queen, the newly-born prince, who was a Roman Catholic, would now inherit the throne on James' death. Moderates and extremists alike, Tories and Whigs, joined to take immediate action to prevent this from happening.

154

Seven men, representing all parties and interests in the nation, jour- The Glorious
neyed to Holland and invited Mary and her husband, William of Orange, Revolution
to bring an army to England and support them against James. William
was tempted by the invitation. He did not desire the English throne for
its own sake, but English arms could help him to defend Holland against
the mighty Louis XIV. After serious consideration William decided
upon the gamble.

Fortune favoured the bold Dutchman. For a month a westerly
wind kept his ships bottled up in Dutch harbours. At last a "Protestant
wind" sprang up to carry him across the Channel while that same wind
held the English fleet motionless in its harbours, powerless to interfere
with the crossing. When his army came ashore in England, "the people
on land, in great numbers, welcomed his Highness with loud acclama-
tions of joy". Deserted by his military leaders, the unfortunate James

THE FLIGHT OF JAMES II

As support for William of Orange steadily increased, James II lost his nerve and decided
to flee from England. He set out secretly from his palace in Whitehall, crossed the Thames
in a small boat, and made his way to the coast, hoping to escape to France. At
Faversham he was captured by some fishermen and returned to London. William of Orange
permitted him to escape again and James thereafter lived in France near the court of
his cousin Louis XIV.

fled to France. A Convention Parliament declared that by his flight James had "abdicated the government" and invited William and Mary to become joint sovereigns. Thus ended the Bloodless Revolution of 1688.

The Bill of Rights 1689 The year 1688 is one of the most important dates in British history. Parliament was determined to make sure that all its hard-won rights were guaranteed by the new rulers, and before William and Mary received the crown they had to accept the provisions of the Bill of Rights, which ranks with Magna Carta and the Petition of Right as the third great document in English constitutional development. In this way it was clearly established that the monarch owed his throne to a Parliament which represented the nation. The Bill of Rights listed King James II's misdeeds and pronounced them illegal. It declared that no king could levy taxes, set aside laws, or maintain an army without the consent of Parliament. Parliament was to meet frequently and its members were to be freely elected and have full freedom of debate. Finally, it proclaimed that no Roman Catholic was ever to wear the English crown.

In the next few years the powers of Parliament were further strengthened by additional Acts which, together with the Bill of Rights, **The Mutiny Act 1689** make up what is known as the Revolutionary Settlement. The Mutiny Act of 1689 authorized, for one year only, the use of military law, the law by which discipline was maintained in the army. Thus Parliament had to be called every year to renew the Act. A new clause was intro- **Coronation Oath** duced into the coronation oath which bound the king to "govern . . . acccrding to the statutes in Parliament agreed on and the laws and customs of the same". The Triennial Act of 1694 ordered new elections to be held every three years and so prevented a king from governing with a Parliament he might have bribed into supporting him, as Charles II had hoped to do. In 1691 Parliament won the right to control the expenditure of money it had voted.

Act of Settlement 1701 The Act of Settlement of 1701 added two more important provisions to the Revolutionary Settlement. Henceforth judges were to hold office for life and could not be dismissed except on the request of Parliament. No longer could a king secure favourable decisions in law cases in which he was interested, by threatening to dismiss the judges if they did not rule as he wished. The Act also provided for the succession to the throne.

Since William and Mary had no children, the crown after their death was to pass to Mary's sister Anne and after her, if she had no children,

156

to her closest Protestant relation, Sophia, daughter of the Elector of Hanover, a small German state. England is still ruled under the Act of Settlement, for Sophia's son did become King of England in 1714 and the crown has ever since descended in direct succession.

Elizabeth I had once berated her Parliament for daring to discuss the question of who should succeed her. Less than a hundred years later Parliament was regulating the succession by a statute. Few facts better illustrate the growth in parliamentary power. In those hundred years England had become a parliamentary monarchy.

The Revolutionary Settlement also ended the fierce religious conflicts of the seventeenth century. Anglicans and Dissenters had united to overthrow James II. As a result, the Toleration Act of 1689 allowed the Protestant Dissenters freedom of worship, although they were still excluded from holding public office. They had the right to vote, however, and many Dissenters qualified for public office by attending an Anglican service once a year. _{Toleration Act 1689}

The Toleration Act greatly facilitated the union of England and Scotland in 1707. Although the two countries had had the same monarch since 1603, the governments had remained separate except for the period when Cromwell ruled. It was not friendship that brought the two nations together, but a hard-headed realization that union would serve the interests of both. For England it would remove the threat of Scottish support of the son of James II; for the Scots it would mean participation in the expansion of English trade and commerce. After 1500 years of conflict between the two countries, the northern border was quiet, for the time being at least. _{Act of Union with Scotland 1707}

The Act of Union, enacted by Parliament in 1707, gave Scotland forty-five seats in the House of Commons in London. The Revolutionary Settlement had made that chamber the most important part of the English governmental system. Parliament was clearly the senior partner in government, even if it was not yet completely the king's master.

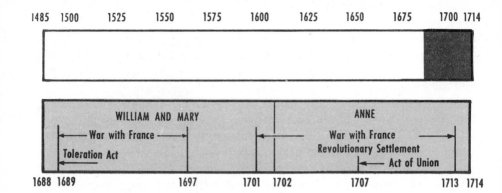

1485 1500   1525   1550   1575   1600   1625   1650   1675   1700 1714

WILLIAM AND MARY
←——— War with France ———→
Toleration Act
←———

ANNE
←——— War with France ———→
Revolutionary Settlement
←——— Act of Union

1688 1689   1697   1701 1702   1707   1713 1714

CHAPTER TWENTY-FOUR

William III
1689-1702

ENGLAND AND FRANCE AT WAR: 1688-1714

Although most Englishmen in 1689 accepted William of Orange as their King, very few liked the cold little Dutchman. From boyhood William had been weak and sickly. Unable to enjoy the ordinary pleasures of youth, as an adult he had become stern and serious. One of his subjects wrote:

> He has a coldness in his way that damps a modest man extremely, for he hears things with a dry silence that shows too much of distrust for those to whom he speaks. . . . If the prince does not, in many things, change his way he will hardly gain the hearts of the nation. His coldness will look like contempt, and that the English cannot bear; and they are too impatient to digest that slowness that is almost become natural to him in the most inconsiderable things.

What William lacked in charm and physical strength, however, he more than made up in determination and ability. For sixteen years he had fought to save Holland and Europe from French domination, at a time when France was Europe's greatest military power. Neither crisis nor disaster had shaken his calm and steadfast courage. Always unpopular with his English subjects, he was, nevertheless, one of England's strongest kings.

William's main reason for accepting the crown had been to gain England's support against France. Before he could move against his enemy on the Continent, however, he had to establish control over Scotland and Ireland, for Highland clans and Irish Catholics rallied to support the exiled James II. By 1692 both countries were subdued and William was able to seek revenge on his old French enemy. The resulting

158

THE BATTLE OF THE BOYNE

On July 12, 1690, William met the Catholic Irish and French forces of the exiled James at the Boyne River in Ireland. The English forces won a complete victory. One contemporary wrote that King William's courage and conduct set a fine example for his troops. Although wounded, he rode "into every body of his army; he charged in many different places; and nothing stood before him." James, in contrast, watched the battle from a safe distance, surrounded by his bodyguard. When he saw his forces beginning to give way, he was the first to flee and actually reached Dublin before the action was quite over.

war marked the beginning of a series of conflicts, which lasted for over a century, between England and France.

In the first war of the series, 1689-1697, England was part of an anti-French alliance which included Holland, Austria, Spain, and Sweden. Most of the action took place in Belgium, the "cock-pit of Europe", where Englishmen have fought many battles through the years. (Because Belgium lies directly across the narrow seas, England since Elizabeth's reign has always regarded the possession of this country by a strong power as a threat to her national security, for it is an ideal base for invasion.) Although William lost most of the battles in this war, he was able to hold the allies together and prevent defeat from becoming disaster. On the seas the allies soon won definite naval superiority and almost ruined French overseas trade.

The war was not fought in Europe only. In North America Frontenac led the French and Indians in savage raids upon the isolated

The War with France 1689-1697

159

frontiers of New England. The English, in return, conquered Acadia and attempted unsuccessfully to capture Quebec. Weary of war, the

The Peace of Ryswick 1697

European nations in 1697 signed the Peace of Ryswick which restored all conquests and left matters much as they had been before the war. Both sides knew the peace was only a breathing spell and that a new struggle was bound to come before long.

The Revival of War 1701-1713

In 1701 the expected war broke out. Louis XIV sent French troops into Belgium and announced that he would support the son of James II as the rightful King of England. William died before he could lead his troops into battle. Since his wife Mary had died eight years earlier,

Queen Anne 1702-1714

William was succeeded in 1702 by the dowdy, stolid, but hard-working Anne. Queen Anne, a thirty-six-year-old invalid, was hardly a Joan of Arc and it was fortunate that in this critical moment in England's history the Queen found in John Churchill a man who was even better qualified than William to lead the nation in war.

The Duke of Marlborough

Better known as the Duke of Marlborough, John Churchill was a military genius, perhaps the greatest general England has ever produced. One of his Dutch deputies wrote this description of him:

> He is a man of birth: about the middle height, and the best figure in the world: his features without fault, fine, sparkling eyes, good teeth, and his complexion such a mixture of white and red as the fairer sex might envy: in brief, except for his legs, which are too thin, one of the handsomest men ever seen. His mind is keen and subtle, his judgement very clear and sound, his insight both quick and deep, with a consummate knowledge of men which no false show of merit can deceive.

In the planning of vast campaigns and battlefield tactics, Marlborough towered above the soldiers of his time. Time and again the boldness and speed of his movements left his enemies gasping and bewildered. Through his patient and skilful diplomacy he won the co-operation of jealous and obstinate allies and held a coalition of European powers together. In the polite salons of European society few could resist the handsome Duke and on the battlefields of Europe no one could withstand him.

The war, which lasted from 1701 to 1713, was in fact a world war.

The War in Europe

It was fought in Belgium and Holland, in Spain, in North America, and on the high seas. For the first few years the fighting was indecisive, but in 1704 France threatened to force Britain's ally, Austria, from the war. Pretending an attack on eastern France, Marlborough marched secretly and with unbelievable speed across Germany to the Danube

160

River. In the little village of Blenheim he completely routed the great French army of 50,000. For the first time Louis XIV's forces had been defeated in the field; from this time on, Britain and her allies had the advantage. During the next five years Marlborough won sensational victories at Ramillies, Oudenarde, and Malplaquet. By 1709 the French had been driven from Belgium. With his treasury empty and his people exhausted and starving, Louis XIV was ready for peace.

Meanwhile the English and Dutch fleets had secured control of the oceans and closed the sea lanes to French shipping. In 1704 an English fleet under Admiral Rooke captured the famous Rock of Gibraltar, the key to the Mediterranean. Four years later Britain seized the island of Minorca and made it a permanent winter naval base. Possession of the huge rock fortress controlling the entrance to the Mediterranean and of the base at Minorca, established Britain as a naval power in the Mediterranean. Control of these strategic locations also played a vital role in the later development of the Empire. *The War Overseas*

THE CAPTURE OF GIBRALTAR

The capture of Gibraltar was the first step in Britain's determination to secure bases from which she could protect and expand her trade. The narrow strait was one of the most crowded sea-lanes in the world and a naval squadron based on it could control the trade of the Mediterranean. The Rock was not well defended and the British captured it easily, but holding it against a French and Spanish siege was more difficult. While prepared to negotiate the return of other conquests, the British refused to surrender Gibraltar.

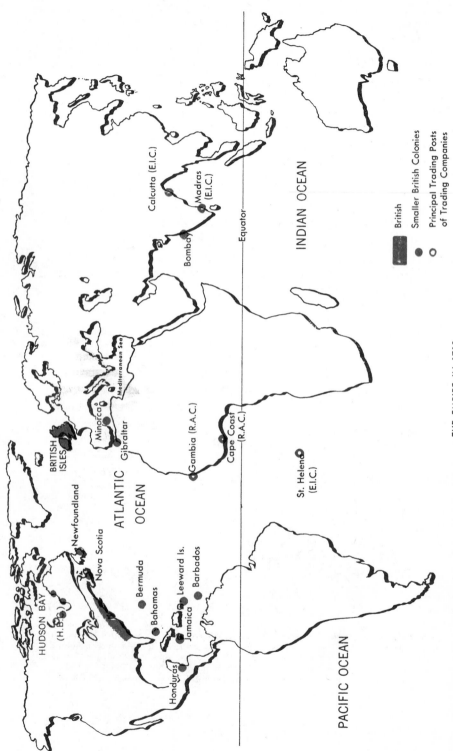

THE EMPIRE IN 1713

British

Smaller British Colonies

Principal Trading Posts
of Trading Companies

HUDSON BAY
(H.B.)

Newfoundland

Nova Scotia

Bermuda

Bahamas

Leeward Is.

Jamaica

Barbados

Honduras

ATLANTIC
OCEAN

BRITISH
ISLES

Minorca

Gibraltar

Mediterranean Sea

Gambia (R.A.C.)

Cape Coast
(R.A.C.)

St. Helena
(E.I.C.)

Calcutta (E.I.C.)

Madras
(E.I.C.)

Bombay

Equator

INDIAN OCEAN

PACIFIC OCEAN

As in the previous war, the English settlers in North America were once again involved in the hostilities. In American history these actions are known as Queen Anne's war. In 1710 a force of New England colonists and British regulars won Acadia which had been returned to France by the Treaty of Ryswick. Henceforth the new possession was to be known as Nova Scotia. In honour of their Queen the New Englanders changed the name of its settlement from Port Royal to Annapolis.

In 1713 the Treaty of Utrecht ended the war and with it the hopes of Louis XIV to dominate the Continent. England had won the first round in her long conflict with France. Although great struggles lay in the future, England had established her supremacy for the time being in naval and colonial affairs. In North America she had won Nova Scotia and was to create a great naval fortress at Halifax. She was given a clear title to the disputed regions around Hudson Bay and in Newfoundland. Possession of Gibralter and Minorca established her position in the Mediterranean. Above all, Louis XIV had recognized the Protestant succession in England rather than the Stuart line.

Even while her statesmen were negotiating the Treaty of Utrecht, England approached another crisis. Queen Anne was dying and the question of the succession to the throne once again became important. Although the Act of Settlement of 1701 had stated that the crown would pass to the Hanoverian line, there was a group in England known as the High Tories who favoured the son of James II. The leader of this group was the brilliant Henry St. John, better known as Viscount Bolingbroke. Bolingbroke had made himself the most powerful figure in the land and was determined to gain for himself the name of "Kingmaker." Knowing something of his plans, however, the Queen did not trust him. As she lay dying, Queen Anne passed the white staff, the symbol of the highest office in the land, to the Duke of Shrewsbury who she knew would follow the Act of Settlement. With her death in 1714 orders were sent throughout the country to make ready for the succession of the Hanoverian heir. Bolingbroke's plot to restore the Stuarts died with the Queen. Eleven weeks later a reluctant, homesick, and bewildered German prince arrived peacefully to be crowned George I and to rule over a people whose language, manners, and politics he did not understand.

TIME CHART

IN THE BRITISH ISLES		ELSEWHERE
POLITICAL	**OTHER**	
1487 Court of Star Chamber Statute against Liveries and Maintenance	1485 Battle of Bosworth	
		1492 First voyage of Columbus 1493 Pope divides New World between Spain and Portugal 1497-98 Cabot in America 1497-99 Voyage of Vasco da Gama
	1509 Henry VIII marries Catherine of Aragon	
		1519-21 Cortez conquers Mexico 1519-22 Magellan sails around the world 1525-35 Pizzaro conquers Peru
1529-36 Reformation Parliament Dissolution of monasteries	1525 Tyndale's English Bible	
1534 Act of Supremacy	1533 Henry marries Anne Boleyn 1535 Execution of Sir Thomas More	1534-36 Cartier in Canada
1554 Restoration of Papal authority in England		
1559 Acts of Uniformity and Supremacy 1563 Thirty-nine Articles	1555-58 Mary's Religious persecutions	
	1564 Birth of Shakespeare	1576-78 Frobisher's search for North-West Passage 1577-80 Drake's voyage around world
	1585 English army to Netherlands	1585-90 Raleigh's colony in Virginia 1585-87 Davis explores Greenland and coast of North America
1587 Execution of Mary Queen of Scots	1588 Spanish Armada	
1601 Poor Law Act		1600 Establishment of East India Company
	1604 Hampton Court Conference	

164

TIME CHART

IN THE BRITISH ISLES		ELSEWHERE
POLITICAL	**OTHER**	
	1605 The Gunpowder Plot	
		1607 First permanent settlement in Virginia
	1611 Completion Authorized Version of the Bible	1608 Champlain founds Quebec
		1613-15 Champlain explores Great Lakes
		1613-1616 British factory at Surat
		1618 Trading post at Gambia
		1620 Voyage of Mayflower
		1627 Company of New France created
1628 Petition of Right		1628-29 Acadia and Quebec captured by English; restored in 1632
		1630 Puritan settlement of Massachusetts begun
1633 Laud Archbishop of Canterbury		
1634 First levy of ship-money		
	1637-38 Hampden's "ship-money" case	
	1638 Scottish National Covenant	
1640 Short Parliament		
1640-60 Long Parliament		
1641 Grand Remonstrance Execution of Strafford		
	1642-48 Civil War	1642 French settlement of Montreal
		1642-44 Explorations of Tasman
		1643-1715 Louis XIV King of France
1649 Abolition of monarchy and House of Lords Execution of Charles I		
		1652 Dutch settlement at Cape of Good Hope
1653 Barebones Parliament Instrument of Government Cromwell Lord Protector		
	1654-59 War With Spain	1654-67 English occupation of Acadia
1658 Richard Cromwell Protector		

TIME CHART

IN THE BRITISH ISLES		ELSEWHERE
POLITICAL	**OTHER**	
1660 Restoration 1661-65 Clarendon Code		
	1662 Royal Society founded 1665 Great Plague 1666 Great Fire	1662 British African Company founded
		1668 Bombay granted to East India Company 1670 Incorporation of Hudson's Bay Company
1673 Test Act	1678 Bunyan's "Pilgrim's Progress"	
1679 Habeas Corpus Act 1688-1714 Revolutionary Settlement		1681-82 LaSalle explores Mississippi 1690-97 War in Hudson Valley and Acadia 1704 Capture of Gibraltar 1710 British and colonials seize Acadia

166

BOOK III

THE RISE OF TRADE AND EMPIRE

25. Georgian England, 1714-1760
26. The Age of Walpole
27. The Road to Empire
28. Pitt and the Great War for Trade and Empire
29. The Loss of the Thirteen American Colonies
30. George III and John Wilkes
31. Church, Chapel and John Wesley
32. The Growth of Industry
33. Reform and Reaction: 1783-1793
34. A Nation in Arms: 1793-1815

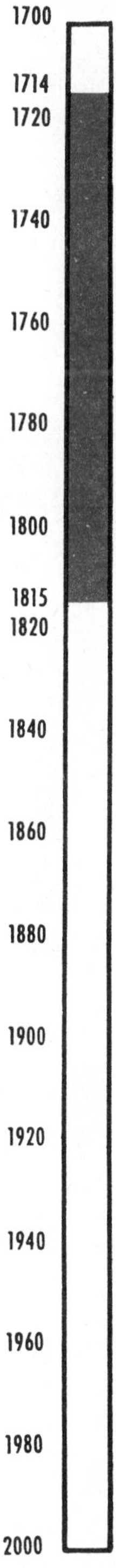

1700
1714
1720
1740
1760
1780
1800
1815
1820
1840
1860
1880
1900
1920
1940
1960
1980
2000

RULERS OF GREAT BRITAIN FROM 1714-1815

1714-1727 George I
1727-1760 George II } Hanover
1760-1820 George III

THE PRINCIPAL PRIME MINISTERS OF GREAT BRITAIN
1714-1815

1721-1742 Robert Walpole

1757-1761
1766-1767 William Pitt, Earl of Chatham

1770-1782 Lord North

1783-1801
1804-1806 William Pitt the Younger

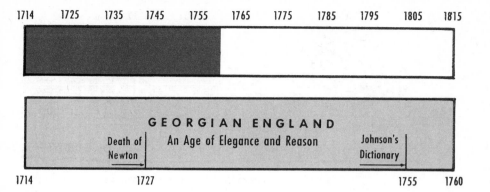

1714 1727 1755 1760

GEORGIAN ENGLAND
Death of Newton | An Age of Elegance and Reason | Johnson's Dictionary

CHAPTER TWENTY-FIVE

GEORGIAN ENGLAND

For fifty years after George I came to the throne in 1714 England enjoyed a stability and contentment she was never to experience again. The bitter political and religious strife of the seventeenth century had spent its fury. New problems, created by industrial and social changes, did not arise till near the end of the century. With the accession of George, the form of government was settled and was to remain so for a century. Although there were great extremes of wealth and Parliament represented only the wealthy, there were few complaints. The ordinary Englishman, in King George's reign, did not believe in political or social equality as we do today. His general attitude was best expressed in the verse:

> God bless the squire and his relations
> And keep us in our proper stations.

Georgian England was the last golden age of the aristocracy. The great families ruled the country and their ranks were constantly being increased by newcomers who could not even trace their descent from the reign of Henry VIII. Many of the newly-created aristocrats had made a fortune out of trade and had bought a title. One of them, Lord Craven, candidly admitted, "I am William, Lord Craven. My father was Lord Mayor of London and my grandfather was the Lord knows who."

The Golden Age of the Aristocracy

Those were the days when the aristocrats lived in lavish splendour. They built spacious town houses and beautiful country palaces that today are showplaces visited by tourists. It was an age of good taste. The aristocrats patronized the arts and encouraged writers and musicians.

169

AN EIGHTEENTH-CENTURY COUNTRY HOUSE

One of the great hobbies of the wealthy in the eighteenth century was architecture. Few men of money could resist the temptation to design and build an elaborate country house. The formal and magnificent style of the period was termed Palladian, for it imitated the buildings of the Italian architect, Palladio. The emphasis was on size and splendour and often little thought was given to comfort. Elaborate gardens, with walks, ponds, and statues of every sort, surrounded the lavish homes. Many men bankrupted themselves trying to achieve the utmost magnificence in design and construction.

Their homes were filled with the paintings of Reynolds and Gainsborough, with Chippendale furniture and Wedgwood china.

Many aristocrats ignored moral conventions. Georgian England has been dubbed "The Age of Scandal". Certainly it was an age of gambling. Rich and poor alike shared the national pastime. The poor gambled on the weather, on cock fights, on how long it would take a criminal to die by hanging. In their fashionable London clubs and salons, the rich gambled on anything at all. Once a man staggered and fell to the ground outside White's, a fashionable London club. Before he hit the ground wagers totalling £100,000 had been placed on whether or not he was dead. Those who bet on his death vigorously objected to restoratives being used on him.

The Age of Reason   Georgian England was seldom stirred by the fierce intellectual debates which raged in other countries during the eighteenth century. Above all, the Georgians disliked enthusiasm and emotion and worshipped reason and common sense. Baron Bielfield, a German visitor, saluted England as the home of practical common sense:

> It reigns in every branch of government, in all the great national institutions, in commerce, in literature, and in everything that constitutes the predominant character of the people.

Literature   As the Baron suggested, Georgian literature reflected the lack of emotion, the absence of great issues, the happy acceptance of life as it

170

was, the belief that "whatever is, is right", or at least is good enough. Like the architecture and painting of the period, the literature was exquisite in design and faultless in structure.

There were, indeed, many great writers in Georgian England. Daniel Defoe and Jonathan Swift raised the art of political satire to a level never since surpassed. Henry Fielding, Laurence Sterne, and others made the novel an accepted form of literary expression. Dr. Samuel Johnson, poet, novelist, satirist, and biographer, compiled a dictionary of the English language and made literary criticism an art in itself.

The spirit of the age was not such as to nourish great poetry, however. Alexander Pope, one of the outstanding poets of the age, de-

A GEORGIAN INTERIOR

The spacious interiors of many Georgian homes matched the size and splendour of the exterior. A description of one such home began: "On the left hand of the hall . . . we go up eight-and-forty steps, ten feet broad." The rooms were often huge; some would contain an average twentieth-century house without any difficulty. The furniture was elegant and sparse, yet not too elaborate or uncomfortable. Today, throughout the world, eighteenth-century antiques are highly prized, and imitation Chippendale chairs are still to be found in every good furniture shop. Clothes, as always, varied with the temperament of the wearer. Wigs were worn by men and women and the men's heads were usually closeshaven. Later in the century men wore their own hair long.

scribed Georgian poetry as "what oft was thought but ne'er so well expressed". Some of Pope's own lines, which have become part of our everyday speech, illustrate his point:

A little learning is a dangerous thing.

Fools rush in where angels fear to tread.

Hope springs eternal in the human breast.

No one would suggest that such lines contain great originality of thought but they do express certain truths very neatly. Perhaps the best-known poet of the time is Thomas Gray, whose melancholy *Elegy Written in a Country Churchyard* is one of the most familiar poems in the English language. His fame, however, rests on the perfection of his lyrics, not the depth of his thought. In the following lines Gray is saying merely that true merit is often unrecognized:

AN EIGHTEENTH-CENTURY BOXING MATCH

Boxing began as a pastime, in the days of George II. By the late eighteenth century it had become a national sport, with 20,000 spectators often assembled to watch, shout, and bet. The boxers themselves were usually the hired champions of wealthy aristocrats who looked after them and bet on them as they would on their horses. The brilliant historian G. M. Trevelyan has written: "Among these sturdy 'bruisers' whose business it was to give and take 'punishment', not a few ruffians could be found, but the real champions, men like Broughton, 'the father of British pugilism' in the reign of George II, and in later times, Belcher, Tom Cribb and Tom Spring were fine fellows and honourable men. Their lordly patrons were proud to be seen driving them to the ring-side in coach or gig."

Full many a gem, of purest ray serene,
The dark unfathomed caves of ocean bear;
Full many a flower is born to blush unseen,
And waste its sweetness on the desert air.

While the age produced few scientists of note, it was a period when **Science** scientific ideas began to challange old superstitions. Before the end of the seventeenth century, scientists had already done much to push back the frontiers of knowledge. Robert Boyle, who has been called the father of modern chemistry, discovered the relation between the volume and pressure of gases, known as Boyle's law. Sir Isaac Newton, one of the world's outstanding scientists, clearly established the law of gravitation as the governing factor in the universe.

Nature and nature's law lay hid in night;
God said, "Let Newton be," and all was light!

Newton also invented differential calculus and discovered the compound nature of light. He became president of the Royal Society, which had been founded in 1662 for the advancement of science. Newton was knighted for his achievements and on his death in 1727 was buried in Westminster Abbey.

Despite the constant growth of trade and industry, England was still **Agriculture** an agricultural country in 1714. Most of her six million people lived on the land, much as their ancestors had done for generations. Village life had changed little over the years. The ordinary farmer worked hard to make a bare living from the land and seldom moved far beyond his village. The narrow twisting roads were unbelievably poor, little more than dust bowls in the summer and mud bogs the rest of the year. Cattle and sheep were driven to market along the roads, contesting for the right of way with the carriages of the rich and the traders' train of pack horses. The few bridges were at the mercy of the smallest spring freshet. Highwaymen waited everywhere to prey on the unsuspecting traveller.

Unless they were evicted by some landlord who wished to consolidate all his land into one enclosure, the villagers had little desire to move. While life was hard, it was not unpleasant. Social life centered on the **Social Life** village inn where the evenings were spent in quiet conversation over a pint of beer and a game of darts. Beer was the national drink. Without it, troops refused to fight and seamen would not put to sea.

For the poor, life in the cities was much less pleasant. Only one out of every three babies born in the cities lived to reach his first birth-

AN EIGHTEENTH-CENTURY ROAD

The growth of internal trade in England made transportation a real problem. Roads had not improved for centuries. Each parish was responsible for maintaining the roads that passed through it. Every farmer was required to labour for six days a year on the roads. One traveller described a twelve-mile piece of road as "so narrow that a mouse cannot pass by any carriage. I saw a fellow creep under his waggon to assist me to lift, if possible, my chaise over a hedge. The ruts are of an incredible depth. The trees everywhere overgrow the road, so that it is totally impervious to the sun, except at a few places. And to add to all the infamous circumstances which concur to plague a traveller, I must not forget eternally meeting with chalk-waggons, themselves frequently stuck fast, till a collection of them are in the same situation, that twenty or thirty horses may be tacked to each to draw them out one by one."

day. Crowded together, the townsmen were easy victims for the epidemics of smallpox and typhoid fever, against which eighteenth-century medicine seemed helpless. There were no country lanes where the poor could walk, or public parks in which they could pass their free time. Their common escape was often the gin tavern, where enterprising barmen advertised "Drunk for a penny, dead drunk for tuppence, clean straw for nothing". Cheap gin was among the greatest killers until Parliament in the 1740's began to pass laws to restrict its sale.

For the upper classes, much of the social life centered about the clubs and the coffee houses. Most men had their favourite club where they met their friends and earnestly discussed matters of common interest. In some, writers and artists gathered; in others, politicians. Merchants and bankers usually met at Lloyd's Coffee-house near the London docks, where the rooms echoed with the fantastic tales told by soldiers and seamen just back from America or India.

London   The life of the nation was centered in London, then the greatest city in the world. By 1714 half a million people were crowded into its narrow streets. The city had no organized police force and Dr.

174

Johnson warned his countrymen to:

> Prepare for death if here at night you roam
> And sign your will before you sup from home.

A common figure in the streets was the ballad singer, whose purpose, according to the poet Edmund Gay, was not entertainment alone:

> Let not the ballad singer's shrilling strain
> Amid the swarm the listening ear detain;
> Guard well thy pocket for these sirens stand
> To aid the labours of the divining hand.

What struck foreigners and visitors from the country most about London was the immense, incessant, unbelievable activity. The Thames teemed with traffic and the docks were lined with ships. The streets,

COFFEE-HOUSE, 1730

By the early eighteenth century it was estimated that there were well over two thousand coffee-houses in London. People went to them not simply to eat and drink, but to discuss, argue, and read. As one visiting Frenchman wrote: "What attracts enormously in these coffee-houses are the gazettes and other public papers. Workmen habitually begin the day by going to coffee-rooms in order to read the latest news. . . ." Another added that men of all ranks and occupations gathered round the tables discussing the daily news. "The government affairs," said he in some amazement, "are as much the concern of the people as of the great. Men condemn, approve, revile, rail with bitter invectives, both in speech and writing. . . . The King himself is not secure from censure. The coffee-houses and other public places are the seats of English liberty. For two pence you have the right to read all the papers for and against the government and take a sip of tea or coffee as well."

175

a perpetual pageant of colour and excitement, were jammed with the brilliant coaches of the rich and heavily laden drays driven by cursing drivers. Stores were bursting with merchandise from all over the world and offices were crammed with busy clerks. Here indeed was the heart of a nation and an empire. The observer, had he been gifted to foretell the future, would have seen in all this activity the signs of the birth of modern England.

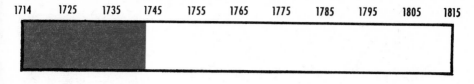

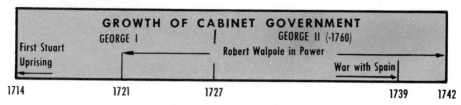

GROWTH OF CABINET GOVERNMENT

GEORGE I | GEORGE II (-1760)

First Stuart Uprising | Robert Walpole in Power

War with Spain

1714   1721   1727   1739   1742

CHAPTER TWENTY-SIX

THE AGE OF WALPOLE

George I's accession marks the beginning of a long period of political stability in England. The Revolutionary Settlement of 1688-1714 solved the problem of government for a century. Yet despite the careful arrangement for the succession to the throne laid down in the Act of Settlement, many Englishmen longed for a return of the Stuarts. James II's son, whose birth had been the immediate cause of the Revolution of 1688, lived in France and after the death of his father took the title James III. In 1715 his followers led an uprising in Scotland, original home of the Stuarts, in the hope of leading the Scots into war against England. The Rebellion of '15 was a dismal failure. Thirty years later, in 1745, there was a more serious uprising, led this time by Bonnie Prince Charlie, the son of James III. Although the colourful and romantic Charles was able to raise the Highlands in revolt and to invade England, his followers were no match for the regular troops that moved against them. The rising of 1745 was the last attempt to upset the Revolutionary Settlement.

For a generation after 1714 English politics was dominated by one man, Sir Robert Walpole. At first glance Walpole, who was short and fat, seemed hardly the type of man to govern England for over twenty years; a second glance, however, showed that he had strength and dignity. His eyes were alert and his mouth habitually wore a rather cynical smile. There was much more to Sir Robert than his contemporaries thought. Many men underestimated his ability and cunning and paid for their mistake.

Walpole was born a member of the governing class. He was not a titled aristocrat but a very wealthy and prominent country squire with

George I 1714-1727

Stuart Uprising 1715, 1745

Sir Robert Walpole

177

BONNIE PRINCE CHARLIE AND "THE '45"

Although the Georgian kings were firmly seated on the throne there were still many Englishmen who dreamt of the return of the Stuarts. In 1745 Prince Charles, grandson of James II, landed in Scotland with only seven friends. The Highlands rose to support him and the British troops in Scotland were roundly trounced. At the head of the Highlanders, Charles moved south to within eighty miles of London. Meanwhile, British troops had been recalled from Europe, where they were then fighting, and Charles was forced to retreat. Pursued by the Duke of Cumberland, often called the "Butcher" because of the way in which he punished the disloyal Scots, Charles was finally caught and defeated at Culloden. Loyal Highlanders and a lady named Flora Macdonald spirited him out of the country and away to safety in France. In 1788 he died in Rome where he had lived for years, a solitary and unhappy man.

friends and relations among the aristocracy. At an early age he sat in Parliament for a seat long owned by his family. By 1714 he was one of the most prominent young politicians in the country; seven years later he had become the leading political figure. From 1721 until 1742 he was without a rival, in an age when selfish politicians were eager to overthrow anyone if, by so doing, they could gain more power for themselves.

The Political System 　Walpole owed his brilliant success to a complete understanding of the political system of eighteenth-century England. He was not truly a party leader, as our Prime Minister is, for in his day there were no real political parties. Two groups, the Whigs and Tories, had arisen late in the seventeenth century, but when the political and religious questions of the time were settled, the original reasons for their existence slowly disappeared and only the names remained. Government was not carried on at that time by two political parties, one in power and the other out. Between 1714 and 1760 power was in the hands of the Whigs, but it should be understood that there were Whigs as well as Tories in opposition to the government.

SIR ROBERT WALPOLE

To understand how eighteenth-century politics worked, we must imagine a Parliament made up of a number of groups, each with an **Parliament** aristocratic leader. In every part of the United Kingdom there were one or two aristocrats or prominent squires who dominated the political scene. The members of Parliament for that region naturally gathered around these leaders. Some men owned a number of seats in Parliament, just as they owned their own homes, for in some constituencies the vote belonged only to owners of certain pieces of property. It was an easy matter for wealthy men to buy up all such property and thereby control all the votes. Seats which were not owned outright by private individuals might be won through bribery; it was common knowledge just how much it cost to bribe the voters in a given constituency. Some voters asked £5 for their vote, others fifty; still others asked only an evening's entertainment.

The largest and most important group in Parliament was the Court **The Court** Party or the "King's Men". It was composed of those who held profit- **Party** able government appointments and were dependent on the good will of the King or Court to keep their positions. The selection of the government still rested with the monarch and the Court Party supported any ministers he picked. The King would choose several leaders of groups to form a government. These men in turn would ask others to join them until they could command a majority of the votes in the Commons. Once in office, they used all the influence of the Court, the power of making appointments to the Church, the Civil Service, and the

179

AN EIGHTEENTH-CENTURY ELECTION

One observer described a London election as follows: "I saw the servants of the Duke of Northumberland, in their showy dress liveries, throwing lumps of bread and cheese among the dense crowd. . . . To see these vagabonds catching the lumps, shouting, swearing, fighting and blackguarding in every possible way, women as well as men . . ." was certainly disillusioning. The Duke had ample refreshments and soon someone suggested that the barrels containing the beer be broken open. "The heads were battered in and the coal-heavers ladled the beer out with their long-tailed, broad-brimmed hats." Many elections were quiet, however, and when we remember that there were no police it is amazing that near-riots were not more common, given the heat generated by the intense political rivalry.

military forces, as well as government money, to maintain and expand their strength.

Reasons for Walpole's Success   Walpole understood every phase of eighteenth-century political life. He knew that he must first keep on good terms with the King and he managed to do so both with George I (1714-1727) and his son, George II (1727-1760). He knew, too, that leaders of the political groups required tactful handling and sometimes profitable positions for themselves and their friends. Above all, he realized that the ability to manage the House of Commons was the real key to success as a parliamentary leader. If he could do that better than anyone else, his other tasks would be much easier. It would be little exaggeration to say that Walpole was probably the first man to see that the House of Commons was the most important branch of Parliament. For this reason he refused the honour of a title which would have sent him to the House of Lords.

Walpole excelled in the political arts this system required. He knew the members of Parliament intimately and could talk to them about their families, their finances, their hopes, and their fears. He was brilliant in debate, not flowery but down to earth, and spoke in a language that all men understood. He was not a venturesome politician and preferred to avoid issues rather than raise them. His motto might

180

well have been "Let sleeping dogs lie", for that was the creed he followed.

Walpole's policy suited the country squires who trooped reluctantly to Parliament every year and who felt that the less the government did the better. They understood Walpole, who had been brought up as they had, and usually gave him their support. They turned against him, however, when he proposed such legislation as the Excise Bill, which would have done much to facilitate trade but would have raised taxes and given government officials the right to inspect houses and buildings for taxable goods. It was an invasion of their privacy, they said! Although the government needed the money which the Bill would have raised, Walpole backed down and withdrew it. Walpole's Policy

Walpole knew that the country needed peace and time to recover from the long wars that ended in 1713. His twenty-two years in power were not marked by any sensational legislation or brilliant strokes of policy; yet he gave the nation sound and stable government. Walpole

THE EXCISE BILL

The above picture, based on a contemporary cartoon, like a popular doggerel of the day reflected the public's reaction to the Excise Bill.

See this Dragon, EXCISE,
Has Ten Thousand Eyes
And Five Thousand Mouths to devour us
And Sting and sharp Claws
With wide-gaping Jaws,
And a Belly as big as a Store-house.

181

has been criticized by some historians for failing to fill the statute books with legislation, but those who criticize him do not realize that the purpose of government in eighteenth-century England was not to pass laws. Its functions were to keep law and order, carry on the foreign affairs of the country, and insure it against attack. These tasks Walpole accomplished admirably.

Walpole and Cabinet Government
In developing techniques of managing the House of Commons, the King, and other members of the Council, Walpole laid the foundations for the growth of cabinet government. He insisted that he was the most important minister and he forced other members of the Council to submit to his will or resign. Since George I had no desire to attend the Council meetings as other monarchs had done, Walpole acted as the chairman and the chief intermediary between the Council and the King. To strengthen his government, he insisted that the Council should act as a unit. Whatever their private disagreements, Walpole insisted that the members should present a united front in Parliament. Sir Robert did not always succeed in this, but he did go a long way

WALPOLE AND THE CABINET

Walpole has often been termed the first "Prime Minister" and the "founder of cabinet government". He was neither, but he did a great deal to establish both the Cabinet and the position of Prime Minister in the English system of government. There were several important differences between the cabinet system then and now: Walpole did not choose all his colleagues, although his word had great influence with the King. The members of the Cabinet did not necessarily present a united front. The support of the King was more important to the Cabinet than the support of Parliament. The Cabinet did not resign as a unit when the government was defeated, as it would today.

towards establishing what we now call the cabinet system of government in which a united Cabinet is responsible to Parliament as well as to the king. Walpole stood so far above his colleagues that he has been described as the first Prime Minister, although at the time he indignantly denied that he held any such position. It is important to realize that Walpole was not deliberately trying to create a new system of government. He was a practical and ambitious politician, interested only in making the existing system work as well as possible.

People are not always happy with an unimaginative and stable government. As the years passed, Walpole faced increasing opposition from other aristocratic leaders who envied his success, and from merchants who felt that greater trade would result from a more ambitious foreign policy. There were some who thought that England owed her great prosperity to past wars and felt that there was much to be gained by a war with the wealthy but weak Spanish Empire. The merchants wanted trade, the adventurers wanted glory, Walpole's enemies wanted power, and the people ached for excitement. **The Growth of Opposition**

The ranks of Walpole's opponents gradually swelled with new recruits till in 1739 he was forced into a war with Spain. Walpole was not by nature a war-time leader and in 1742 he was forced from office. The men who immediately succeeded him are of little importance. None achieved his pre-eminence. All used the same methods of government, however, and the nature of political life did not change. The important events in the story of eighteenth-century Britain after 1742 were to take place outside the country, from India to the West Indies and from the North Sea to the South Pacific. **Walpole's Downfall**

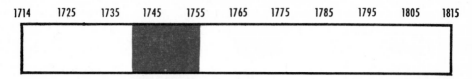

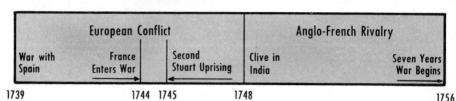

European Conflict			Anglo-French Rivalry	
War with Spain	France Enters War	Second Stuart Uprising	Clive in India	Seven Years War Begins
1739	1744 1745	1748		1756

CHAPTER TWENTY-SEVEN

THE ROAD TO EMPIRE

War with Spain   When Sir Robert Walpole was forced into the war with Spain in 1739 the bells of London rang out in jubilation. Mobs milled through the streets joyously celebrating the news. From his windows Sir Robert could see and hear the tumult. Now an old man, he shook his head in sorrow. "They are ringing their bells now," he observed; "they will be wringing their hands soon." Three years later, with the war going badly, Walpole was forced to resign. It was not his war and in many ways he was glad to be out of it.

Like other statesmen, this master craftsman in the art of politics had outlived his usefulness. For almost twenty years he had given England the kind of government she needed after the long wars with France. Peace and prosperity had strengthened the hands of those who were to defeat him. The wealth of the country had increased and Reasons for War the merchants were looking ambitiously around the world for sources of additional profit. They and the country as a whole had taken on a new confidence. The English were tired of peace and, stimulated by the chorus of envious politicians anxious to take Walpole's place, they clamoured for war.

The immediate enemy was Spain, whose rich, sprawling empire lay outstretched as a prize for the country that chose to take it. Spain had long since lost the strength to defend her possessions. In 1713 Great Britain had secured from Spain the exclusive right to supply the Spanish colonies with the slaves so necessary to work the West Indies plantations and the mines of Mexico and Peru. England had also gained the privilege of sending one ship a year to trade at Vera Cruz, a busy Spanish port in Mexico. But English mechants were not content with this

184

JENKINS' EAR

Captain Jenkins was one of the many whose tales inflamed the war spirit in England. In 1738 he appeared before the House of Commons and told the members that in 1731, while on his way back from Jamaica, his ship had been intercepted by Spanish guarda-costas, pillaged and turned adrift. Although many believed that both ears were safely tucked away under his wig, Jenkins had an ear, carefully preserved in a bottle, which, he said, had been cut off by the Spaniards while he was tied to the mast. When asked what he did then, the Captain replied that he had committed his soul to God and his cause to his country.

legitimate commerce. English smugglers constantly cruised in Spanish waters and the slave traders carried goods for illegal trade. Sometimes, it has been said, the one ship allowed to enter Vera Cruz sailed not between England and Mexico but between the harbour and a number of heavily stocked ships lying just off shore.

To stop this illegal trade, Spain resorted to severe measures. Spanish coastguard vessels stopped British merchantmen and searched them for contraband goods. Sometimes harsh treatment was meted out to the guilty. When this occurred, the aggrieved law-breakers went back to England, perfect pictures of innocence, to report on the misdeeds of the cruel Spaniards. One such complainant was Captain Robert Jenkins who claimed that the Spaniards had cut off one of his ears. As a result, the war is sometimes called the War of Jenkins' Ear. Gradually the demand for war was stimulated. The people felt outraged by accounts of Spanish cruelties; the merchants saw that a war with Spain might increase the Empire and their trade; and the politicians sensed a chance to defeat Walpole. In October 1739, amidst general enthusiasm, George II formally declared war on Spain.

The desire for war and the ability to wage one successfully were very different things, however. During the long years of peace Britain's army and navy had fallen into a sorry state. Ambitious British attacks

185

LOUISBOURG FROM THE INNER HARBOUR

Louisbourg had been started by the French a few years after Acadia (or Nova Scotia) had become British in 1713. Its purpose was to guard the entrance to the St. Lawrence and provide protection for the French fishing vessels and the commerce between the West Indies and New France. The American colonists looked upon it as a menace to their own fishing fleets and commerce, for a French fleet based on Louisbourg could easily create havoc in the North Atlantic. Thus in 1745 a British force, largely composed of Americans, moved north from Massachusetts to capture the fortress. After it was returned to France in 1748 the British built Halifax to offset Louisbourg. Again in 1758, although it was supposed to be impregnable, British forces besieged and captured the fortress before moving up the St. Lawrence to take Quebec.

were dismal failures and for several years the war drifted along. Meanwhile, a general war had broken out on the Continent, and the conflict between Britain and Spain soon became part of the more general con-

The Entry of France 1744 flict. By 1744 Great Britain found herself fighting a world-wide war with both Spain and France. France, the senior partner, was by far Britain's most dangerous enemy.

From 1744 to 1748 the war raged back and forth, as Britain and France competed for trade and power in every corner of the globe. In North America British colonists from New England took the French fort of Louisbourg on Cape Breton Island. In India, the French under Dupleix captured the British post at Madras. The French attempt to capture England from within by supporting the invasion of Bonnie Prince Charlie in 1745 failed. The Highlanders of Scotland answered the call of the Stuart grandson of James II and marched into England, but the army sent against them was too strong and Scotland paid a heavy penalty for her treason.

"Peace": Treaty of Aix-la-Chapelle 1748 Though France won striking victories on the Continent, the British navy, brilliantly reorganized by Admiral Anson, destroyed the French fleets and swept French and Spanish trade from the seas. With taxes increasing and trade hampered by war, both England and her enemies

186

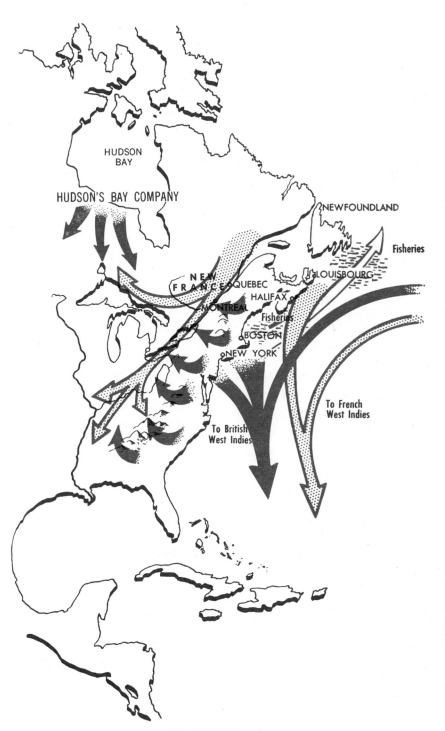

ANGLO-FRENCH RIVALRY IN AMERICA

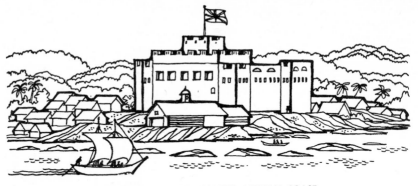

A SLAVE-TRADE FORT ON THE AFRICAN COAST

By the middle of the eighteenth century the British had a number of forts along the Gold Coast in west Africa to protect the slave trade. So important was the trade for the plantations in the West Indies and the southern United States, that the British government gave the Royal West African Company £10,000 a year to maintain the forts and protect the trade against French and Dutch competitors. The Gold Coast, the original centre of the British slave trade, is now a member of the Commonwealth of Nations.

had had enough for the moment. The Treaty of Aix-la-Chapelle in 1748 called a halt to the fighting. Britan returned Louisbourg to the French, the French returned Madras, and the Spanish Empire was left intact as an inviting prize. But there were men who learned much from this inconclusive war. One man, William Pitt, saw that France was indeed Britain's principal enemy, that control over the world's trade was the real stake in the conflict, and that only a nation strong on the sea could hope to win it. The world was to hear and remember much of this man.

The Treaty of Aix-la-Chapelle only ended the war; it did not bring peace. It was a truce, a breathing space, during which the two main combatants gained new strength for the decisive clash that both knew was coming. Indeed, before the ink was dry on the treaty, reports were reaching London and Paris of new encounters in different parts of their scattered colonial possessions.

Anglo-French Rivalry: West Indies In the West Indies where both countries had wealthy sugar islands, smugglers and illegal traders from Britain's American colonies defied the authority of France and bargained for French sugar, molasses, and rum. The French planters were only too willing to trade with the hardy Boston merchants who paid good prices. Nests of privateers or pirates could be found in the sheltered harbours of the unsettled islands that abound in the Caribbean. Seizures and arrests constantly created tense situations where the line between war and peace was often very slim.

188

Rivalry on the west coast of Africa was also strong. The economy **Africa** of the West Indies was dependent upon slaves, and British merchants alone carried twelve thousand Negroes a year from Africa to America on the horrible "slavers". Both Britain and France had posts on the west coast of Africa and slave traders of both countries fought incessantly to expand their trade in human beings at the other's expense. Rival squadrons of warships sailed along the coast determined to protect this profitable trade. Battles on both land and sea were common, even though the two countries were technically at peace.

Africans who sold their fellows into slavery did so for colourful cottons and calicoes from India. For well over a century Britain and France had maintained trading posts, or factories, on the coast of India. **India** By the middle of the eighteenth century, thoughts of trade had grown to thoughts of conquest, as the once powerful Mogul Empire in India collapsed from within. While there was room for two to trade, there was not room for two to rule. Under Dupleix the French traders had expanded their possessions and the British, with Robert Clive at their head, did likewise. Each man acted in alliance with rival Indian leaders and long before the war broke out officially in 1756, England and France were at war in India. Although the Indians did not realize it, the outcome of the conflict between two trading companies was to determine the future of that gigantic nation.

By far the most important centre of conflict was in North America, **North** where the century-long rivalry between the French in Canada and the **America** British in the thirteen American colonies was rapidly reaching a climax. As the population of the British colonies grew, settlers moved westward from the seaboard, slowly and irresistibly. Meanwhile the enterprising voyageurs and empire-builders of New France had extended their trading routes from the St. Lawrence to the Ohio and Mississippi Rivers. From Montreal to New Orleans stretched one great French waterway connecting the colonies of Quebec and Louisiana. Thus when the British colonists pushed over the Alleghenies in their restless search for new land, they found further expansion stopped by the presence of the French. French forts stood in their way. American leaders like Colonel George Washington, aided by British forces, were determined to clear the way for the settlers to follow. Conflict on this North American frontier had been going on for two years when, in May 1756, England and France formally began the war which has been called the Seven **The Seven** Years War. **Years War**

with France These Anglo-French commercial and imperial rivalries came to a **1756-1763**

189

crisis just as events in Europe once more led to a Continental war. England was allied with Frederick the Great of Prussia against France and Austria. For a year the war went badly for the British. In India Calcutta was lost. In North America the British general, Braddock, was defeated by French troops under Montcalm. The island of Minorca was captured by the French and Lord Byng, the British admiral, was executed as a scapegoat for the defeat. It appeared as though the war on which so much depended would end in disaster for Britain. The people turned angry eyes on the government leaders who seemed pitifully inadequate for the task of waging war. But in Parliament there was one man cast in the mould of a national hero, a man who had boasted: "I know that I can save the country and I alone can." Now he was to have his chance.

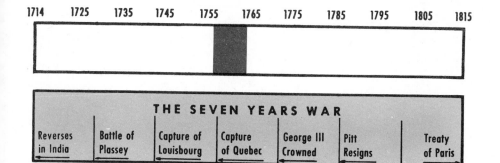

CHAPTER TWENTY-EIGHT

PITT AND THE GREAT WAR FOR TRADE AND EMPIRE

William Pitt, later known as the Earl of Chatham, was one of the   William Pitt
most striking figures in eighteenth-century England. Like Winston
Churchill in 1940, Pitt had been called to save the nation from disaster
and turn defeat into victory. Like Churchill, too, he stood far above his
fellows in Parliament. Even in his own day Pitt was a remarkable,
exciting, and unusual man. His grandfather was the famous "Diamond"
Pitt who, sword in hand, had helped to carve out a trading empire in
India and in so doing had made his own fortune. Pitt inherited much
of his grandfather's indomitable will, his belief that England's future lay
in trade, and his conviction that in strength lay success. Through his
grandfather, Pitt came to know the merchants of Britain and to share
their views.

Pitt entered Parliament at the age of twenty-eight as a member for
Old Sarum, a family borough owned by his grandfather who had
acquired it by the simple process of buying the seven houses that possessed votes. He soon became a leader of the "boy patriots", a group
of young members of Parliament, who had forced on Walpole the war
with Spain in 1739 and brought about his downfall in 1742. Pitt's eloquence was unequalled and his enemies came to dread the very sound
of his voice. In Parliament and out, he hypnotized his audience who
felt, as they listened, that here was the voice of Britain's destiny. Thea-
trical, truculent, and moved by fiery passion, Pitt stirred the entire
nation.

Pitt's oratory was inflamed by the insanity that pursued him throughout his career. His life was a succession of extremes. Periods of tremendous energy and exhilaration were followed by weeks of despair

191

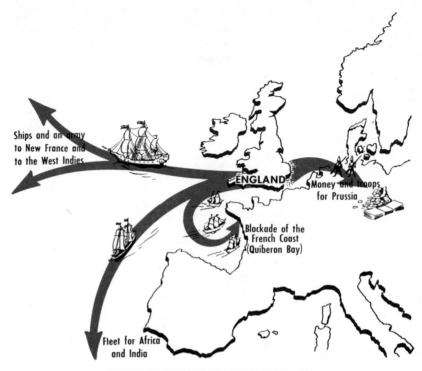

Ships and an army
to New France and
to the West Indies

ENGLAND

Money and troops
for Prussia

Blockade of the
French Coast
(Quiberon Bay)

Fleet for Africa
and India

PITT'S STRATEGY FOR THE SEVEN YEARS WAR

when, closeted in his room, he spoke to no one and ate only the food pushed in through a transom. This instability, this semi-madness, gave a sense of intense urgency to everything he did.

For years Pitt had sounded a warning against those who did not see that a great future for Britain lay in trade and empire. "When trade is at stake," he cried, "it is your last retrenchment—you must defend it or perish." Pitt had long regarded France as the principal enemy of Britain, not because of her European ambitions but because she was a great maritime and commercial power. This obsession with trade and empire, not unmixed with the wish for personal glory and prestige, dominated all his thoughts and gave to his actions a crystal-clear purpose. In 1757 the time had come to put his beliefs into practice.

Pitt's Policy and Strategy   Once in power, Pitt reorganized the army and the navy. His ability to select men was excellent. Young, new leaders, such as James Wolfe who was chosen as one of the army commanders in North America, replaced the exhausted warriors of an earlier day. With these new military leaders he discussed the course the war was to take and outlined

192

THE BATTLE OF QUIBERON BAY, NOVEMBER 20, 1759

For a year the French had been building ships and flat-bottomed boats and collecting troops for an invasion of England itself. Although small British squadrons were sent by Pitt into the Channel ports to destroy French shipping, the French plans still might have succeeded if the French Mediterranean and Atlantic fleets had ever joined forces and gained control of the English Channel. In November a great French fleet of twenty-six ships slipped out of Brest, but Sir Edward Hawke, despite heavy adverse winds, was soon upon it and drove it into Quiberon Bay. Overcoming the dangerous winds and ignoring the rocky shore, Hawke moved in and routed the French fleet, destroying seven ships and forcing others to ground themselves on the beach. The battle was fought so near the coast that one officer reported, "Ten thousand persons on the shore were sad witnesses of the white flag's disgrace."

his brilliant strategy. To keep the French army occupied in Europe, he supplied men and money to his European ally, Frederick the Great of Prussia. Constant raids by the British along the French coast kept others of the famed French regiments at home, while English forces seized control of the French Empire abroad. A strong naval blockade lying off the main French ports made hazardous, if not impossible, any attempt by the French to reinforce and supply their armies overseas. Flying squadrons of the English navy swept the seas of French merchantmen, while the British army and navy seized the key points of France's commercial empire.

193

The Fear of Invasion   In this strategy, however, there was one grave danger. Might not France stake all on an invasion of England? To do so she would have to gather all her naval forces together to transport her troops over the rough, twenty-mile-wide English Channel and to support them after the landing. In August 1759, Pitt's navy, on permanent watch, fell upon the French Mediterranean fleet off the coast of Portugal and destroyed it. Three months later another British squadron defeated a French fleet in Quiberon Bay as it moved out of Brest to support the intended invasion. These two decisive strokes ended for England any fear of invasion. With France's army occupied in Europe against Frederick the Great and the remnants of her fleet bottled up in French harbours, the issue was no longer in doubt.

North America 1758-1760   In Pitt's mind North America was the important theatre. The conquest of Canada would please the American colonists and disrupt the whole system of settlement which the French had established from the West Indies almost to Hudson Bay. In 1758 a combined naval and military force fell on the French fortress of Louisbourg which commanded the approach to the St. Lawrence. While James Wolfe was landing troops in the heavy surf off Louisbourg, another British army was moving slowly towards Montreal by the Hudson River-Lake Champlain route. Louisbourg was captured and the British sailed up the St. Lawrence as soon as the ice went out in the spring. British soldiers and sailors looked on the imposing citadel of Quebec, the centre of France's North American empire.

The capture of Quebec is an old and familiar tale to Canadians, for it was then that the future of Canada was determined. To William Pitt must go much of the credit for the success of the venture. He had personally selected Wolfe for the command; he had ordered Captain James Cooke, later famous as an explorer and the discoverer of Australia, to survey the St. Lawrence so that the giant British force could move without pilots to Quebec; and he had given Wolfe a large and powerful fighting machine. The Heights of Abraham were scaled and in a brief encounter on the plain above, British regiments held their line while the French broke and fled. Wolfe and the French leader, Montcalm, were both killed in the fighting, and Canada became British.

The West Indies   Elsewhere British arms secured similar success. In the West Indies, Guadeloupe was captured in 1759 and Martinique surrendered in 1762, when Admiral Rodney appeared off shore with nineteen warships. **Africa** Dakar, the French centre for the gum and slave trade of West Africa, was taken in 1759. Supported by a British fleet and troops, Robert

194

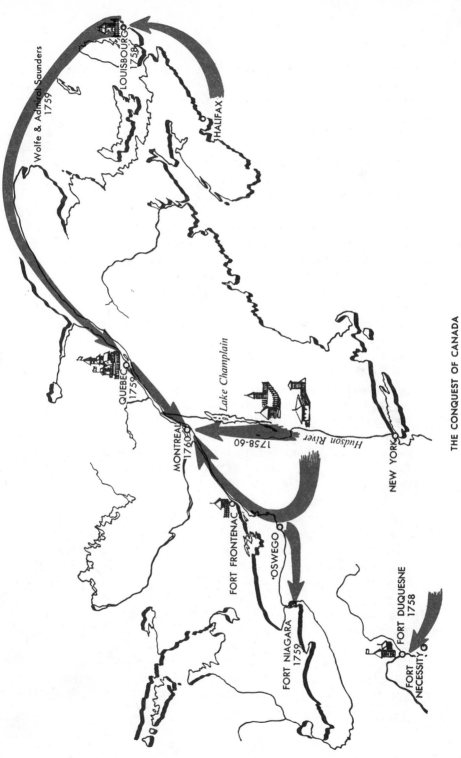

THE CONQUEST OF CANADA

India Clive expelled the French from India. At the battles of Plassey (1757) and Wandiwash (1760) the British won victories over the French and their Indian allies. Britain ended the war no longer simply a nation trading in India, but the governor of large sections of that immense land. This British empire in India was to grow until it included the whole country; it was not to end until 1947 when India and Pakistan became independent members of the Commonwealth.

Pitt's Resignation   In 1761 Pitt was watching the triumphant progress of the war from the shadow of the Opposition. A new king, George III, had come to the throne in 1760 determined, as we shall see, to get rid of the Whig aristocrats who had held power ever since 1714. Members of the Cabinet were conspiring against Pitt even as British forces carrying out his strategy were gaining victory after victory. In fact, some cautious members of the government were frightened by the sensational success of the war. The immediate cause of' Pitt's downfall was the question of war with Spain. He had long known that Spain would eventually join in the war on the side of France, for if the British decisively defeated France, the Spanish knew that, sooner or later, they would turn their attention to her rich and defenceless Empire. Pitt wished to anticipate the Spanish entry into the war and attack Spain before she was ready, not after she had finished her preparations. George III and the peace group within the Cabinet refused to sanction this policy, and Pitt resigned in 1761. Nevertheless, the war machine he had put into operation continued to function with spectacular success even after his fall. Spanish ships were chased from the seas and Spanish trade was taken over by English merchants. Havana in the West Indies and Manila in the south Pacific fell before the English onslaught.

The Treaty of Paris 1763   Meanwhile the new government was seeking peace. So eager were the British statesmen that in the Treaty of Paris in 1763 they undid at one stroke much of what had been accomplished. The rich sugar islands of the West Indies, Martinique and Guadeloupe, were returned to France. So too was Dakar. The profitable Newfoundland fisheries were opened once again to French fishermen. British forces left the Spanish colonies. But Canada was kept and France never again was restored to her old position in India. Nevertheless a triumphant war had ended in what seemed almost a humiliating peace. Well might observers wonder whether Britain had won or lost.

When the treaty was being debated in the House of Commons, the sick and crippled Pitt was borne in on the arms of his servants and crawled to his seat with the help of a crutch. Some of his eloquence

196

was gone, but the members listened for over three hours to his denunciation of this humiliating peace. "We retain nothing although we have conquered everything," he cried. By restoring all the French possessions, Britain had restored the French power: "We have given her the means of recovering her prodigious losses and of becoming once more formidable to us at sea." It was a speech to be remembered and yet his hearers scarcely realized that they were hearing a prophecy that in their own lifetime was to come true. Fifteen years later France was to assist the American colonies in their war of independence. After that, for a quarter of a century, France and England were to be locked in mortal combat. In that later epic struggle it was William Pitt's son who was to be the leader of the British people.

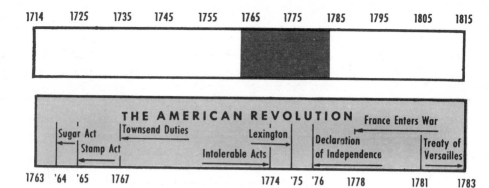

CHAPTER TWENTY-NINE

THE LOSS OF THE THIRTEEN AMERICAN COLONIES

The Beginning of the American Revolution 1775   In the grey light of early morning on April 19, 1775, a small troop of red-coated British soldiers marched along a country lane leading out of Boston in the colony of Massachusetts. General Gage had heard that the American colonists at Concord were collecting ammunition and he had decided to seize the stores and arrest their leader, Samuel Adams. The troop had left in secrecy after dark and had marched all night, but the soldiers had been seen and the colonists were forewarned. As they entered the small village of Lexington, a company of Massachusetts militia was formed up on the lawn outside the town hall. The British commander ordered the militia to disperse. Outnumbered, the colonists were preparing to follow the order when a shot rang out. No one knows whether the shot was fired by a British or an American soldier, but it was the opening gun in the American Revolution, a revolution that was to see thirteen of the fifteen British colonies in America emerge as the independent United States of America.

Causes of the Revolt   Just twenty years after Pitt had raised the British Empire to dazzling heights, its very heart and centre was to break away. This event, the American Revolution, is one of the great stories of modern history. If everything written about the Revolution were gathered in your classroom, the books would line every wall and lie scattered about the floor; but many of these books would be bad books, for there has been much written about the Revolution that is not true. We should keep firmly in mind that whatever the causes of the American Revolution, it was not a fight against the supposedly despotic and tyrannical George III of Britain; George III was neither a despot nor a tyrant.

198

Most of the American Colonies had been founded in the seventeenth century. Many of the colonists were Puritans or Anglicans, who had fled from England in order to be free to worship as they pleased. During the next century these Colonies grew in population and expanded westward from the ocean until, as we have seen, they came into conflict with the French in Canada.

These Thirteen Colonies, stretching from the Gulf of Mexico to the St. Lawrence River, were part of what is called the Old Colonial System. This system rested on two basic facts which few people ever questioned. First, each colony belonged to an economic system directed by the Mother Country and operated for the benefit not of the colony alone, but of Britain and the Empire as a whole. Secondly, while the colonies had some degree of self-government they were, in all important matters, controlled by the British government. As the years passed, the American Colonies developed economically and matured politically, and the colonists began to challenge both of these facts. Children obey and profit by their obedience; young teen-agers complain and secretly try to escape some of the regulations; twenty-year-olds, although not yet men, often rebel. So it was with the American Colonies. *The Old Colonial System*

Economically the Old Colonial System had been of immense benefit to the Colonies. Even before the days of Cromwell, Britain's object had been to create a strong and self-sufficient empire. She encouraged the Colonies to produce goods that Britain could not produce and assured them of ready markets. Fish and furs, coffee, tobacco, and rice moved in increasing quantities from America to Britain or to the British West Indies. Returning ships carried British manufactured goods to the colonists. The growth in size and wealth of the Colonies showed how valuable this policy, known as mercantilism, was to them. *Economic Causes*

In time, however, the American Colonies outgrew the mercantilist system. They were producing more goods than Britain and the other British colonies could absorb and yet they were forbidden by British laws to trade elsewhere. Many defied the regulations and a vigorous and profitable smuggling trade grew up in the ports of Boston, New York, and Philadelphia, usually ignored by the British Customs and Admiralty officials. In addition, as the Colonies grew in population they sought to produce goods that Britain also manufactured and the colonists resented the British laws that restricted such production. Although the Colonies were increasing their exports, Britain sold more to America than America did to Britain. This unfavourable balance of trade meant that the colonists were always in debt, a situation which they found intolerable.

199

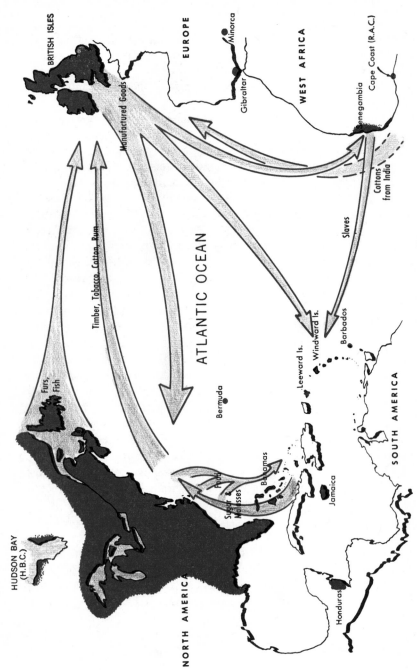

THE NORTH ATLANTIC TRADING COMMUNITY

BRITISH ISLES

EUROPE

Minorca

Gibraltar

WEST AFRICA

Senegambia

Cape Coast (R.A.C.)

Manufactured Goods

Cottons from India

Slaves

ATLANTIC OCEAN

Timber, Tobacco, Cotton, Rum

Furs, Fish

Bermuda

Leeward Is.

Windward Is.

Barbados

Rum

Sugar & Molasses

Bahamas

Jamaica

SOUTH AMERICA

HUDSON BAY (H.B.C.)

NORTH AMERICA

Honduras

Colonial economic growth paralleled a growing unwillingness on the **Political Causes** part of the colonists to accept the restrictions on their self-government. Throughout the eighteenth century, the elected Legislative Assemblies in the Colonies demanded more and more power, and the governors of the colonies, appointed by the British, found it exceedingly difficult to restrain them. A similar situation was to develop later in Canada and was to cause a minor rebellion in 1837, as every Canadian knows. In Canada a solution was found, happily, as it turned out. But no solution was found in the American Colonies seventy-five years earlier.

All this may be summarized by saying that by the middle years of the eighteenth century the American Colonies were growing up. They looked upon themselves as a country different from England, whose interests were no longer served by the Old Colonial System. One brilliant American historian says that the Americans rebelled out of a narrow self-interest. Their growing nationalism and their desire for self-rule made some change necessary. The British may have lacked wisdom in not seeing this, but they were not the despots they have been painted so often.

History is full of strange tricks. Before 1763 the American Colonies had not ventured on any movement for independence, for although the old system had become unsatisfactory in its economic and political aspects, the Americans very much needed Britain to protect them against the French. By his success in the Seven Years War, Pitt had destroyed the French menace. In building one empire he had unknowingly helped to destroy another. Moreover, the war against France had cost a great deal of money. British troops were still needed on **Defence and** the Indian frontier of the American Colonies and to keep them there **Taxation** would cost more. Since Canada was conquered and the West acquired, partly because of American insistence, the British felt that the Thirteen Colonies should pay some of the expenses of defending the country. The Americans refused, and when the British government tried to tax them to pay for their own defence, the train of events leading up to the Revolution began.

In 1764 the British government passed the Sugar Act. Actually, this **Sugar Act** Act lowered the duty on molasses from which the Americans made rum, **1764** but the smugglers who had once brought the molasses in without paying duty were now prevented from operating by the vigorous activities of the navy and the Customs. In the following year, the Stamp Act was **Stamp Act** passed. A tax of five cents for a stamp on all legal documents and **1765** newspapers was not going to ruin the Colonies, but the Americans

201

refused to pay it. The Act threatened their liberty as Englishmen, they said, for it amounted to direct taxation without representation. That is, they were paying a tax which they had not voted in their own legislatures. A tremendous agitation against the tax arose. Church bells were muffled and Americans wore black arm bands on the day the Act came into force. A mob in New York burnt the house of the commander of the British troops there. Young ladies refused to associate with men who agreed to pay for the stamps. Societies, known as the Sons of Liberty, were formed throughout the Colonies and dangerous talk began to be heard of winning independence from Britain. A meeting of the representatives of seven colonies—the Stamp Act Congress of October 1765 —approved of a boycott on all British goods. This meant that all seven colonies would refuse to purchase goods imported from the United Kingdom.

The British were amazed at this response to a tax which they themselves paid. However, the boycott on trade hurt the merchant community of England, and at its request the Act was repealed. In 1767, **The Townshend Duties 1767** Charles Townshend, the Chancellor of the Exchequer, tried a different way of raising money for the defence of America. He put duties on

OPPOSITION TO THE STAMP ACT, 1765

With the opposition to the Stamp Act, political protests turned into violence. Inflamed by Samuel Adams, mobs paraded the streets of Boston and pillaged the Governor's mansion. "Our presses have groaned, our pulpits have thundered, our legislatures have resolved, our towns have voted; the crown officers have everywhere trembled, and all their little tools and creatures have been afraid to speak and ashamed to be seen," wrote the excited John Adams. Opposition to the Stamp Act also forced the colonists to offer some constitutional reason for their action. The Stamp Act Congress in New York declared that there could be no taxation without representation and that the Act had a "manifest tendency to subvert the rights and liberties of the colonists".

glass, lead, paint, paper, and tea imported into the Colonies. By this time radicals of the Colonies, men like Samuel Adams and Patrick Henry, were rapidly gaining control and the boycott on British goods was again imposed. The British gave way again but kept the duty on tea as a stern reminder that in principle the British government had the power to do as it pleased in the Colonies.

The Colonies continued to smoulder. When in 1773 the government permitted the East India Company to take its tea directly to America, where before it had been handled by American merchants or smuggled in by Dutch traders, the smouldering embers burst into flames. Only slightly disguised as Indians, well-to-do Bostonians threw the tea from the cargo of a recently arrived ship into the harbour. Weary of the disobedience and lawlessness of which this so-called Boston Tea Party was evidence, the British took firm action. The port of Boston was closed; the constitution of Massachusetts was drastically reformed to allow fewer liberties to the colonists. These Acts of 1774, quickly named the Intolerable Acts by the colonists, united the Colonies in opposition to Britain. Delegates from the Colonies to a Continental Congress assembled in Philadelphia in September 1774; in the Congress grievances against Britain were recited and it was agreed that the boycott of English goods should be intensified.

The Boston Tea Party 1773

The British Reaction 1773-1774

A clash between British troops and the American colonists was practically inevitable. It was only a question of when and where. When General Gage sent his small troop to Concord from Boston to seize the arms and supplies stored there, colonial horsemen, among them a famous silversmith called Paul Revere, rode about the country warning the colonists of the movement of British troops. The colonial militia gathered at Lexington town hall, and there the shot was fired that was "heard round the world". On July 4, 1776, delegates to the Continental Congress signed a Declaration of Independence that was fashioned largely by the brilliant pen of Thomas Jefferson. The Declaration announced that the American colonies were free and independent states.

The Declaration of Independence 1776

By this time war between the Colonies and Britain had been going on for two years. No one expected the Americans to win; they were poor and divided. The British had an army that, properly led, could have easily and quickly defeated them. But British commanders in America bungled operations when once they undertook them and the British government was indecisive. Under the brilliant leadership of George Washington, there slowly came into being an American

The War 1775-1783

Entry of
European
Nations into
the War

army, which won several important battles. In 1778, France, later joined by Spain and Holland, all seeking revenge on Britain for past defeats, entered the war on the American side. Soon the war was being fought in every part of the world. The British were more concerned about the West Indies, India, and Gibraltar than about America. The French and Spanish fleets momentarily secured command of the American coastline and when the British general, Cornwallis, moved back to the port of Yorktown to maintain contact with the British fleet which was supplying his army, he found the port controlled by the French. Surprised, and cut off from his supplies, he surrendered without a fight. With the surrender of Cornwallis in 1781, the American War of Independence was virtually over.

The following year the British regained naval supremacy and Admiral Rodney smashed the French fleet in the West Indies. The British could have fought on and possibly regained control of America, for her forces still occupied the most important sections of the Thirteen Colonies.

THOMAS JEFFERSON AND THE DECLARATION OF INDEPENDENCE

On July 4, 1776, the American Colonies adopted the Declaration of Independence written by Thomas Jefferson of Virginia. The second paragraph has become immortal: "We hold these truths to be self-evident, that all men are created equal, that they are endowed by their Creator with certain unalienable Rights, that among these are Life, Liberty, and the pursuit of Happiness. — That to secure these rights, Governments are instituted among Men, deriving their just powers from the consent of the governed, — That whenever· any Form of Government becomes destructive of these ends, it is the Right of the people to alter or to abolish it, and to institute new Government, laying its foundation on such principles and organizing its powers in such form, as to them shall seem most likely to effect their Safety and Happiness." Here was the justification for the Revolution. In many ways the Declaration was not too different from the Bill of Rights of 1689 by which the Glorious Revolution was justified.

LOYALISTS EMBARKING FOR NOVA SCOTIA

Some historians have described the American Revolution as a civil war. There were thousands of colonists who remained loyal to George III. Over 70,000 of them left during the Revolution, but the great majority stayed in America, partly because they had no place else to go. Fifty years later there were still Americans who celebrated the king's birthday and pulled their curtains on July 4, Independence Day. Many Loyalists moved north to what was still British North America to provide the nucleus for the new colonies of New Brunswick and Upper Canada (now Ontario). Some returned to England, some eventually made their way to Australia. A large number of the Loyalists were of the wealthy upper classes, although there were a good many less well-to-do men among those who moved to Upper Canada.

The navy was now in first-rate condition for the first time and the army was larger and under better leaders. But the British had no taste for further fighting. There were many Englishmen who had never approved of the war. They argued that there was little point in trying to keep the Colonies within the old economic and political system and that to grant them independence would be the best solution to all problems.

Thus, with the signature of the Treaty of Versailles in 1783, the independence of the United States of America was recognized by Britain. The British Empire was split in two. The old Empire was to continue to grow, to expand, and in time to find solutions to the problems that drove the Americans to revolution. Out of that solution was to come the modern Commonwealth of Nations, in which countries as different as Canada and India would be independent of Britain yet members of a British community of nations. The new United States of America was also to become an empire expanding from east to west and north to

The Treaty of Versailles 1783

205

south until it became the strongest nation in the world. Despite the trials of the past, these two empires, sharing a common language and common traditions, were in time to ensure between them the future of the free world and Western civilization.

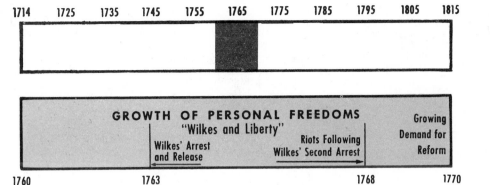

CHAPTER THIRTY

GEORGE III AND JOHN WILKES

While discontent in America was growing and the War of Independence was being fought, many Englishmen were more concerned about the behaviour of their new King and the escapades of a rogue named John Wilkes than they were about the American Revolution. On the death of his grandfather in 1760, George III had come to the throne, at the age of twenty-two. It is often said that this young King set out to break the English constitution, destroy the power of Parliament, and become an absolute monarch. Nothing could be further from the truth. George had no designs upon either the powers of Parliament or the liberty of his subjects.

George's father had never been gifted mentally and there is every reason to believe that the son took after him. The young prince was dull and backward; he could not read properly until he was eleven. Nevertheless he was shrewd and determined and he made up in hard work what he may have lacked in intelligence. But determination can often become stubborness and so it was with George III. Once he had decided on a matter, nothing could make him change his mind.

King George was honest, but not always frank. Of other characteristics one of his teachers said:

George III
1760-1820

> His religion is free from all hypocrisy but it is not of the most charitable sort; he has rather too much attention to the sins of his neighbour. His has a kind of unhappiness in his temper which, if it be not conquered before it has taken too deep a root, will be a source of frequent anxiety. Whenever he is displeased, his anger does not break out with heat and violence; but he becomes sullen and silent, and retires to his closet; not

207

"GEORGE, BE A KING"

Generations of historians repeated the legend that George III came to the throne determined to follow his dominating mother's advice to "be a king" by overthrowing the
system of government established after 1688 and taking power into his own hands. Within
the last twenty-five years this has been proven to be a myth. The influence of his mother,
a German princess, was strong but it was not directed towards upsetting the constitution.

to compose his mind by study and contemplation, but merely
to indulge the melancholy enjoyment of his ill humour.

The modern psychiatrist might see in this behaviour the early symptoms
of mental illness. Throughout his life the King was plagued with fits
of insanity and though he reigned for sixty years, he was completely mad
and incapable of governing during the last two decades.

The young prince's accession to the throne was popular. Unlike his
grandfather and great-grandfather, he had been born and brought up
in England, was accustomed to the English way of life, and "gloried in
George III's the name of Briton". The young man was determined to be king in fact
Policy as well as in name. He desired to restore to the monarchy the loyalty
and reverence of his subjects that earlier kings had possessed and to
exercise the full powers that properly belonged to the monarch.

Between 1714 and 1760 the powers of the king had been steadily
taken over by the Whig aristrocrats who, among them, ruled the nation.
These Whig aristrocrats had convinced George I and George II that if
the Tories were to win power they would restore to England the Stuarts
and Roman Catholicism. By 1760, however, this myth had long since

outlived its usefulness. George III recognized it as a Whiggish story to frighten young kings and keep politicians in office. He was determined to free the monarch from captivity. The king, he felt, should be free to choose his own ministers as the constitution provided. Men should be selected according to their ability, their concern for the national interest, their willingness to work with the king, and their support in Parliament.

For ten years after he came to the throne, one minister after another held office,

JOHN WILKES

Despite his scandalous private life John Wilkes charmed even his opponents with his quick wit. The following exchange took place during the Middlesex election. "Vote for you, Sir! I'd sooner vote for the Devil," said one of the Middlesex electors. "But in case your friend should not stand?" enquired Wilkes.

but failed to please the King, Parliament, or the people. Finally, in 1770, George III found in Lord North a man who pleased all three. North **Lord North 1770-1782** was to remain Prime Minister until 1782 when the American disasters drove him from office. In those twelve years George successfully broke the political power of the Whig aristocracy. Lord North's successor after a short interlude was William Pitt the Younger, the commoner son of the great Earl of Chatham.

George III and his ministers were unfortunate enough to have to **John Wilkes** deal not only with the troublesome Americans but also with John Wilkes, who was to be a thorn in their side for twenty years. Wilkes played an important part in the growth of British democracy, because of the causes he represented rather than because of who he was. By 1760 people in England were beginning to question the system of government and the structure of society. This was the first stirring of the movement for a more democratic form of government. It was Wilkes' fate to create issues around which democratic forces could gather. Among these issues were freedom of speech, freedom of the press, freedom from unlawful arrest, and the privileges of a member of Parliament.

Wilkes himself was a rogue. The son of a wealthy distiller, he profited by a university education at least to the extent that he learned to write well. Personal interest led him to marry a woman much older than himself, but after squandering her fortune he left her. His free time, and the young rake had plenty of it, was spent with a group of wealthy young men whose favourite hobby was writing crude poetry. One of his friends spent over fifty thousand dollars getting Wilkes elected to Parliament where the ambitious young man hoped to further his own fortunes.

Wilkes' Attack on the Government

Meanwhile, Wilkes had become the editor of a newspaper, *The North Briton*, and in Number 45 he attacked the King and the government in an outrageous manner. The authorities had Wilkes arrested on a general warrant and promptly locked him in the Tower. There was reason to believe that the government acted unlawfully in making the arrest. Then, as now, a warrant for arrest was supposed to specify the person and the crime for which he was being taken into custody. A general warrant did not name the person wanted. Moreover, a member of Parliament was supposed to be immune from arrest. On the latter ground the judges freed Wilkes. Knowing that a scandalous story which he had written had been discovered among his papers, and that this might lead to his being arrested again, Wilkes fled to France. The courts declared him an outlaw and Parliament expelled him.

After four years of luxurious living on the Continent, Wilkes returned to England where he was immediately elected to Parliament. Now that he was a member of Parliament, he believed he would be free from the danger of being imprisoned and surrendered himself to the authorities. Yet he was immediately sentenced to twenty-two months in jail. When the House of Commons met, the members expelled him again and ordered a new election for his seat.

"Wilkes and Liberty"

The people were outraged by the imprisonment of Wilkes and made his cause their own. Cries of "Wilkes and liberty" echoed through the London streets. Mobs raced up and down the fashionable districts demanding that lights be put on for Wilkes. Stones smashed through the windows of the hesitant. Lawlessness and disorder were the rule of the day in London. A news item of July 1768 stated:

> At the sessions of the peace at Guildhall, a woman was tried for assaulting Mr. Emmerton, a constable. He had taken her into custody for bawling, "Wilkes and liberty!" when, for his folly, she said, she would take the liberty to break his head, which she accordingly did.

The jury found her guilty and the court fined her a shilling.

Wilkes was elected again and for the third time the House of Commons expelled him. After his fourth election Parliament gave in, however, and Wilkes took his seat. It had been a victory for the people

WILKES AND LIBERTY

A prominent Englishman described Wilkes' election campaign for the County of Middlesex. "The election came on last Monday. By five in the morning a very large body of Weavers, etc., took possession of Piccadilly, and the roads and turnpikes leading to Brentford, and would suffer nobody to pass without blue cockades, and paper inscribed, 'No. 45, Wilkes and Liberty!' They tore to pieces the coaches of Sir W. Beauchamp Proctor, and Mr. Cooke, the other candidates. . . . They stopped every carriage, scratched and spoilt several with writing all over them 'No. 45', pelted, threw dirt and stones, and forced everybody to huzza for Wilkes."

over the government. However scandalous and unprincipled his private life, John Wilkes had become a symbol of good causes. He was one of a great many Englishmen who had stood for freedom of speech, freedom of the press, the right of the individual to live free from fear of imprisonment without cause, and the privileges and independence of Parliament against the government. He arrived on the scene at a time when the system of government in England was first coming under attack. In the years following the famous "Wilkes and liberty!" excitement, other men turned their attention to the cause of reform. After many hundreds of years the English Parliament was ceasing to reflect the interests of the English people. It was to be another century, however, before even half of the people in the country had some voice in their own government.

Wilkes' Contribution to Reform

The American Revolution intensified this feeling of dissatisfaction with the government as it was. Some Englishmen felt that the Americans were also fighting against an unrepresentative and sometimes tyrannical Parliament and government. In the late 1770's and 1780's demands for reform were heard from many sides. Great changes were overtaking England, but not until these changes had worked for several generations, as yeast works in the dough, was the bread of reform ready to be baked and served.

CHAPTER THIRTY-ONE

CHURCH, CHAPEL, AND JOHN WESLEY

Religion in Eighteenth-Century England   Since 1530 England had been disturbed and then torn asunder by religious conflicts. With the revolution of 1688 and the accession of the Hanoverian kings in 1714, religious struggles gave way to religious tolerance. Eighteenth-century Englishmen had no wish to be disturbed again by such matters and, in fact, they often wondered, like an eighteenth-century poet, what the fuss and furor created by their fathers had been about:

> I would by no means Church and King destroy,
> And yet the doctrine, taught me when a boy
> By Crabb the Curate now seems wondrous odd,
> That either came immediately from God.

As the poet implied, there seemed to be little of God in eighteenth-century religion in England. Both Anglican churches and Nonconformist or Dissenting chapels had settled down after 1714 to a long, deep sleep from which it took the genius of a clergyman named John Wesley and his brother Charles to rouse them.

The eighteenth century was the Age of Common Sense, of Reason and of Science and its voice was hostile to emotional religion. The **The Church of England** Church of England was directed by bishops who mingled with the aristocracy and sat in the House of Lords, often caring little for religious work. The principal concern of many bishops was to further their own ambition. As one playful poet wrote:

> What makes all doctrines plain and clear?
> About two hundred pounds a year.
> And that which was proved true before
> Proved false again? Two hundred more.

212

The ordinary parsons were of two types. Some were younger sons of country gentlemen who chose the Church rather than law or the army as a profession, not because they felt any deep religious impulse, but because it was a pleasant life. The papers often carried advertisements of parishes for sale, which usually pointed out that there was good hunting and good fishing amid pleasant scenery and elegant society. Yet

TO BE SOLD by auction by Hoggart and Philipps, Old Broad St., London. A most valuable living in one of the finest sporting counties. The vicinity affords the best coursing in England, also excellent fishing, extensive cover for game, and numerous packs of fox hounds, etc. The surrounding country is beautiful and healthy and the society elegant and fashionable.

A NEWSPAPER ADVERTISEMENT ADDRESSED TO CLERGYMEN

many parsons were poorly paid men who farmed on week-days and preached on Sundays. Poorly educated, if well meaning, they were hardly the type to arouse the religious enthusiasm of their congregations.

The Nonconformist congregations were no better. They had settled down after the wars of the seventeenth century to enjoy their hard-won independence. Their chapels soon tended to become dominated by the well-to-do middle class. Prosperous and complacent, most Nonconformists soon came to care nothing for the mass of the people. *The Nonconformists*

Two things were lacking in the religious life of the century. Religion had no real spiritual content and did not appeal to the emotions or the hearts of men. Moreover, while people were moving from country to city because of growing industrialism, the churches and chapels did not follow them. Large churches in the country had small congregations, while large cities were often without a church. Tens of thousands of men and women went years without having the opportunity to hear a minister. Even if they did hear one there was likely to be little in the sermon to appeal to them. *The Need for a Religious Revival*

Thus Great Britain was ready for the religious revival led by John Wesley. As a young Church of England minister, Wesley had felt the need for a closer relationship with God. He believed that religion existed to save men from sin and to offer them hope of salvation. To him, every man was a battleground between the forces of God and the Devil. If the battle were to be won by the forces of good, men had to live an earnest, religious life, battling every day against temptation. Because of his emphasis on a methodical religious life, Wesley and his supporters became known as Methodists. *John Wesley 1703-1791*

A METHODIST PREACHER

The Methodists sought out an audience wherever one could be found, particularly among groups not usually served by any Anglican or Nonconformist minister. Equal to John Wesley in the fervour of his preaching was George Whitefield. On one occasion Whitefield addressed a body of sailors and used a raging storm at sea to illustrate his message. In brilliant tones he pictured the violent gale, tossing the small ship about like a piece of kindling. The heavens lowered, the thunder clapped, and the lightning flashed. The waves rose and dashed furiously against the ship. The sky darkened. The masts were falling. The ship began to buckle. "What next?" cried Whitefield. So entranced were his audience that as one man they shouted, "Take to the boats, to the boats, take to the boats."

Instead of staying in their churches for the people to come to them, Wesley and his followers went out into the countryside and into the cities, speaking in halls or on hillsides to crowds as large as ten and twenty thousand. His audiences listened with terror and fascination as he pictured the war going on within them and the grave dangers that threatened them all. In his journal Wesley has described one such meeting:

> I heard many cry out, especially children, whose agonies were amazing. While poor sinners felt the sentence of death in their souls what sounds of distress did I hear. Some shrieking, some roaring aloud. And, indeed, almost all the cries were like those of human creatures dying in bitter anguish. Great numbers wept without any noise; others fell down as if dead; some sinking in silence; some with extreme noise and agitation.

John Wesley's brother Charles wrote beautiful hymns through which the Methodists could express the religious feelings welling up within them. Many of these hymns are still sung in the Protestant churches of Canada.

Here was a vital faith which touched the very heart and soul of human beings. It reached hundreds of thousands who had previously had no religion at all. John Wesley himself travelled over five thousand miles a year on horseback to preach to the people and when he moved on, Methodist "societies" were left behind to continue his work.

The Wesleyan movement was of great importance. The idea of a Christian life was revived. As a result of Methodist teaching, Sunday became a day of rest and of prayer in countless English homes, rather than a day for cock-fights and gambling. Methodists convinced the working class of the importance of a good life, of frugality and hard work, and that cleanliness was in some ways next to godliness. By the end of the eighteenth century, through the activities of the Methodists, both the Church of England and the Nonconformist chapels were roused to action. Some of their members began to concern themselves with the outrageous abuses of the times, and with remedying them. Such men were known as Evangelicals, or humanitarians. One of them, John Howard, spent a lifetime trying to improve the scandalous conditions in the English prisons. William Wilberforce, a wealthy member of Parliament, and Thomas Clarkson, a tireless propagandist, after a long battle secured the abolition of the slave trade in 1808. Missionaries sailed from Britain to the colonies to convert the Africans, the Indians, and the Chinese to Christianity, and religious life was quickened everywhere that English was spoken. Methodism was to have a great influence in Canada and the United States.

John Wesley should also be regarded as one of those who influenced the movement for democracy. Though he was conservative himself, by uplifting the lower classes he helped them to value their political rights and to make use of them. He preached that every man was equal before God. From this doctrine it was but a short step to the belief that every man was equal socially and politically, although it took a hundred years to make that step. These teachings, however, caused many to disapprove of Wesley and the Methodists. As one duchess exclaimed, "It is monstrous to be told that you have a heart as sinful as the common wretches that crawl on the ground." Yet however hostile people of the upper classes might be, the Wesleyan movement was too strong to be

The Importance of the Wesleyan Movement

The Evangelicals

Wesley and Democracy

215

defeated. Before his death at the age of eighty-eight, Wesley saw the triumph of the religious movement that he had started more than half a century earlier.

THE SLAVE TRADE

For many years the slave trade was looked upon as an essential part of British overseas trade. Fabulous profits were made by those in the trade, for a slave purchased for £3 on the African coast was sold for £15 in the West Indies or America. Between 1783 and 1793 British ships carried over 300,000 slaves across the Atlantic. The Negroes were unwilling captives; many of them leaped out of the boats and drowned themselves to avoid being put on board the slavers. Life on shipboard was hideous and many failed to survive the crossing, known as the "Middle Passage". One captain reported to a committee set up on the insistence of the Evangelicals: "We spent in our passage . . . two months eleven days . . . in which time there happened much sickness and mortality among my poor men, and Negroes, that of the first we buried 14, and of the last 320." Another skipper declared that he "made the most of the room and wedged them in. They had not as much room as man in his coffin either in length or breadth. It was impossible for them to turn or to shift." Once having arrived in America or the West Indies the slaves were "put on the block" and sold to the highest bidder. The slave sale was anxiously awaited: "All being in readiness, the slaves were brought in, one at a time, and mounted upon the chair before the bidders, who handled them and inspected them with as little concern as if they had been examining cattle. . . . They turned them about, felt them, viewed their shape and limbs, looked into their mouths, made them jump and throw out their arms, and subjected them to all the means of trial as if dealing with a horse or any other brute animal." Such reports as these gave the humanitarians ample proof that the trade should be abolished.

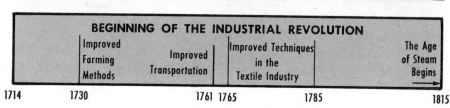

1714 1725 1735 1745 1755 1765 1775 1785 1795 1805 1815

BEGINNING OF THE INDUSTRIAL REVOLUTION

| Improved Farming Methods | Improved Transportation | Improved Techniques in the Textile Industry | The Age of Steam Begins |

1714   1730   1761 1765   1785   1815

CHAPTER THIRTY-TWO

THE GROWTH OF INDUSTRY

The England of George III and Samuel Johnson, John Wilkes, and John Wesley was experiencing great changes by which the whole face and nature of the country was being transformed. Historians commonly call these changes the Industrial Revolution, but the word "Revolution" is poorly chosen. The movement was not one that sprang up suddenly and changed England overnight. It was a slow movement which began imperceptibly, early in the eighteenth century, picked up speed as it went along, and did not reach its first climax for a century. It should be compared not to a waterfall but to an unbroken stretch of rapids which continues to seethe; for the Industrial Revolution is just beginning in some countries today.

The Industrial Revolution: A Definition

In 1714 England was still largely an agricultural country, with poor dirt roads as the principal means of communication. Not until 1850 was it an industrial country, criss-crossed by railways. Some time between 1714 and 1850 the Industrial Revolution may be said to have begun in England, and what we must do here is to examine its gradual emergence and its origins.

Before any country can become industrialized it must have a labour force to man the factories, over and above that needed to keep the people fed. Eighteenth-century England was rapidly increasing in population. In 1714 there were roughly 6,000,000 people in England, and by 1760 still only 6,500,000. But by 1815 the figure had leaped to 10,500,000 and was to continue to grow thereafter. There are many reasons for this rapid increase in population in the second half of the century. Better and more plentiful food, improved medicine, some knowledge of how to control disease and of the importance of sanitation,

Population Growth

217

TULL'S SEED DRILL

Jethro Tull was an Oxford graduate who did much to modernize English farming methods. After a close study of European agricultural practices, he wrote his famous book, "Horse Hoeing Husbandry". He claimed that soil could be made more productive by frequent hoeing even after the grain began to grow. Since hoeing was impossible if the seed had been scattered by hand, it was necessary to find some way of sowing it in rows. Tull's ingenious seed drill was the solution. It made the channels, sowed the seed and covered the rows all in one operation. To their amazement English farmers discovered that with Tull's drill a reduced amount of seed would produce more grain to the acre.

the curbing of the deadly gin trade, and the development of hospitals led to a fall in the death rate. More children lived to be adults and in turn had families. Rapidly increasing prospects of employment encouraged people to have more children, for the youngsters could start to bring in wages at a very early age.

Agriculture　　Improved farming methods made it possible for fewer farmers to produce the food necessary for the growing population, and to do so at an increased profit. Viscount Townshend, known as "Turnip" Townshend, instead of following the old method of enriching the land by letting it lie fallow, began to grow turnips to provide winter feed for cattle, and clover to replenish the soil with needed nitrogen. Jethro Tull developed a seed drill which permitted rapid and more efficient sowing. Thomas Coke used manure as fertilizer, with amazing results. These new methods proved to be much more profitable if the farms were large and operated by the owner. The old open-field system, dating from

218

Anglo-Saxon times, gave way to modern farms, as landowners bought out or evicted their tenants, who moved off to swell the labour force in the cities. Oliver Goldsmith's poem, "The Deserted Village", lamented the decline of the peasantry:

> Ill fares the land, to hastening ills a prey,
> Where wealth accumulates, and men decay.

An industrial country needs raw materials to convert into manufac- Raw Materials tured goods and markets in which to sell them. England had both in abundance. Her coal and iron had been used for a long time, but seemingly endless wealth still lay hidden underneath the soil. Her overseas empire provided her with growing markets for the products of factory and mine. But money or capital is necessary to gather the materials together, to build factories, and to get the product to market.

THE BANK OF ENGLAND
The Bank of England, the most famous of world banks, was started in 1694. Until 1946 it was a private organization and for a long time was really the government's banker. In the last half of the eighteenth century many other smaller banks were established, thus making possible the rapid and easy flow of money and credit which was necessary to finance the great economic changes that were taking place. The Bank of England, however, remained the greatest bank in the country and its bank notes were the chief currency in London and in many other parts of England. By 1800 its notes were honoured throughout the world. Napoleon used it as a model when he established the Bank of France.

A TOLL-GATE OR TURNPIKE

In an attempt to improve the roads the toll system was adopted in England. Often a stretch of road was given over to a "turnpike trust", a group of men who guaranteed to keep the roads in good repair and in return were permitted to levy a toll on all traffic. Although very unpopular, the system was reasonably successful. It was many years before the government itself assumed responsibility for the maintenance of the roads. Not until the nineteenth century, when men like McAdam and Telford adopted adequate drainage techniques and the practice of topping the roads, was the science of road-building developed to anything like a modern level.

Capital Eighteenth-century England possessed large amounts of surplus capital. The expansion of trade and the profits resulting from the new farming methods created wealth. The development of an efficient banking system helped to make it available to the would-be manufacturer.

Transportation An industrial society demands a good transportation system. Raw materials, finished products, orders, and payments have to be moved quickly and cheaply. In the second half of the century, the English began to improve their roads. The Duke of Bridgewater built a canal that could transport heavy goods and his example was soon followed by others. Before long the rivers were deepened and connected by a network of canals that made possible the movement of goods from one end of England to the other. Ship-building was improved and new cargo-vessels appeared which could move coal cheaply by sea to other parts of England, while fast merchantmen carried English products throughout the Empire and the world.

Inventions Finally, men with education and inventiveness are needed to develop new means of production. Great Britain in the eighteenth century had these men in abundance, particularly among the Scots whose educational system ranked with the best in Europe. The inventions of James Hargreaves (spinning jenny), Richard Arkwright (water frame), Samuel

220

ECONOMIC GROWTH 1714-1850

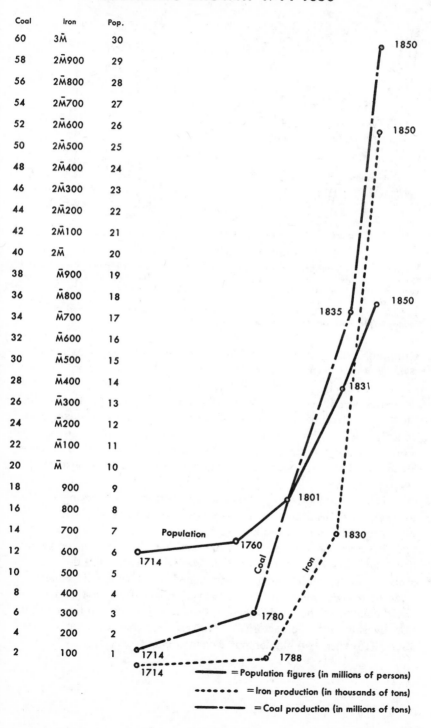

Coal	Iron	Pop.
60	3M̄	30
58	2M̄900	29
56	2M̄800	28
54	2M̄700	27
52	2M̄600	26
50	2M̄500	25
48	2M̄400	24
46	2M̄300	23
44	2M̄200	22
42	2M̄100	21
40	2M̄	20
38	M̄900	19
36	M̄800	18
34	M̄700	17
32	M̄600	16
30	M̄500	15
28	M̄400	14
26	M̄300	13
24	M̄200	12
22	M̄100	11
20	M̄	10
18	900	9
16	800	8
14	700	7
12	600	6
10	500	5
8	400	4
6	300	3
4	200	2
2	100	1

1850

1850

1850

1835

1831

1801

Population

1760

1714

Coal

Iron

1830

1780

1714

1788

1714

——— = Population figures (in millions of persons)

••••••• = Iron production (in thousands of tons)

—·—·— = Coal production (in millions of tons)

JAMES WATT AND THE TEA KETTLE

For many years historians have scoffed at the tales of young Watt and the tea kettle. Recently, however, one historian went through Watt's note books on his experiments and concluded that it would indeed be a rash man who would flatly deny "the story of a small Scots boy watching a kettle-lid rise and dreaming, by his fireside, of steam pressure and the steam engine". Watt did not invent the steam engine but followed and vastly improved the work of Newcomen and Savery.

Crompton (the "mule"), and Edmund Cartwright (power loom) revolutionized the textile industry. Other men developed improved techniques of mining, smelting, and forging. The most famous inventor of the period was James Watt,who developed the first effective steam engine. Steam was of prime importance; with engines powered by steam, mines could go deeper, machines could go faster, heavy work could be done more easily, and tasks performed that men alone could not have done. Steam, coal, and iron became the foundations of English industrial society.

The Rate of Change   Throughout the century these forces were slowly working together to create an industrial nation. So gradual were the changes that many of George III's subjects did not even know they were taking place. The pace became faster during the 1770's and 1780's. During the twenty-five years after 1790 England was at war with France and the need for arms, clothing, and equipment stimulated great economic expansion. Even by the war's end in 1815, however, England was not an industrialized country. The old putting-out system of Elizabethan times existed side by side with the factories. The greatest changes were to come after 1815 when two momentous developments took place.

222

The first of these developments was the increasing use of the steam engine in many forms of industry. So successful was the change-over that by 1850 the factory system, based on steam, had completely replaced other forms of enterprise. The second development was the application of steam to transportation. Beginning in the 1840's steam ships built of iron competed with the old sailing vessels and gradually drove them from the seas. In 1828 when George Stephenson's steam locomotive, *The Rocket,* attained the amazing speed of almost thirty miles an hour, the Railway Age had arrived. Ten years later there were still only five hundred miles of railway in operation in England, but by 1848 over five thousand miles had been built. With the locomotive, the iron ship, and the large factories and huge machinery required to construct them, England had become an industrial country. Iron and coal production and population growth took tremendous leaps in the 1830's and 1840's. In 1850 the English found that for the first time in their history half of the people lived in cities.

The industrialization of England created grave political and social problems, however. Men skilled in the old crafts and farmers evicted from their lands often found themselves unemployed and their families sometimes starving. The new cities were slums such as Canadians have never seen. The factories were manned by children, many scarcely more than babes. Men, women, and children worked unbelievably long hours under the merciless eye of the factory owner or his foremen. The middle class, made wealthy by the Industrial Revolution, became the most powerful group in the country and was to fight with the aristocracy for political power. The new working class slowly became organized and demanded political and social reforms. In time these two groups were to alter radically the nature of English government. Political democracy and social equality were, in the long run, the two consequences of the Industrial Revolution which were to have the greatest influence on British life. The faint beginnings of both can be seen in the careers of Wilkes and Wesley, but the story of their full development belongs to the nineteenth and twentieth centuries.

Industrial Growth 1815-1850

Industrial and Social Problems

Industrialism and Politics

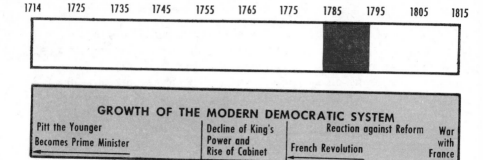

CHAPTER THIRTY-THREE

REFORM AND REACTION: 1783-1793

When the disasters suffered by Britain in the American Revolution forced Lord North from office in 1782, George III tried several Prime Ministers before he found a man to replace him who pleased both King and Parliament. In 1783 his choice fell on William Pitt, son of the great Earl of Chatham, and in the election of 1784 Pitt won a large majority. With the exception of the years from 1801-1804, Pitt remained Prime Minister until his death in 1806. Only Walpole could boast of a longer period in office.

William Pitt the Younger

Pitt's rise to power was astonishing. Born in that triumphant year, 1759, as his father's generals and admirals in the Seven Years War brought France to her knees, young William Pitt soon showed remarkable ability. At fourteen he entered Cambridge University and while still only twenty-one took his seat in the House of Commons. Three years later he was Prime Minister of England. He died at the age of forty-six, exhausted by the task of governing England in peace and war.

Pitt the Younger owed much to his father, particularly the famous name he bore, which undoubtedly helped the young man get ahead. He inherited his father's eloquence, the ability to command attention and make an audience wait on every word, an ability to manage Parliament, an unquestionable honesty of purpose, and sound judgement. It required limitless courage and self-confidence for a young man of twenty-four, delicate and sickly, to take the office of Prime Minister in such troubled times. Though a gay blade in his youth, Pitt became more reserved and withdrawn as he grew older, and his later portraits show an anxious and troubled man.

224

WILLIAM PITT

A sight to make surrounding nations stare,
A Kingdom trusted to a schoolboy's care.

Many tasks lay before the new Prime Minister. After the American Revolution England's trade was stagnant and her finances disorganized. Pitt tried to make the financial system of the country more efficient, by simplifying the system of taxation and making it less costly to operate. While some new forms of taxation helped to balance the budget, Pitt knew that the best and only permanent solution to the problem of finance was a flourishing trade which would bring wealth to the country and taxes into the treasury. He wished to increase British trade with her Empire, with her former American colonies, and with Europe. Long before the idea of free trade between nations, without the imposition of customs duties, was generally accepted, he set about seeking means of freeing trade from restraints. He even negotiated a commercial treaty with England's enemy, France, in 1786. These measures by themselves were enough to earn for Pitt a reputation as one of England's greatest peacetime Prime Ministers. *Financial Reform*

Pitt's long stay in office did much to further the development of the cabinet system of government. Even yet the office of Prime Minister and the position of the Cabinet were not clearly defined. By the end of Pitt's life it was quite clear that he was the Prime Minister and led his own Cabinet. The King still took a great interest in every aspect of *Pitt, the King, and Cabinet Government*

THE FALL OF THE BASTILLE, PARIS, JULY 1789

The initial British reaction to the tumultuous beginning of the French Revolution varied between enthusiasm and indifference. Ignorant of the causes of the revolt, most Englishmen assumed the French were simply imitating the British in establishing a free government. Sir Samuel Romilly, a lawyer and member of Parliament, informed a friend: "I rejoice at the Revolution which has taken place. I think of nothing else. . . . It will perhaps surprise you, but it is certainly true, that the Revolution has produced a very sincere and very general joy here. It is the subject of all conversation; and even the newspapers, without one exception . . . join in sounding forth the praises of the Parisians, and in rejoicing at any event so important for mankind." William Wordsworth was inspired to write:

> Bliss was it in that dawn to be alive,
> But to be young was very heaven!

Before long, however, the rejoicing had turned to shock and horror.

government and exercised a good deal of influence on policy and on the forbidding of measures such as the one which would have permitted Roman Catholics to hold offices in the government. Nevertheless, the King's influence slowly declined, particularly after the November day in 1787 when George III jumped out of his carriage and addressed an oak tree as the King of Prussia. From then on bad health and increasingly frequent bouts of insanity removed the King from day-to-day concern with government. Under these circumstances the Prime Minister became more important in the government of the country.

In 1789, however, the British people turned their attention from matters of finance and trade and the state of the King's health, to **The French Revolution 1789** momentous events occurring in France. On July 14, 1789, a discontented French people rose in arms against government by a King who had absolute power over his people. A mob in Paris stormed the

Bastille, a great fortress-prison in which political prisoners were supposed to be lodged. In succeeding months the French revolutionaries abolished the feudal rights and privileges of the aristrocracy and began to set limits to the powers of the King, establishing a limited constitutional monarchy similar to that which existed in England. Most Englishmen hailed the event with enthusiasm. France, it seemed, had at long last seen the excellence of the British constitution and was attempting a revolution similar to the English Revolution of 1688. The immediate effect of the French Revolution was to stimulate the reform movement in England.

But English enthusiasm soon waned as the French Revolution went from one excess to another. The impetus given by the Revolution to

A RADICAL MEETING

The early years of the French Revolution stimulated the radical movement in England. Many societies were formed, some upper class, some middle-class, and some working-class. One of the most important was the London Corresponding Society, the first distinctively working-class political body in English history. Its leader was Thomas Hardy, a shoemaker, and its object was to spread radical ideas by leaflets, pamphlets, and correspondence with workers throughout England. Since the government adopted severe repressive measures against such bodies the meetings were held in secret. The government adopted the practice of planting spies in the radical associations, however, and on the basis of their reports the authorities moved quickly, in May 1794, to stamp out these "subversive" organizations and throw their leaders in jail.

227

the reform movement in England soon changed into a hostility on the part of the governing classes to anything that smacked of reform or democracy. As revolutionary France overran her borders and sought to "liberate" other peoples, distaste turned into alarm.

Late in 1792 French troops moved into Belgium. Everyone knew that Holland would be the next country to be occupied. To Britain a strong power in control of the Netherlands was intolerable. Alarm was coupled with revulsion as the French revolutionaries began to guillotine those French aristocrats unfortunate enough not to have escaped from the country. Finally, in January 1793, the guillotine removed the head of King Louis XVI, as toothless, hawk-faced, and blood-spattered old women chortled and knitted while they watched. The following month France recognized the inevitable and declared war on Britain.

English Reaction to the French Revolution By this time the French Revolution had killed any idea of reform in England, where the governing class tended to assume that any demand for reform would take the direction of the radical movement in France. Among the working class there was much admiration for the French revolutionaries and some hotheads even held France up as an example for England to follow. This attitude made the governing class more hostile to reform than ever. Thus throughout the war with France, and for some years after it, the movement for reform in England was ended and any sign of unrest on the part of the people was quickly put down.

Eighteenth-century England, as we have seen, was governed for many years by a group of aristocrats who called themselves Whigs. Pitt had **Toryism and Burke** been called a Tory because he had opposed them, but it was the reaction to the French Revolution that really created a Tory Party and a Tory philosophy. In general it may be said that Tories were men afraid of change or reform and fearful of radical movements. The Tories had a spokesman, Edmund Burke, one of the world's most brilliant political philosophers. Burke argued that society and government were like living plants and as such must grow naturally. It is true, he said, that there may be things wrong with the government or the law, but if you cut off a branch the whole plant may die. That was what had happened in France, said Burke.

Burke himself was not an extreme Tory, nor were men like Pitt and his followers. But many of the members of the governing classes were. Lord Eldon, long a member of the Cabinet, was an example of the so-called "Diehards" who were blind and deaf to the crying need for reform in England. As one man said of him:

228

As for Lord Eldon, it is the most difficult thing in the world ever to believe that there was such a man. He believed in everything that it was impossible to believe in—in the danger of Parliamentary Reform, in the danger of Catholic emancipation, in the danger of altering the Court of Chancery, in the danger of abolishing capital punishment for trivial thefts, in the danger of making landowners pay their debts.

During the long war with France that began in 1793, and for a decade after it ended in 1815, this hostility to reform on the part of men like Lord Eldon dominated the government of England.

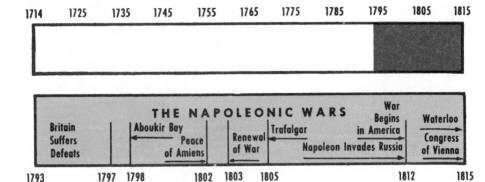

1714 | 1725 | 1735 | 1745 | 1755 | 1765 | 1775 | 1785 | 1795 | 1805 | 1815

THE NAPOLEONIC WARS

Britain Suffers Defeats | Aboukir Bay ← Peace of Amiens | Renewal of War | Trafalgar ← | War Begins in America → Napoleon Invades Russia | Waterloo ← Congress of Vienna →

1793 | 1797 1798 | 1802 1803 1805 | 1812 | 1815

CHAPTER THIRTY-FOUR

A NATION IN ARMS: 1793-1815

Pitt: War Minister   In 1793 the thirty-four-year-old Pitt, who had already shown himself a great peacetime Prime Minister, found himself forced to lead his country in war. Only a year earlier, while the continent of Europe seethed with unrest and revolutionary France was engaged in creating a monster army, he had declared that war was unlikely! The younger Pitt did not have the grasp of war strategy nor that single-minded concentration that had made his father a great war minister. But he had faith, confidence, and courage. These qualities were to carry his nation through one of its toughest ordeals since Harold's failure to halt the Norman invasion at Hastings.

Causes of War with France   Britain had gone to war mainly because France planned to conquer Belgium and Holland, which would place a powerful hostile army almost on Britain's doorstep. There were many people in England who regarded the war a battle against revolutionary ideas which threatened to upset the world they knew and loved. It was soon obvious, however, that this conflict was one more in the long series of Anglo-French wars for trade and empire.

Britain's Strategy   At the beginning of the war Britain's strategy was what it had been in the Seven Years War. Pitt set out to strengthen Britain's finances in order to provide money for his European allies. The navy was to defend the country, blockade France, and destroy French trade, while the army seized the French Empire overseas. In 1793, however, Britain faced a new France, one inspired by an almost religious enthusiasm for its revolution. The first four years were tragic for Britain and her allies.

The First Coalition 1793-1797   A coalition of European countries—Prussia, Russia, Spain, and Holland —was soon broken up by the might of the French armies. English

230

MUTINY AT SPITHEAD, 1797

In 1797 two serious mutinies in the British navy broke out at the Nore and at Spithead. The sailors had many grievances. Pay was low and often badly in arrears; food was disgraceful; punishments were often incredibly brutal. Many sailors were in the navy against their will, having been forced into service by the notorious Press Gangs. When the Channel Fleet was ordered to sea, mutinous sailors at Spithead, off Portsmouth, hoisted the red flag of defiance and refused to sail until their pay was raised. Although Parliament redressed some grievances, the mutiny spread to many sections of the Fleet. In the same year, however, many ships which had been involved in the mutinies won decisive victories against the French.

attacks on the West Indies were pitiful failures, and French fleets forced the British to withdraw from the Mediterranean. Bad crops, high prices, and unemployment led to serious unrest among the British people, while Ireland seized the opportunity to revolt against England. In the spring of 1797, English sailors mutinied and refused to put to sea. Never before in her history had the outlook been so bleak for England.

Meanwhile a brilliant general, Napoleon Bonaparte, had risen to power in France. Napoleon thought seriously of invading England in 1797-98, but decided that she could be crushed in the East. If he were to capture her vast Indian empire, he reasoned, England would be forced into a humiliating surrender. Quickly he moved across the Mediterranean to Egypt, the first step on the road to India. Here for the first time Napoleon met his match in the person of Admiral Nelson. **Napoleon Bonaparte**

Horatio Nelson had gone to sea as a midshipman at the age of fourteen. He loved the sea and knew his ships and seamen as few admirals had ever done. Like other great men, Nelson was arrogant and supremely confident of his own ability. Like Napoleon, he believed that he was a man of destiny. Given to reckless heroism, he had lost an eye at Corsica and an arm at Santa Cruz, both in daring attacks. Nelson, now an admiral of the British navy, was determined to re-enter the Mediterranean, find Napoleon's fleet, and destroy it. After a long search he found the French ships in Egypt's Aboukir Bay. Disregarding **Admiral Nelson**

231

NAPOLEON PLANS THE INVASION OF BRITAIN

the treacherous waters, he sailed in, caught the French off-guard, and destroyed their fleet. Napoleon got back to France in a small ship which managed to sail through the British blockade. The army which he had abandoned, its communications with France cut off, was forced to surrender to the British. The Mediterranean was once again a British lake. Overnight the spirit of the English people revived. They knew they would survive and might in time be victorious.

The Second Coalition 1798-1802   The European powers formed a second coalition against France, once again financed by Pitt's taxation. Napoleon immediately launched a series of lightning attacks which defeated the allied countries and brought much of Europe under French domination. To oppose the French and Napoleon, who by now was the real ruler of France, and the countries France had conquered, there remained Pitt, Admiral Nelson, and the British people.

Fearing that Denmark would soon be at war with Britain, Nelson moved his ships to Copenhagen and captured the Danish fleet, depriving France of invaluable sea power. By 1802 a deadlock between the two countries had been reached and France and England signed the Peace of Amiens. Both countries realized that the treaty provided only a breathing space; it did not end the war.

Peace of Amiens 1802

232

Pitt had resigned in 1801 as Prime Minister. In an attempt to quench the flames of revolt in Ireland he had carried through Parliament an Act of Union which united that turbulent and unhappy land with Britain and gave the Irish representation in the Parliament at Westminister. He also pressed for Roman Catholic emancipation. Roman Catholics were still debarred by their faith from holding public office, and Pitt believed it essential that this state of affairs should be ended. The King refused to accept such a policy and Pitt resigned. *Pitt's Resignation 1801*

In 1803 the war with France began again. Nelson spoke for Britain when he exclaimed, "It is really shocking that one animal should disturb the peace of Europe." Napoleon planned to invade England, believing that only in this way would his most persistent enemy be destroyed. He assembled thousands of flat-bottomed boats in the harbours of the Channel towns of France and began to train an army of half a million men for the invasion. In this emergency the English people demanded the return of Pitt as Prime Minister. George Canning, later a brilliant Foreign Secretary, expressed their feeling when he said, "Whether Pitt *The Renewal of War 1803*

ENGLISH COAST DEFENCES

Napoleon's invasion plans presented a greater threat to England than any since the Spanish Armada. However, in the crisis Englishmen did not lose their sense of humour. "As for the spirit of the peasantry," wrote the humorist Sydney Smith, "in making a gallant defence behind hedgerows, and through plate-racks and hen-coops, highly as I think of their bravery, I do not know any nation in Europe so likely to be struck with panic as the English; and this from their total unacquaintance with the science of war. Old wheat and beans blazing for twenty miles round; cart mares shot; sows of Lord Somerville's breed running wild over the country; the minister of the parish wounded sorely in his hinder parts; Mrs. Plymley in fits; all these scenes of war an Austrian or Russian has seen three or four times over; but it is now three centuries since an English pig has fallen in a fair battle upon English ground, or a farm-house been rifled."

233

will save us, I do not know, but surely he is the only man that can."
Though he was exhausted and ill, Pitt returned to office in 1804.

The Defence of England

Under his inspiration the nation prepared for Napoleon's attack.
Civilian troops were organized and armed with pikes and clubs, trenches
were dug along the shoreline, Martello towers—small circular forts—
were built all along the coast, and the navy on which everything might
depend was ordered to maintain a vigilant watch. Napoleon instructed
his admirals to slip out to sea, draw the British fleet into the Atlantic in
hot pursuit, elude it, and return to control the Channel for the few
days necessary to move the French army across. The French fleets
slipped out, joined forces, and raced westward. Nelson gave chase. To
the West Indies and back, he stayed on the heels of the enemy ships.

NELSON AT TRAFALGAR, 1805

The Battle of Trafalgar was England's greatest naval victory. Of thirty-three enemy ships,
eighteen were captured, four surrendered later, and twenty thousand prisoners were
taken. Just before the battle Nelson made his famous signal to the fleet: "England expects
every man to do his duty." A naval lieutenant described the reaction upon some crew-
men when they were told the Admiral's message. "There were murmurs from some,
whilst others in an audible whisper, murmured, 'Do our duty! Of course we'll do our
duty! I've always done mine, haven't you? Let us come alongside of 'em and we'll
soon show whether we'll do our duty.' "

Forewarned, another British squadron awaited their return and forced the enemy fleets into the Spanish harbour of Corunna.

Nelson was not to be denied his last victory. Catching the enemy fleet off Cape Trafalgar his ships moved in, not in the traditional line ahead, but in two columns. The French fleet was cut in half and then annihilated. A bullet from a sniper high on the rigging of one of the enemy ships lodged in Nelson's spine. But as Horatio Nelson lay dying on the deck of his ship, *Victory,* he knew that the day was his. England was saved from invasion, but the nation was too stunned by Nelson's death to rejoice. _{Trafalgar 1805}

With much of Europe still under Napoleon's heel, England again stood alone against him. Pitt now had only a few months to live but he still gave his courage to the nation. "England has saved herself by her exertions and will, as I trust, save Europe by her example," he said. Two months later, on January 23, 1806, he died.

In 1804 Napoleon had crowned himself Emperor of France. His attempt to invade England had failed and he now sought to bring that country to her knees by other means. Shrewdly, he decided to attack and destroy her trade. A series of Napoleon's orders, known as the Continental System, forbade any European state to trade with Britain. Britain countered with a blockade of Europe to prevent any neutral power from shipping goods to the Continent. The question was: who would suffer most? In Europe defeat followed defeat for Britain's allies and from 1806 to 1812 she once more stood virtually alone against the French Empire. _{Economic Warfare}

Only in Portugal and Spain did Britain find friends. Here the people had risen against Napoleon, and Britain had sent Sir Arthur Wellesley, a general who had fought brilliantly in India, to organize their resistance. Later famous as the Duke of Wellington, the "Iron Duke", Wellesley practised the tactics of "hit and run". For several years, while he was building up strength, he kept up a running fight with the best armies Napoleon could send against him. With his base in Portugal, Wellesley could easily be reinforced and supplied by sea from England, while French army supplies had to come through a hostile country whose inhabitants kept up a savage guerrilla warfare against the invader. Wellesley avoided a pitched battle and when it appeared that he might be outnumbered he withdrew his army behind the great defensive works which he had built in Portugal. His campaign in Spain seriously weakened the great Emperor and kept French armies operating in Spain when they might usefully have been employed elsewhere in Europe. _{Wellesley in Portugal and Spain}

The War of 1812 in North America

In 1812 the United States decided to enter the war against Britain. There were two reasons for this. First, Britain's blockade of France led to the frequent search and seizure of American ships which had tried to break the blockade and deliver American goods to Europe. In the life or death struggle with Napoleon, Britain was in no mood to listen to American complaints. Secondly, a group of politicians in the United States wanted war with Britain as an excuse to invade and capture Canada, which many Americans believed should be part of the United States.

As every Canadian student knows, the war in North America was fought mainly in the Great Lakes area. Sir Isaac Brock, who commanded the British troops in Canada, quickly captured Detroit and the American army defending it. Later Brock lost his life in the heroic, successful counter-attack at Queenston Heights, where an invading American army was hurled into the Niagara River and back across the border. While American ships secured temporary command of the Great Lakes, British and Canadian soldiers fought side by side to prevent any conquest by land. The battles of Stoney Creek, Lundy's Lane, and Chateauguay still recall the success of Canadian arms. The War of 1812 was a distraction for Britain but the main theatre of operations was still in Europe. The tide had at last begun to turn against Napoleon.

The French Invasion of Russia 1812

In 1812 Napoleon invaded Russia, one of the few countries in Europe that he had not conquered. The great distance his army had to cover, the winter snows, and the courage of the Russian defenders defeated him. In the spring of 1813 broken French troops trudged wearily back across Europe. In their rear rose the peoples of Europe, tired of an alien rule and hopeful that this time the conquerer might be defeated. The British Foreign Secretary, Lord Castlereagh, organized a fourth coalition of European powers against France, and from all sides the pressure on Napoleon increased. By the end of 1813 Wellington

Victory 1814

was poised on the Spanish border of France. In March, 1814, Paris was occupied by the Allied Army and the war was apparently over. Napoleon abdicated the Imperial throne and was sent to the island of Elba.

The Return of Napoleon 1815

While the statesmen of Europe were gathered at Vienna to discuss the arrangements for a permanent peace, Napoleon escaped. The French army sent to oppose him, joined him. The French people rushed to support him and, once again at the head of a large army, he made a last deperate bid for victory. On June 18, 1815, he met the Allied Armies led by the Duke of Wellington at Waterloo, not far from the Belgian capital of Brussells. For hours the outcome of the battle

236

was uncertain, but eventually the French lines broke while the British, despite thousands of casualties, held firm. The Battle of Waterloo, one **Waterloo** of the most decisive battles in the history of the world, ended in victory for Britain and her allies.

Napoleon was sent off in a British ship to the island of St. Helena where he died six years later. The statesmen returned to the problems of a peace settlement. Lord Castlereagh was determined to see that

THE PINCERS CLOSE, 1814

THE BATTLE OF WATERLOO

With the news of the French defeat and Napoleon's capture, the London "Times" wrote: "Our paper of this day will satisfy the sceptics, for such there were beginning to be, as to the capture of that bloody miscreant, who had so long tortured Europe, Napoleon Buonaparte. Savages are always found to unite the greatest degree of cunning to the ferocious part of their nature. The cruelty of this person is written in characters of blood in almost every country in Europe and in the contiguous angles of Africa and Asia which he visited." It had been an expensive victory. Of the 67,000 men under his command (24,000 of whom were British), Wellington lost 15,000. So fierce was the fighting that by the day's end 45,000 killed and wounded lay in an area of less than three square miles.

France was weakened but not ravaged by the victors, for he wanted to create a balance of power in Europe that might keep the peace for generations. On the whole he was successful. The peace established at the Congress of Vienna in 1815 was to last for fifty years.

Congress of Vienna 1815

Although Britain, as the principal and most persistent opponent of Napoleon, had been chiefly responsible for the victory, she wanted very little for herself in the peace settlement. In Europe she supported the union of Belgium and Holland in the hope that union would make them strong enough to keep out the French in the future. Although the union later broke up, Britain supported the general agreement that Belgium would be permanently neutral in the future. In 1914 she was to go to war against Germany when that nation failed to respect Belgium's

British Objectives

238

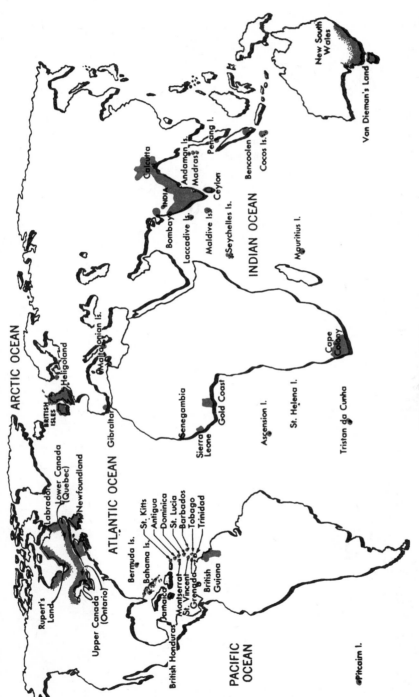

ARCTIC OCEAN

BRITISH ISLES

Heligoland

Malagonian Is.

Labrador

Lower Canada (Quebec)

Newfoundland

Rupert's Land

Upper Canada (Ontario)

British Honduras

Jamaica

Bermuda Is.

Bahama Is.

Montserrat

St. Vincent

Grenada

British Guiana

St. Kitts

Antigua

Dominica

St. Lucia

Barbados

Tobago

Trinidad

ATLANTIC OCEAN

Gibraltar

Senegambia

Sierra Leone

Gold Coast

Ascension I.

St. Helena I.

Tristan da Cunha

Cape Colony

PACIFIC OCEAN

Pitcairn I.

Calcutta

INDIA

Bombay

Madras

Andaman Is.

Laccadive Is.

Maldive Is.

Seychelles Is.

Ceylon

Penang I.

Bencoolen

Cocos Is.

INDIAN OCEAN

Mauritius I.

New South Wales

Van Dieman's Land

THE BRITISH EMPIRE IN 1815

neutrality. Other than that, England wished only some colonial possessions to safeguard her Empire. The Cape of Good Hope in South Africa, previously owned by the Dutch, was kept by Britain to guard the ocean lifeline to India, for the Suez Canal had not yet been built. The island of Malta was kept to assure control of the Mediterranean. Mauritius, off the coast of Africa, and Ceylon, off the southern coast of India, were likewise added to the Empire, for strategic reasons.

By 1815 the French threat to dominate Europe and the world had been ended. With the restoration of the brother of the executed Louis XVI as King of France, the French Revolution appeared to have been extinguished. Britain had taken few spoils of battle, but they were crucial spoils. In 1815 Britain and her empire were supreme in the world.

TIME CHART

IN THE BRITISH ISLES		ELSEWHERE
POLITICAL	**OTHER**	
1715 First Stuart Uprising 1721 Walpole becomes leading minister		1715 Death of Louis XIV
		1731-38 LaVerendrye's explorations in North America
	1738 Conversion of John Wesley 1739 War with Spain	
1742 Fall of Walpole		1743 Clive goes to India
1745 Second Stuart Uprising	1744 France enters war	1745 Capture of Louisbourg
	1748 Treaty of Aix-la-Chapelle	1748 Louisbourg returned
		1749 Halifax founded to offset Louisbourg
	1756 Seven Years War	1755 Braddock and Washington defeated Expulsion of Acadians
1757 Pitt enters the government		1757 Battle of Plassey
1761 Resignation of Pitt		1758 Capture of Louisbourg 1759 Capture of Quebec 1760 Capture of Montreal
1763-68 "Wilkes and Liberty"	1762 Spain joins France 1763 Treaty of Paris	1763 Treaty of Paris—retention of Canada
	1764 Hargreaves' spinning jenny	1764 Sugar Act
	1769 Watt's pumping engine Arkwright's water frame	1765 Stamp Act 1769 Prince Edward Island made separate colony Birth of Napoleon
1770 Lord North becomes leading minister		1771 Hearns reaches Arctic 1773 Boston Tea Party 1774 Quebec Act 1775 The American Revolution.
	1776 Smith's "Wealth of Nations" 1778 France enters the war 1779 Crompton's spinning mule Spain and Holland enter war	1776 The Declaration of Independence
1783 Pitt the Younger becomes Prime Minister	1783 Peace of Versailles	1783 Independence of American Colonies Beginning of Loyalist immigration into Canada

TIME CHART

IN THE BRITISH ISLES		ELSEWHERE
POLITICAL	**OTHER**	
	1784 Cartwright's power loom	1784 North West Company organized 1787 American constitution drawn up 1788 First (convict) settlement in Australia 1789 Outbreak of the French Revolution Washington first President of the United States 1791 Constitutional Act — representative government to Upper and Lower Canada Creation of Upper Canada 1792-94 Captain Vancouver charts the north-west coast
	1793 France declares war	1793 Mackenzie reaches Pacific
	1798 Battle of the Nile	
1800 Act of Union with Ireland 1801 Pitt's resignation		1800 Jefferson President of the United States
	1802 Peace of Amiens	
1804 Pitt's return to office		1804 Napoleon becomes Emperor of France
	1805 Trafalgar	
1806 Death of Pitt		1807 Aboltion of slave trade
	1808 Wellington to Portugal and Spain	1808 Fraser explores the Fraser River 1811 Selkirk settlers leave for Red River 1812 War of 1812 Queenston Heights Napoleon invades Russia
	1815 Waterloo Congress of Vienna	1815 British immigration into Canada begins Britain keeps Cape Colony and Ceylon

242

BOOK IV

TOWARDS DEMOCRACY

35. The Beginning of Reform
36. The Reform of Parliament: 1832
37. Working-class Unrest and Social Reform: 1832-1848
38. The Middle-class Victory: 1832-1849
39. Queen Victoria's Middle-class England
40. The Mid-Victorian Empire
41. The Age of Palmerston
42. Gladstone and Liberalism: 1866-1874
43. Disraeli and Tory Democracy: 1874-1880
44. Gladstone and Ireland: 1868-1898
45. Labour Enters Politics
46. The Climax of British Imperialism
47. The End of an Era

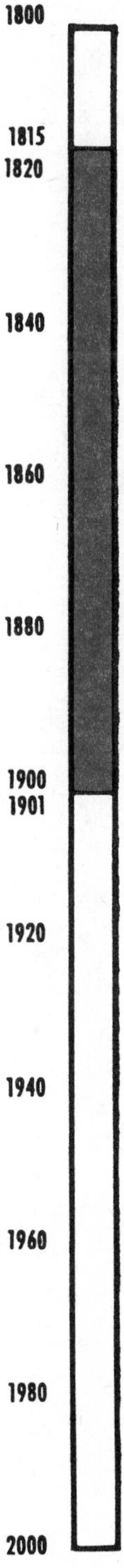

1800
1815
1820
1840
1860
1880
1900
1901
1920
1940
1960
1980
2000

RULERS OF GREAT BRITAIN FROM 1815-1901

1760-1820 George III ⎫
1820-1830 George IV ⎪
1830-1837 William IV ⎬ Hanover
1837-1901 Victoria ⎭

THE PRINCIPAL PRIME MINISTERS OF GREAT BRITAIN
1815-1901

1828-1830 Duke of Wellington

1830-1834 Earl Grey

1834
1835-1841 Lord Melbourne

1834-1835
1841-1846 Sir Robert Peel

1846-1852
1865-1866 Lord John Russell

1855-1858
1859-1865 Lord Palmerston

1868
1874-1880 Benjamin Disraeli

1868-1874
1880-1885
1885-1886 William Ewart Gladstone
1892-1894

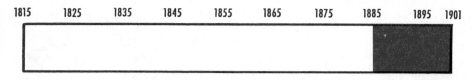

DEMANDS FOR POLITICAL REFORM

Peterloo |———————————— Minor Tory Reforms ————————|
                                    Catholic Emancipation Act —|

1815   1819   1829 1830

CHAPTER THIRTY-FIVE

THE BEGINNING OF REFORM

On a warm August day in 1819 six troops of the Fifteenth Hussars, *"Peterloo"* wearing their Waterloo medals, faced an army of a kind they had never before encountered. Fifty thousand working men, with their wives and children, all dressed in their Sunday best, had gathered on St. Peter's Fields just outside Manchester. The crowd was peaceful and orderly. They had come to St. Peter's Fields to hear the great radical orator, Henry Hunt, discuss the need for reform of Parliament. Nervously watching the proceedings were magistrates, the protectors of "law and order", who were themselves privileged members of the old England whose position seemed to be threatened by the activities of men like Hunt, and by their appeal to the working classes.

Never before had the magistrates seen such a demonstration. The great crowd was not the rabble of the nation but was composed of sober and respectable men. Their very determination and organization was frightening. Might not Hunt's eloquence stir them beyond peaceful protest to insurrection? It was not likely, for that was not his purpose. Yet the magistrates were determined to arrest Hunt, and to assist them they had assembled a military force. Before the day was over the troops had moved against the people, reluctantly, with no enthusiasm, and using the flats of their swords rather than the edge. But so congested was the field that bloodshed could hardly be avoided. When the crowd had been dispersed and Hunt captured, St. Peter's Fields was littered with the hats and coats, the banners and placards of the fleeing multitude, and among the litter stretched the bodies of eleven dead and many hundred injured. St. Peter's had become a battlefield: it was Peterloo.

HENRY HUNT AT PETERLOO

The radical reformer, Henry Hunt, was an English farmer, and like his counterpart, William Cobbett, whom he resembled, was pugnacious and devoted to the cause of reform. At a series of public meetings and dinners his brilliant and fiery eloquence won for him the name Orator Hunt. The white hat he wore at Peterloo, which was said to have been battered in by a sword, became the symbol of reform. While serving a two-and-a-half-year prison sentence he wrote "A Peep Into a Jail" which played a part in promoting prison reform in England.

In the history and legend of the British working class this "Massacre of Peterloo" has become famous. It was followed by severe repression of the demands for reform. The government quickly passed a series of Acts which tried to cripple the organized power of the working class by prohibiting large public meetings and limiting the freedom of the press. The future looked bleak; yet the government could not long turn a deaf ear and a blind eye towards the workers. The fifty thousand men who had gathered at St. Peter's Fields represented the new Britain—the Britain of the factory and the mine, the slums and often the bread-line; they had claims which could not for long be denied.

Working-class Discontent By the time of Peterloo the working class had found leaders to champion its cause. Under the leadership of men like Henry Hunt and Francis Place, an intelligent, self-educated tailor and trade-union organizer, the wage earners were ceasing to be the uncontrolled and ill-disciplined mob of the eighteenth century, who knew no other way of expressing their grievances than by rioting. The workers were becoming better organized and better educated. They knew that industrialization meant a great increase in the wealth of the country; but they saw just

246

as sharply the tremendous inequalities of its distribution between themselves and the well-to-do factory owners for whom they worked. They wanted many reforms: shorter hours and better wages, protection against unemployment, and some voice in the government of the country.

Despite the government's stern repression of its demands in 1819, the working class soon realized that in its criticism of the industrial system and in its demands for political reform it was beginning to have powerful allies. Perhaps the most eloquent of these was William Cobbett, son of a Surrey farmer, who had moved to the city and become a brilliant journalist. In his paper, *The Political Register,* Cobbett wrote of the vanishing past of what he called "Merrie England", the England of contented yeomen and simple village craftsmen (which, of course, had never really existed). He hated the England of factories and slums. In some ways Cobbett was a tragic figure, for no man can turn back the clock, and return to an agricultural England was impossible. Yet Cobbett saw the evils of uncontrolled industrialism and wrote of these eloquently in his paper. **William Cobbett**

The Romantic poets were also out of sympathy with the new England. Loving beauty above all else, these men stood for the country **The Romantic Poets**

COBBETT

William Cobbett rode on horseback through many sections of England and with his mighty pen depicted in his "Rural Rides" the ills of the countryside. "Between Holbeach and Boston, even at a public house, neither bread nor meat was to be found, and while the landlord was telling me that the people were become so poor that the butchers killed no meat in the neighbourhood, I counted more than two thousand fat sheep lying about in the pastures in that richest spot in the whole world. Starvation in the midst of plenty; the land covered with food, and the working people without victuals: everything taken away by the tax-eaters of various descriptions."

247

against the city, for God had made the country and man had made the city. The beauties of nature, the rhythm of the countryside where men worked according to nature's laws and told the time by the sun and the stars, gave a purpose to life that was lost in the city. William Wordsworth bitterly lamented that:

> The world is too much with us; late and soon,
> Getting and spending, we lay waste our powers:
> Little we see in Nature that is ours;
> We have given our hearts away, a sordid boon!
> This Sea that bares her bosom to the moon;
> The winds that will be howling at all hours,
> And are up-gathered now like sleeping flowers;
> For this, for everything, we are out of tune;
> It moves us not.

The mighty pens of Samuel Coleridge and Lord Byron laboured in the same way. Although the Romantics were not working-class champions they did, at least, direct men's attention to some of the shortcomings of the new industrial order.

Yet peaceful reform by Act of Parliament could come only from the middle and upper classes, since it was they who sat in Parliament and controlled the government. Among them, too, the demand for reforms of many kinds was growing, for they began to find the old order more and more intolerable for their own reasons. Two men in particular, whose following grew as the years passed, had made a powerful case **Adam Smith** against the old order. As early as 1776, Adam Smith had argued in his book, *The Wealth of Nations,* that the system of mercantilism which protected British agriculture and regulated trade artificially was out of date. Sweep away all the laws regulating wages and prices, trade and commerce, agriculture and industry, he declared, and make competition the key-note of the new age. The weak might falter but the strong would survive. After the Napoleonic Wars Smith's arguments began to have a strong appeal for the new manufacturers who felt that they were strong enough to survive.

Jeremy Bentham Another philosopher, Jeremy Bentham, saw the hopelessness of trying to govern nineteenth-century England by means of institutions that had been devised in mediæval times. "What is needed is government and institutions that work," he said; "but looking at the Law, at Parliament, at the Church or anything else, ask yourself just two questions: How well does it work? Can it be made to work better?" Because of his policy of examining the usefulness or "utility" of everything, Bentham

248

and his followers were called *Utilitarians*. Many nineteenth-century reforms began in the fertile mind of Jeremy Bentham and his followers.

Even in Parliament itself the demands for reform were increasing. The Whig aristocrats once again awoke to the need for change, as they *The Whigs* had in 1688. The Whigs had been out of office for a long time, partly because their mild reform policy after 1760 had not found favour with the British people during the wars with revolutionary France. Now the wind had shifted. After 1815 the Whigs took up the reform cause with new fervour, partly on principle and partly in the hope of regaining power. In the end they were successful.

The Tories were less enthusiastic for reform. It was a Tory government that had taken a strong line after Peterloo. Yet in the 1820's the blind hostility to change of any kind gave way to a new and cautious *Tory Reform* approach to reform. Younger men, like Sir Robert Peel, who created the London Police (often called Peelers or Bobbies after him), and William Huskisson, who started to reform the mercantilist system, showed that the former Tory resistance to change was on the way out. From 1820 to 1830 the Tory government picked piecemeal at abuses needing reform. They carried out one really momentous reform in 1829 when Roman Catholics, after almost three hundred years, were granted the right to hold public office and sit in Parliament.

Yet despite these gains the greatest abuse of all remained untouched. The movement for reform could make only minor advances until the House of Commons, the guardian of the old England and the most important branch of the legislature, was itself reformed. By 1830 the energy of all reformers was concentrated on the reform of Parliament.

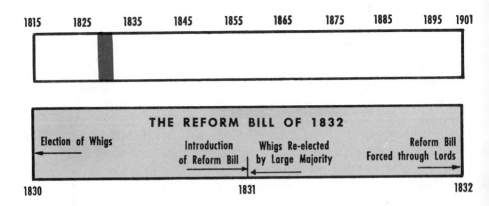

CHAPTER THIRTY-SIX

THE REFORM OF PARLIAMENT: 1832

The Unreformed Parliament   Well might the reformers demand changes in Parliament. The method by which the various parts of England were represented in the House of Commons was outdated and confusing. The system was never planned; like Topsy it had "just growed". The House of Commons represented the freeholders of the shires or counties (men who owned a life-interest in property which they passed on to their heirs) and the citizens of the boroughs or towns. Each county, regardless of size and population, sent two members to the House of Commons. The county representatives made up less than a quarter of the members of the Commons. Most of the members came from the borough constituencies which usually had the right to send two representatives each. It was in connection with borough representation that the greatest faults were found.

Representation   When representatives from boroughs were first summoned to Parliament, hundreds of years before, there were few boroughs in northern England because most of the people lived in the south and east. However, as manufacturing developed in northern England, many people moved from the agricultural south to work in the factories of the new industrial cities. But nothing was done to make the system of representation more efficient. Although Lancashire had increased in population from 166,200 in 1700 to 856,000 in 1801, it was still represented by the same number of members in the House of Commons. While great industrial cities like Manchester, Leeds, and Birmingham had no representatives, the village of Dunwich, which had almost disappeared under the North Sea, still sent two members to the Commons. The village of

250

Scotland
Returned only 45 out
of the 558 members

Newcastle

Leeds
Hull
Blackburn Bradford
Manchester
Sheffield

Stoke
Derby

Wolverhampton
Birmingham
Dunwich

WALES
24 seats

70% of the members of
the House of Commons

Bristol

London
Returned
10 members
Old Sarum
Gatton
Included 1/10
population of country

25%

Dense population

Large unrepresented cities

Boroughs disfranchised 1832

PARLIAMENTARY REPRESENTATION IN 1830

Old Sarum, now just a hilltop, and Gatton, an ancient wall, still sent their spokesmen to Parliament.

The Franchise In both county and borough constituencies the franchise, or right to vote, was restricted to a very few. It has been claimed that the majority of the House of Commons was elected by fewer than 15,000 persons. In the counties a statute of 1430, still in force, gave the vote to freeholders or men whose land would yield a rent of 40 shillings a year. Most farmers, however, were tenants who did not own their land and therefore could not vote. Those who could vote were usually dominated by the great aristocratic landholders.

In the boroughs, the franchise varied greatly. In 53 boroughs a wide franchise enabled most men to vote, but in many others only the mayor and town councillors voted. Some borough seats were owned outright by wealthy aristocrats. These were sarcastically called "pocket" boroughs and could be awarded or sold to a candidate. People who traded in such seats were called borough-mongers. Other boroughs, known as "rotten" boroughs, had very few voters and these could be easily bullied or bribed by the great men of the districts. In 1793 an investigation showed that 154 men actually controlled 307 seats out of a total membership in the Commons of 658.

Bad as this system was, it was tolerated as long as the main centres of population and the major interests in the community were represented in Parliament. By 1830 neither was adequately represented. England's economic development had outgrown her political institutions. The middle class, who dominated the economic life of the nation, had little voice in its government. Wise men saw that unless this situation was remedied by peaceful means, it might be done by force.

The Demand for Reform By 1830 demands for parliamentary reform were more intense than ever before. Discontented workers in the cities were persuaded that the only solution to their problems lay in a reform of Parliament which would give them political power. Political thinkers, like Jeremy Bentham and his followers, argued convincingly that reform was necessary in the interests of good government. Merchants, bankers, and industrialists demanded the vote. Northern England, where the new industries, and consequently the new cities, were concentrated, insisted on being represented in Parliament. Whig aristocrats, out of power for almost sixty years, saw their chance and championed reform, in the hope of regaining office. The Whig argument that without reform there would be revolution was strengthened by outbursts of violence in southern England in 1830. There, desperate, under-paid, and unemployed farm workers, in a blind reaction against their misery, destroyed threshing machines which they blamed for putting them out of work, burned hay ricks, and sent threatening letters to landowners signed "Captain Swing". They did not know just what they wanted, but their violence was evidence of what might happen in England if reform was not achieved.

When George IV died in 1830 a new election was called. The great issue was the reform of Parliament. "Down with rotten boroughs and borough-mongers" was the cry on every street. After an exciting campaign, the voters returned a Whig majority. The Whig Cabinet was led by Earl Grey, one of the greatest aristocrats in England, and was composed almost entirely of nobles; it seemed an unlikely instrument of parliamentary reform. In March 1831, however, Lord John Russell, who was heir to a dukedom, introduced a Reform Bill in the House of Commons. The excitement throughout England was tremendous. As one observer wrote:

The Election of 1830

Earl Grey

The First Reform Bill

> Nothing talked of, thought of, dreamt of, but Reform. Every creature one meets asks, What is said now? How will it go? What is the last news? What do you think? And so it is from morning to night, in the streets, in the clubs, and in private houses.

The Bill passed its second reading in the Commons by one vote. When the result was announced the members went wild. Not since the Grand Remonstrance had passed in 1641 had the Commons witnessed such pandemonium.

> We set up a shout that you might have heard to Charing Cross, waving our hats, stamping against the floor, and clapping our hands. . . . The house was thronged up to the table, and all the floor was fluctuating with heads like the pit of a theatre. . . . We shook hands, and clapped each other on the back, and went out laughing, crying and huzzaing into the lobby. . . . I called a cab and the first thing the driver asked was, "Is the Bill carried?" "Yes, by one." "Thank God for it, Sir."

Grey realized that since the Bill had passed the Commons by such a narrow margin, the House of Lords would probably throw it out. He therefore dissolved Parliament and called a new election, to get a clear statement of the will of the people. This time the Whigs were returned with an overwhelming majority. The Reform Bill was again introduced in the House of Commons and passed by a large majority. It then went to the House of Lords, where it was discussed and abruptly rejected.

The Election of 1831

253

Feeling in the country rose to fever pitch. Mass meetings and torch-light processions were the order of the day in London, and many of these demonstrations were close to riots. For three days the city of Bristol was controlled by a mob. The jail in the city of Derby was broken open and the prisoners freed. The bishops, who had all voted against the Bill in the Lords, were afraid to venture from their homes or conduct services. There was ominous talk of abolishing the House of Lords, which had acted so clearly against the will of the people. Young John Stuart Mill, one of the most brilliant men of his day, wrote that "If the minister flinch or the Peers remain obstinate, I am firmly convinced that in six months a national convention chosen by universal suffrage will be sitting in London."

In May 1832 Earl Grey, the Prime Minister, asked the new King, William IV, to exercise his right and create enough peers as members of the House of Lords to enable the Bill to be passed. The King refused and Earl Grey resigned. William then summoned the Duke of Wellington, the hero of Waterloo, to form a new government.

Revolution had never seemed so close as in these "Days of May". By making the Duke of Wellington Prime Minister, the King seemed to be calling in the army to suppress the people and destroy Parliament. Working-class "Political Unions", formed by such men as Francis Place, paraded threateningly throughout London. Placards reading TO STOP THE DUKE GO FOR GOLD urged people to take their money out of the bank and in this way bring the economy and the government to a halt. Radical agitators talked of an armed revolt and risings were planned

POLITICAL UNREST
Rioters storm the Derby jail, 1831.

GREY ASKS THE KING TO CREATE NEW LORDS

Faced with the unrelenting opposition of the House of Lords, Grey concluded that only William IV could provide a solution to the problem. The King alone had the right to appoint new members to the House of Lords, and Grey asked him to use this power to create enough new lords favourable to the Reform Bill to secure its passage. This unusual request was refused by the King who felt that such an action on his part would go a long way to destroying the power of the House of Lords. Nor was the King particularly sympathetic to the reform cause itself. After Wellington failed to form a government, however, and as public demands for the Bill grew more insistent, the King consented. Knowing that their continued opposition was hopeless and would only bring a flood of Lords into their ranks, many Tory nobles absented themselves and allowed the Bill to pass.

in London and the north of England. Realizing that opposition to the Reform Bill was hopeless, Wellington advised the King to recall Grey as Prime Minister and agree to appoint new peers if necessary. Grey was recalled but, rather than see the House of Lords swamped with new appointments, members opposed to the Reform Bill stayed away, and the Bill passed. The crisis was over.

The Reform Act of 1832 was one of the most important measures in British history. It did not establish democracy in Great Britain but it cleared the way and in time made the modern democratic system possible. The old haphazard method of representation was swept away. Fifty-six boroughs lost the right to send members to Parliament and thirty others had their representation reduced to one member. One hundred and forty-three seats were redistributed, mainly among the large towns. The larger counties were also given additional representation. However, no attempt was made to establish equal electoral districts.

The First Reform Act, 1832

Representation

255

"TO STOP THE DUKE—GO FOR GOLD"

Grey's resignation after the King refused to create fifty new lords upset the whole country. As the Duke of Wellington tried to form a Tory ministry, church bells tolled, workers refused to work, and mobs hooted as the King's coach passed. Some political unions declared against paying taxes; others prepared to use force. Francis Place put out placards, "To stop the Duke—go for gold", which echoed his suggestion that depositors remove all their money from the banks. Such an action would have dislocated the financial life of the country since banks, then as now, loaned out the money that was deposited and never had enough on hand to pay all their depositors. While Wellington was not afraid of such threats, the obvious popularity of the reform movement convinced him, and many other Tories, that a measure of reform was necessary and that it would be foolhardy to refuse it.

Franchise   In the boroughs the vote was given to any man who owned a house that could be rented for £10 a year and to any man who paid £10 a year rental. This meant that the middle class and the most prosperous members of the working class now had the vote. In the counties the freeholder who owned land valued at forty shillings, or more, retained his vote, but the franchise was extended to include certain other groups who leased or rented land.

Although four-fifths of the adult males in England still could not vote, a great forward step had been taken. The new industries were now represented in the House of Commons, where their representatives

256

sat side by side with those of the old agricultural England. The Commons was now to become an arena in which these two groups would compete for power and control. The workers were left wondering what part they were to play in the scheme of things.

The method employed to secure passage of the Reform Bill—forcing it through the House of Lords by the threat to create new peers—was, in itself, important. It had been clearly demonstrated that when a Prime Minister and his Cabinet had the support of a House of Commons backed by the people, neither the king nor the House of Lords could stand in their way. Another milestone in the history of parliamentary government had been passed.

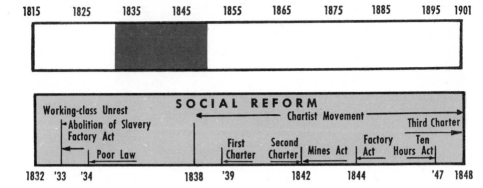

| 1815 | 1825 | 1835 | 1845 | 1855 | 1865 | 1875 | 1885 | 1895 | 1901 |

SOCIAL REFORM

Working-class Unrest
◄—Abolition of Slavery
Factory Act
◄—— Poor Law

◄———— Chartist Movement ————►

First Charter Second Charter Mines Act Factory Act Ten Hours Act Third Charter

| 1832 | '33 | '34 | | 1838 | '39 | 1842 | 1844 | '47 | 1848 |

WORKING-CLASS UNREST AND SOCIAL REFORM: 1832-1848

The Reform Act and the Working-Class   The British working class regarded the Reform Act of 1832 as a great betrayal. It had been their agitation, their threat of violence that had turned the scales in 1831-32, yet they had gained nothing for themselves. The rotten boroughs had gone; the middle class had received the vote; but working men still remained without a voice in government. Nor was there any reason to believe that the new Parliament in which factory and mill owners had a strong voice would be more sympathetic to their demands than one dominated by the aristocracy and the country squires. In 1833 Parliament abolished slavery in the British Empire and this was hailed as a great humanitarian victory. What about slavery in England? asked the working man, the slavery of unbelievably long hours, fantastically low wages, and frequent unemployment? Should not this, too, be abolished?

The Evils of Industrialism   His questions were understandable. In the England of the first half of the nineteenth century, men, women, and children left their drab and crowded homes in the bleak hours of darkness at four or five o'clock in the morning, six days a week, to go to the factories or mines where their every action was dictated by the owner's bell or the foreman's whip. The machinery at which they worked was unshielded and dangerous and injuries to the labourer were common, particularly towards the end of a fifteen- or sixteen-hour day when the exhausted worker toiled mechanically. In the mines, men dug the coal while women on their hands and knees pulled the heavily-laden carts along the tunnels, mumbling oaths in the darkness at the young children who opened and closed the shaft doors.

    At the end of such a day the workers staggered out in the dark to

258

the disease-infested, crowded quarters that they called homes. A whole family, a large one if many of the children survived, was often crowded into one room. Outdoor lavatories were primitive and streets were littered with rotting garbage. Hungry children haunted every alley, begging or stealing to keep themselves alive. Under such conditions, the lives of the labourers were short and physical deformity was common among them. A sixteen-year-old boy called Benjamin told this story to a Committee of Investigation:

What age did you go into the mill? About 9 years old.
What sort of a position do you stand in? (Here the witness showed the position in which he worked.)
Have you always to bend your body? Yes, always.
Were you a healthy and strong boy before you went to the mill? Yes.
Could you walk well? Yes.

WORK IN A TEXTILE FACTORY
Tired children were often kept at their work only through their dread of being beaten. A Committee of Investigation asked the following questions: "How are they beaten?" "That depends on the humanity of the slubber or billy-spinner; some have been beaten so violently that they have lost their lives . . . and even a young girl has had the end of a billy-roller jammed through her cheek." "What is the billy-roller?" "A heavy rod of from two to three yards long. . . . I have seen them take the billy-roller and rap them on the head, making their heads crack, so that you might have heard the blow at a distance . . . in spite of the din and rolling of the machinery."

259

Without pain or difficulty? Yes.

How long did you work at that mill for those long hours before you found your limbs begin to fail? About a year. Did it come on with great pain? It did.

Have you ever been beaten? Yes, till I was black and blue on my face; and have had my ears torn.

Will you have the goodness to show the Committee your limbs? (The witness did so, and they appeared to be excessively crooked.)

Can you stand at all without crutches? Not without crutches or a stick, or something to lean against.

Can you walk at all? No.

Can you get up stairs? Perhaps I might creep up.

Must it be upon your hands and knees? Yes, or backwards way.

Do you get up stairs backwards way? Yes, every night.

Such was the cost of industrial progress to one young life.

The reports of the Commission which heard Benjamin's story in 1832 shocked many members of Parliament, most of whom had never seen the inside of a factory. Led by Lord Shaftesbury, a conservative **The Factory Act** aristocrat who hated all forms of cruelty, a small group of men pressed the government to pass the Factory Act of 1833. This Act prevented owners of textile factories from employing children under nine and limited the work of children under thirteen to nine hours a day. People in Parliament who watched as the Bill was debated noted a general lack of enthusiasm among the members, even for this limited amount of reform.

The temper of the government and the first Parliament elected after the passage of the Reform Bill can best be seen in two events which occurred in 1834. By this time many workers had concluded that their welfare could best be improved and their demands made known through **Trade Unions** the organization of trade unions. Most attempts to form unions had failed when, in 1833, Robert Owen, a well-meaning factory owner, organized a nation-wide union of all working men which he called the Grand National. Employers immediately opposed the Grand National and retaliated by dismissing or "locking out" any of their employees **Tolpuddle Martyrs** who joined it. The government was equally hostile. At Tolpuddle in Dorset six harmless farm labourers were arrested for taking the secret oath of membership in a union. After a hurried trial they were sentenced to seven years' exile in Australia. Despite widespread protests, the Whig government refused to change this ruthless sentence.

The second event to reveal the spirit of the new Parliament was the

260

ROBERT OWEN

Owen was born in 1771, the son of a saddler, and when only ten was sent out to work as a draper's apprentice. By the age of nineteen the intelligent and ambitious young man had become a partner in a cotton factory and within another decade owned one of the largest factories in Scotland. As a factory owner, Owen saw the evils of the industrial system, but he did not think they were incurable. Industrial progress, he believed, could lead to a better life for all. His model factory at New Lanark was designed to prove his point. He lessened the hours of work and increased wages without lowering his profits. He built good clean homes for his workers and encouraged them to lead orderly, thrifty, and temperate lives. Appalled by the evident demoralization among the 500 children in the factory, he started a school for them. A company store sold goods at much less than the usual market price. All attempts to get other factory owners to follow his methods failed, however, as did his efforts to have Parliament pass Acts to improve factory conditions. As a result, Owen came to believe that the factory system would have to be abolished. He became a socialist and argued that the workers would have to take over control of the factories and machinery, and work them for their own benefit. In 1824 he went to America and tried to establish his ideal society there, but without success. When he returned to England he became the leader of the trade union movement and of the co-operative movement, an organization in which workers sold directly to one another.

passage of the Poor Law in 1834. Previously the poor, aged, and crippled had been given food and other assistance by the local authorities in their own parish. Under the new Act those who needed relief would have to enter poorhouses, or workhouses, to get it. In these work-houses life was deliberately made so miserable for the occupants that few people would seek assistance. Families were broken up; there was insufficient food and bedding; and, once inside, the pauper could not get out even to go to church on Sunday. The inmates were kept under lock and key and treated like prisoners. To those who framed the Poor Law of 1834 poverty was regarded as a crime, not a misfortune. ^{The Poor Law 1834}

The new poor houses opened just as hard times threw large numbers of men out of work. The workers turned with hatred on the Poor Law and Parliament. One radical exclaimed: ^{Opposition to the Poor Law}

> You can see yonder factory with its towering chimney; every brick in that chimney is cemented with the blood of women and little children. Sooner than wife and husband and son

261

should be surrendered and dungeoned and fed on skilee—
sooner than wife and daughter should wear the prison dress—
Newcastle ought to be and should be one blaze of fire with only
one way to put it out, and that with the blood of all who supported this abominable measure.

This was strong talk. There were others, however, who concluded that
the only solution to the wretched working and living conditions lay in
getting the working class represented in Parliament. In London the
tireless Francis Place formed the London Working Men's Association to
agitate for political reform. From Leeds, Feargus O'Connor, a brilliant

WORKHOUSES

Few writers were more influential than Charles Dickens whose novels often depicted the
social evils of nineteenth-century England. One book, "Oliver Twist", illustrates some
features of the notorious workhouses. Oliver Twist was born in a workhouse; and on
the day that he was born his poor young mother died. Nobody knew where she came
from or who she was. A woman took the baby out of the blankets in which he had
been rolled and dressed him in old calico robes that had grown yellow from long service;
for dozens of babies born in the workhouse had worn them too. The parish authorities
sent him to a branch workhouse, three miles off—a baby farm, where an old woman
named Mrs. Mann took charge of him, for sevenpence-halfpenny a week. There he
rolled about the floor with twenty or thirty other workhouse babies like himself, with
not too much to eat and very little to wear. Only the strongest babies lived to grow
up at Mrs. Mann's.

but unstable Irishman with great oratorial and literary power, thundered against Parliament and the Poor Law in his paper, *The Northern Star*, and on any platform he could find.

While northern radicals talked of using force, the London group *Chartism* drew up a document known as the People's Charter demanding wholesale political reform. They asked for the vote for all adult males, removal of property qualifications for members of Parliament, payment of members of Parliament, the secret ballot, annual elections, and electoral districts with equal population. Only when these demands had been met, it was felt, could the working class be assured of some political power. Supported by many members of the middle class, earnest Chartists, as the supporters of the Charter were called, canvassed for signatures for a petition to Parliament, to back up their demands. These demands do not nowadays strike us as extreme, but when the Petition, containing a million or more signatures, was laid before the House of Commons in 1839 the members were obviously unimpressed and refused to consider it.

Radical Chartists talked of a general strike or a "National Holiday". Others revived the plan of having everyone withdraw their money from the banks, while still others advocated a boycott of all unsympathetic merchants. A few openly urged "arms for freedom" and a revolution. The government moved quickly to end such agitation. Leading *The Government's Reaction* Chartists were arrested and cast in prison. These actions only encouraged the radicals further. In the south Wales town of Newport, miners armed themselves with pikes and marched on the city. Soldiers swept the streets with gun fire, the miners were dispersed, and their leaders arrested and sentenced to exile in Australia for life.

The Chartist movement was driven underground by these savage measures, but Feargus O'Connor, who had been among those arrested, kept it alive from his prison cell. When he was released in 1841 another Petition was circulated. Said to contain over three million signatures, the Petition was carried to Parliament in a procession over two miles long. While Chartists milled expectantly outside, the House of Commons coldly rejected their Petition by a vote of 287 to 49. Thomas Macaulay, the great Whig orator and brilliant historian, declared that the doctrine of "one man, one vote" would bring about the end of civilization, and Lord John Russell, who in 1832 had introduced the Reform Bill, dismissed the idea as too ridiculous to be discussed.

In the following years conditions improved for the working class. Once again urged by Lord Shaftesbury, Parliament passed several Acts

The Mines and Factory Acts designed to end the worst practices in factories and mines. In 1842 the Mines Act stopped the employment of women and girls underground and prohibited the employment of boys under the age of nine. Two years later another Act secured a six-and-a-half-hour day in factories for children between nine and thirteen and included provisions for fencing dangerous machinery. In 1847 the Ten Hours Act further limited the working hours of women. Men gained by these measures, too, for some factory owners found it inconvenient to have the men working longer hours than the women. Other owners, however, used a relay system of women and children and kept the men at work from 5:30 a.m. to 8.30 p.m., as the law permitted.

The Revival of Chartism In 1847 and 1848 hard times revived Chartism. Much of the inspiration for agitation during these years came from foreign revolutionaries then living in London, among whom were two Germans, Karl Marx and Frederick Engels, who wrote the *Communist Manifesto* in England in 1848. That year revolutions broke out in France, Prussia, Italy, and other European countries. The excitement and example of the European revolutionaries aroused some old Chartists to talk of revolution, while more moderate men circulated a third Petition. When the Petition, said to have over five million names, was brought to London, the government feared the worst and made preparations in case the giant demonstration on Kensington Common got out of hand. The aged Duke of Wellington was called out of retirement to command the army; troops and artillery were stationed all over the city; 150,000 special policemen were enrolled, civil servants were armed, and government offices were barricaded.

Nothing happened. Parliament again rejected the Petition and the Chartists dispersed. The discovery that many of the signatures on the Petition, including that of Queen Victoria, were forged, did not help their cause. Chartism as a movement had failed, and the return of prosperous times took the edge off working-class discontent for thirty years. During this time, wages rose, working conditions improved, and stronger trade-union organization gave added protection to the workers. Political agitation faded into the background for more than a generation.

Conclusion The Chartist movement is important, however, even though it failed. The Chartists' demands for complete democracy were far too radical for the England of the 1840's; yet in time they triumphed. "One man, one vote", the payment of members of Parliament, and the secret ballot were eventually adopted and are now the basis of democratic government not only in Great Britain but in Canada as well.

264

CHAPTER THIRTY-EIGHT

THE MIDDLE-CLASS VICTORY: 1832-1849

While the Chartists scoured the nation for signatures for their Petitions, leaders of the middle class were creating the Anti-Corn Law League, one of the most powerful and effective organizations that England has ever seen. The Chartist leaders proclaimed that the nation's ills could be cured only by the achievement of political democracy; middle-class leaders replied that all the nation needed was cheap food. Feargus O'Connor denounced the factory owners as the cause of all the sufferings of the working class; spokesmen for the Anti-Corn Law League condemned the landowners who, they claimed, kept the nation in a state of bondage and distress by their support of laws which restricted trade and kept cheap food out of England. Here was a three-cornered conflict between the workers, the middle class, and the landowners. Each claimed to act in the national interest, each had a different point of view, and each accused the others of selfishness. Conflict of Interests

Members of the middle class charged that the country's economic system was as unsatisfactory as its political system had been before 1832. They argued that the mercantile system which had regulated and controlled trade for two hundred years was no longer desirable. They wanted to be able to buy raw materials in the cheapest market and sell manufactured goods anywhere for the highest price they could get. Above all, merchants and manufacturers objected to having tariffs, or customs duties put on foreign goods imported into England, partly because they believed that the more other nations sold to Britain, the more they would buy. Many came to agree with Adam Smith, the author of *The Wealth of Nations,* that trade among all countries should be free. Those who believed in this theory were known as Free Traders. The Growth of Free Trade

265

CONFLICTING ARGUMENTS, 1839

The Corn Laws The struggle centered on the Corn Laws, passed by Parliament to protect English agriculture by placing a high tariff on imported foreign grains. While such an Act helped English farmers and landlords by keeping up prices, it meant that the rest of the people had to pay dearly for their food. This point was seized on by the Free Traders, who argued before working-class audiences that they suffered from expensive food, not low wages. Although the tariffs on many goods had been reduced or abolished in the 1820's, a Parliament dominated by landlords naturally refused even to consider any tampering with the Corn Laws. The conflict soon became one between agricultural and industrial England. As one fiery Free Trader proclaimed, "The quarrel is between the bread-eating millions and the few who monopolize the soil."

The Anti-Corn Law League To promote their ideas and to convince the British people that the cure for the nation's ills lay in free trade, Free Traders formed the Anti-

JOHN BRIGHT AT EXETER HALL

A man who had heard Bright speak wrote that he was obviously a man of singular force and firmness of character. "The broad shoulders, the bulk of the figure, the solid massiveness of his masterful individuality, the immovable grasp of his feet upon the fine earth, his uprightness of bearing, the body knit to the head as closely as capital to column—all together made the least careful observer feel that here was one in whose armour the flaws were few."

Corn Law League in 1839. The League's most outstanding leaders were Richard Cobden and John Bright. Cobden, born in a Sussex farmhouse, was a wealthy Manchester textile manufacturer. Energetic and devoted to the cause of free trade, he was the brains of the League and did more than anyone to organize and promote its activities. Richard Cobden

Cobden's chief lieutenant was the remarkable John Bright, a Quaker mill owner. One of the greatest orators in nineteenth-century Britain, Bright spoke with a burning and simple eloquence that often lifted his audiences to a fever pitch. His scathing criticism of the rich stirred the emotions of many working men and drew them away from Chartism and into the ranks of the Anti-Corn Law League. Cobden's clear, well-reasoned speeches appealed to the intellect. Bright's tactics were rougher. As he once remarked, "I used to get up and do a little prize fighting." John Bright

> The Corn Law has scourged you with thongs [he shouted] it has lashed you with scorpions. It has made your trade fluctuating and hazardous. It has deprived you of political independence. It has surrounded you with discontented and impoverished labourers. . . . The League is the foe of aristocratic injustice.

To the landowners' charge that the factory owners, like Cobden and Bright, wanted cheaper food to enable them to lower wages, League

267

preachers replied with thundering Biblical quotations: "Blessed is he that giveth the corn and cursed is he that withholdeth it," was a common text. More than once, Jacob's advice to his sons was used with telling effect: "Behold, I have heard that there is corn in Egypt; get you down thither and buy for us there that we may live and not die." To a nation of Christians who knew their Bible the message seemed clear: trade should be as free as the winds of heaven!

League Strategy The League was tremendously successful. Under Cobden's direction it raised large sums of money, no less than £525,000 in 1845-46. In 1840 cheap postage was introduced into Britain, permitting letters to travel anywhere in the country for a penny. This enabled the League to send circulars and pamphlets all over the country. Nine million tracts flooded every corner of the land. Petitions poured into Parliament. An army of preachers and speakers held meetings in hundreds of centres and hammered away at a few simple ideas. The landowners were pictured as bread-stealing aristocrats who alone stood in the way of cheap food and employment for all. In Cobden's words, the aristocracy was "the bread-taxing oligarchy, unprincipled, unfeeling, rapacious, and plundering".

The Irish Although the League agitation won the support of many workers and Famine middle-class Englishmen, it failed to convince Parliament until 1845. 1845 That year bad harvests in England and the failure of the potato crop in Ireland produced a serious crisis. In Ireland, where potatoes were the staple food of more than eighty per cent of the people, the situation was unbelievably desperate. The British census described the conditions:

> The disorganization of society became marked and memorable by the exodus of over one million of people, who deserted their homes and hearths to seek shelter in foreign lands, of whom thousands perished of pestilence and hardships endured on shipboard. . . . Generally speaking, the actually starving people lived upon the carcasses of diseased cattle, upon dogs and dead horses, but principally upon the herbs of the field, nettle tops, wild mustard and water cresses, and even in some places dead bodies were found with grasses in their mouths.

The only solution for these conditions was to import food. Yet it was doubtful whether the British Parliament would take action, for the Tory Party, dominated by landlords, was in office in 1845. Although Peel and the Prime Minister, Sir Robert Peel, was a manufacturer, he had been Repeal elected in 1841 as an opponent of free trade. Peel, however, was a man whose mind was open to the logic of every argument. Between 1841

268

and 1845 he had become convinced that freer trade was desirable and he had even reduced the duties on some articles. By 1845 he was almost persuaded that the Corn Laws should be abolished, but he hesitated to act because he realized that most of his party did not agree with him. The Irish famine ended his hesitation. The welfare of the people triumphed over party politics. Deserted by most of the Tories, Peel gratefully accepted the help of a number of Whigs and Radicals and the Corn Laws were repealed in June, 1846. Three years later, a Whig government, led by Lord John Russell, swept away the Navigation Acts, which had been first passed in Cromwell's time, and other remnants of the mercantile system. With this, the battle between the agricultural and the industrial interests was over and the victory of free trade, of industrial England, and of the middle class was complete.

The Middle-class Triumph

Britain could embark safely on a policy of free trade because she had become the world's leader in industry and commerce. There were no competitors to fear. By 1850 Britain stood on the brink of a great prosperity and expansion. There were to be stirring economic and political battles in the future, but for the time being the major battles had been fought, the issues had been settled, and Britain in the 1850's and '60's was prepared to sit back and enjoy its prosperity.

1815   1825   1835   1845   1855   1865   1875   1885   1895   1901

VICTORIAN ENGLAND
An Age of Progress and Materialism

Accession of Victoria

Penny
Postage

The Great
Exhibition

Iron Steam-
ships in
Operation

Darwin's
"Origin
of Species"

Atlantic
Cable

1837   1840   1851   1858 '59   '66 1867

CHAPTER THIRTY-NINE

QUEEN VICTORIA'S MIDDLE-CLASS ENGLAND

The Great
Exhibition

On May 1, 1851, the young Queen Victoria, who had come to the throne fourteen years earlier, at the age of eighteen, opened the Great Exhibition at the Crystal Palace. The Palace, a gigantic structure of iron and glass, specially built to house the Exhibition, was a symbol of Victorian England in the middle of the nineteenth century. It was large and solid and it reflected perfectly the taste and mood of the English middle class, which by 1851 had achieved unchallenged economic, social, and political supremacy. It represented the triumph of industrialism and its thirteen thousand exhibits proclaimed England's leadership in manufacturing. In his "Mayday Ode", written to celebrate the opening of the Palace, William Thackeray boasted that England was the workshop of the world and also its master:

> Look yonder where the engines toil;
> These England's arms of conquest are,
> The trophies of her bloodless war;
>   Brave weapons these.
> Victorious over wave and soil
> With these she sails, she weaves, she tills
> Pierces the everlasting hills,
> And spans the seas.

Middle-class
Optimism

The English middle class in 1851 was proud, confident, and optimistic. Railways and telegraphs had linked the country together during the past twenty years. Penny postage made correspondence fast and cheap. The iron steamship and the Atlantic cable, finished in 1866, joined Britain with her empire and the world and made communication with

270

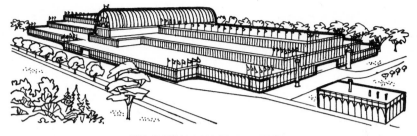

THE CRYSTAL PALACE EXHIBITION

The Great Exhibition of 1851 symbolized the material progress of Victorian England. It was begun and largely carried through by the Prince Consort, Albert, against great opposition. . Sir Joseph Paxton, a self-made man, designed the great glass house, known as the Crystal Palace, which housed the Exhibition in Hyde Park. The skill and craftsmanship of the 13,000 exhibits excited widespread wonder and praise. The Exhibition, visited by over 6,000,000 people, had a great influence on the general standard of design and decoration. To proud Englishmen it seemed to mark the beginning of new and happier times. Later, the Crystal Palace was dismantled and re-erected in another part of the city where it became one of London's main recreation centres until it was destroyed by fire in 1936.

them easy. London had become the centre of the civilized world. Most Englishmen saw nothing ahead but continued progress and prosperity. Alfred, Lord Tennyson, their most popular poet, caught the general mood of optimism in his poem, "Locksley Hall":

> For I dipt into the future, far as human eye could see,
> Saw the Vision of the world, and all the wonder that would be;
> Saw the heavens fill with commerce, argosies of magic sails;
> Pilots of the purple twilight, dropping down with costly bales.

The tone of English society was set by the middle class whose chief interest lay in money-making:

Middle-class Materialism

> *Wealth! wealth! wealth! Praise be to the god of the nineteenth century! The golden idol! The mighty Mammon!* Such are the accents of the time, such the cry of the nation.

A man was judged by his material success and prosperity. A large home, stocked with obviously expensive furniture, fine clothes and jewellery, a country estate, and a handsome carriage were the certain signs of success. Yet success, as the Victorians well knew, did not come easily. It demanded hard work, thrift, and sobriety. It is not surprising that their favourite author was Samuel Smiles, who wrote on this theme, and 20,000 of them bought his *Self-Help* when it was first published in 1859.

The writer Thackeray heaped sarcasm on the ruthless ambition of his countrymen:

271

"THE NORTHUMBRIAN", ONE OF THE FIRST STEAM LOCOMOTIVES

Before the invention of the steam locomotive, horses were sometimes used to pull wagons on railways. The use of steam power in factories inspired the development of steam locomotives. In 1825, George Stephenson, a collier worker with a gift for engineering, built the Stockton-Darlington Railway and persuaded the dubious owners to use his newly-invented steam locomotive to pull the truck-loads of coal. The engine did the work of forty teams of horses and the price of coal in Stockton was cut in half. The first major railway was the Liverpool-Manchester line, opened in 1830. The promoters of the scheme offered a prize for the best locomotive, which was won by by Stephenson's improved "Rocket". Fanny Kemble, the famous actress, wrote this account of her first ride. "We were introduced to the little engine which was to drag us along the rails. . . . This snorting little animal, which I felt rather inclined to pat, was then harnessed to our carriage. . . . [The engine] set off at its utmost speed, thirty-five miles an hour, swifter than a bird flies (for they tried the experiment with a snipe). . . . My spirits rose to the true champagne-height, and I never enjoyed anything so much as the first hour of our progress. [My mother, however,] was frightened to death, and intent upon nothing but devising means of escaping from a situation which appeared to her to threaten with instant annihilation herself and all her travelling companions."

If a better place than yours presents itself just beyond your neighbour's, elbow him and take it. . . . If your neighbour's foot obstructs you, stamp on it; and do you suppose he won't take it away?

Another author, Beatrice Webb, wrote that her father, like most Victorians, believed that it was "the bounden duty of every citizen to better his social status; to ignore those beneath him, and to aim steadily at the top rung of the social ladder".

Middle-class Respectability The Victorian middle class believed in social respectability as well as social success. Its firm belief in morality was strongly tinged with Puritanism; middle-class Victorians hated any suggestion of evil and

272

frowned on harmless frivolity. Some of them, we are told, even draped the legs of their pianos! The home was the centre of middle-class life, where the Bible was read daily and Sunday was a quiet day of rest and prayer. Father was supreme in the home; mother stayed quietly in the background and the large brood of children was meekly submissive to its parents. Queen Victoria and her husband, Prince Albert, were models of the popular conception of the ideal family. Court life might be dull, but the royal family was large and the royal couple was extremely respectable and hard-working.

The word "Victorian" is often used today to describe something that is pompous and dull. The constant emphasis on thrift and industry, success and respectability tended to stifle the imagination. Yet Victorian England produced a host of excellent writers and critics, as only **The Great** a great age can. The most famous of these were men who looked **Critics** beneath the surface of English life and criticized or rebelled at what they saw.

Matthew Arnold, a poet and critic, vigorously attacked the material- **Matthew** ism of the time. In his book, *Culture and Anarchy,* published in 1869, **Arnold** he deplored the lack of imagination and good taste among the British

LAYING THE ATLANTIC TELEGRAPH
Before the days of the transatlantic cable it took weeks for messages to pass between Canada and Great Britain. In 1850 a cable was laid between Britain and France and men began to think of a transoceanic cable. The first attempt to span the Atlantic, in 1857, was a failure, as the cable broke at a depth of 2000 fathoms and could not be recovered. The following year a cable was laid that joined Ireland and Newfoundland, but it too broke after three months' use. The task seemed hopeless. An American named Collins started to build a line from San Francisco to Alaska, via British Columbia, and then under the Bering Sea to Russia and by land to the great cities of Europe. His line had reached a spot in northern British Columbia, known appropriately enough as Telegraph Creek, when word reached him in 1866 that the "Great Eastern" had arrived at Heart's Content Harbour in Newfoundland having successfully laid an Atlantic cable. Four years later an oceanic cable bridged the gap between Britain and India. Later still the Pacific cable went from Vancouver Island to Australia.

273

people of his day. The sprawling, hideous industrial cities were a discredit to the nation, he lamented. The middle class, whom he called the Philistines, were interested in nothing but making money. "What is the purpose of making a fortune," he asked, "if it does not lead to a fuller life? What is the point of being able to read, if you read only the cheapest literature?" Others repeated Arnold's criticisms. "The Victorians," said John Ruskin, "had horrible taste in painting and architecture." Good art, he argued, could come only from a society that was not dominated by a narrow commercial and materialistic spirit.

John Ruskin

Brilliant writers like Charles Dickens, Thomas Carlyle, and Benjamin Disraeli charged over and over again that this triumphant and wealthy middle-class England of 1850 rested on the exploitation of a great part of the people. Once a poor boy himself, Dickens painted vivid pictures of the poverty and misery of the working class in his many novels. Carlyle spoke scathingly of England's division into the "dandies and the drudges, the rich and the poor". Disraeli echoed the accusation that England was not one nation, but two, "the Privileged and the People".

Dickens Carlyle Disraeli

John Stuart Mill, the genius who could read Latin and Greek before he was six, turned his penetrating pen on all aspects of English life. He championed political democracy, free education, and the equality of women with men. The greatest danger to English society, he believed, was social conformity, with everybody acting and thinking alike. Was the herd complex to drive men as it drove cows? he asked. Above all, thought must be free. "One person with a belief," Mill said, "is equal to ninety-nine who have only interests."

John Stuart Mill

More disturbing than the criticisms of these writers was the book, *The Origin of Species,* published by the scientist Charles Darwin, in 1859. After many years of study and research Darwin concluded that animals had not been created in their present form, but had evolved from simpler forms of life. This process of evolution, he argued, had grown out of a permanent conflict between species and continued adjustments to environment. Species that were strong and adjusted survived, those that failed became extinct. Apart from casting doubt on the biblical story of creation, already being questioned by the geologists, Darwin shocked the Victorians by his picture of life as a perpetual and merciless struggle, often against overwhelming odds.

Darwin's "Origin of Species"

Victorian England was a country of contradictions. On the surface it seemed a contented age. The mood of middle-class England was one of optimism, aggressive materialism, and an unquestioning belief in

Summary

274

progress. Yet underneath there was anxiety and doubt. Was the optimism justified? Was the progress worth while? Was the materialism and worship of wealth not cramping man's spirit, imagination, and sense of beauty?

CHAPTER FORTY

THE MID-VICTORIAN EMPIRE

In 1837, the year young Princess Victoria became Queen of England, some Ontario farmers marched down Yonge Street, the principal highway to the north, with the intention of capturing the capital city of Toronto. The same year, the roads out of Montreal echoed with the tramp of soldiers' boots as a small army moved to put down another uprising. These events made an unpleasant beginning for a new reign, for the rebellions suggested that other colonies might follow the lead of the United States and break away from Great Britain. That this did not happen is to the credit of both Englishmen and Canadians. Together they found a solution to the problem of the relations between a mother country and her colonies which was to have important consequences for Britain and the world.

British North America By 1837 there were five British colonies in North America. Quebec, Nova Scotia, and Prince Edward Island had remained loyal in 1775 when the other British colonies in North America had rebelled against the Mother Country. American loyalists, who took Britain's side in her quarrel with the Thirteen Colonies, made their way to Canada after the Revolution and founded two new colonies, New Brunswick in 1784 and Upper Canada, later known as Ontario, in 1791. In the years following the wars with Napoleon, Englishmen, Scots, and Irishmen moved across the Atlantic in ever-increasing numbers. British North America grew and flourished.

The colonists, however, soon expressed the same desire for self-government that had led the Americans to revolt. Members of the elected Legislative Assemblies in the colonies resented the privileged position held by the appointed Governor and his appointed Council. The latter was usually composed of the wealthy members of society and was disparagingly called the Family Compact in Upper Canada and the Chateau Clique in Lower Canada, or Quebec. Protests against this system of government reached a climax in the rebellions of 1837, led by William Lyon Mackenzie in Upper Canada and Louis Joseph Papineau in Lower Canada. Although the rebellions were easily put down, the revolts were a timely warning that all was not well in the colonies.

The Rebellions of 1837

Lord Durham was sent out from England to investigate the trouble in Canada and to suggest a solution. After talking to prominent Canadians, Durham recommended that the colonists be given responsible government and be allowed to govern themselves in all matters that did not concern the Empire as a whole. Although his advice was not followed immediately, the reformed Parliament in Great Britain soon showed a more liberal attitude towards the Canadian colonies than its predecessors had done. Moreover, after the triumph of free trade, there seemed less reason for Britain to continue her strict control of the colonies. In 1846, therefore, Lord Elgin was sent out to Canada to put responsible government into effect. In agreeing to this change, long demanded in Canada, Britain saved her Empire from breaking up and laid the foundation of the modern Commonwealth of independent, equal, self-governing nations.

Lord Elgin

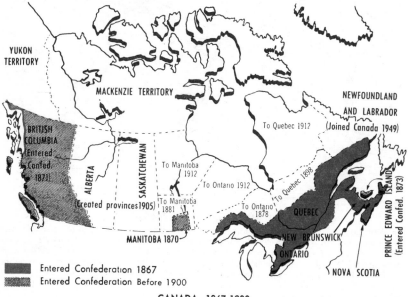

CANADA, 1867-1900

Entered Confederation 1867
Entered Confederation Before 1900

Other British colonies profited from Canada's achievement of responsible government. After the American Revolution, two new colonies had been founded. In 1770, the same Captain James Cook who had been with Wolfe at Quebec had discovered New Zealand and had **Australia** mapped the eastern shore of Australia. For some years thereafter the British did not follow up his explorations. After the American Revolution, however, the British had to find a new place to send prisoners sentenced to transportation beyond the seas. Botany Bay in Australia was selected and the colony of New South Wales was established in 1788.

Convicts were soon followed by more willing emigrants, especially after 1796 when John McArthur started sheep farming and gave Australia its major industry. Other settlements grew up, particularly after 1851 when the discovery of gold in Australia turned the trickle of immigrants into a flood, as prospectors from all over the world came in search

THE AUSTRALIAN GOLD RUSH, 1851

In February 1851, E. A. Hargraves, who had returned from the California gold fields, discovered gold in Australia. By May four hundred miners had raced to the new El Dorado. In succeeding months tens of thousands poured into Australia from the ends of the earth and headed for the gold fields, "some armed with picks, others shouldering crowbars and shovels, and not a few strung round with wash hand basins, tin pots and cullenders [strainers]". As a result of the rush the population of the Australian colonies rose from 405,000 in 1851 to 1,168,000 in 1861.

THE SETTLEMENT OF AUSTRALIA

of treasure. In the 1850's the Australian colonies won responsible government and before Victoria's long reign ended in 1901, they had united to form the Commonwealth of Australia, just as the Canadians had formed the Dominion of Canada in 1867.

The islands of New Zealand had been settled in the 1840's. The growth of the colony had been largely the work of Edward Gibbon Wakefield, an Englishman who felt that the colonies offered the English worker a better life than did the farm and factory of the Mother Country. In 1840, Great Britain annexed New Zealand and gave it institutions like those of Canada and Australia. During the next thirty years there were land disputes and wars with the Maori inhabitants, but the colony eventually resolved its difficulties and grew to become one of the senior members of the modern Commonwealth of Nations. *New Zealand*

A more troublesome imperial problem arose in South Africa. Originally settled by the Dutch, Cape Colony had been captured by the *South Africa*

279

British during the Napoleonic wars and had been kept by Britain in 1815. At that time the colony was simply a small coastal settlement, known as the Cape of Good Hope, which the Dutch sailing ships used as a provisioning depot on the long voyage to India. The Dutch inhabitants, known as Boers, soon tired of British rule and British missionaries who sought to protect the natives from land-hungry whites. In 1836 and 1837 they trekked inland from the Cape to a part of Africa where they believed they were free from British control. Here they formed two new colonies, the Orange Free State and the Transvaal. The new colonies resented any British interference, but eventually Britain acquired some control over them, which she retained until the Boer War of 1899-1902, when she took them over completely. In time, all the British

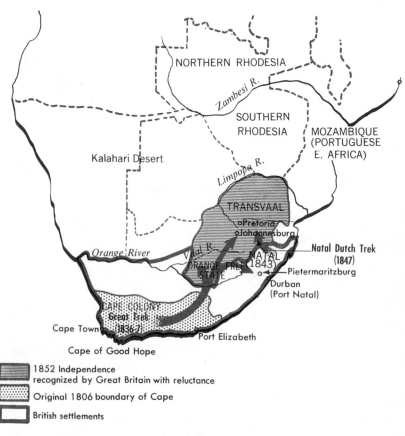

SOUTH AFRICA

THE BOERS TREK NORTH
As early as 1835 the Boers, or Dutch inhabitants of Cape Colony, began to pack up their belongings and move north and east, although the main group was not to leave until 1837. They moved in groups of from 50 to 400—enough for defence against hostile natives, but not too many for adequate pasturing of flocks and herds. About 12,000 had trekked by the early 1840's. Some were prompted by the desire for more land, but the principal reason for the move was the liberal, sympathetic, and protective attitude taken by the new British rulers towards the natives. The Boers believed that the Africans or coloured peoples were born to serve the whites and they accused the British of being dangerously "colour blind".

colonies in South Africa united to form the Union of South Africa, until 1961 a member of the Commonwealth.

Perhaps the brightest gem in the mid-Victorian empire was India where, over the previous century, Britain had expanded her influence until she governed or controlled most of the country. In 1857 the Indian army, composed of Indian soldiers, rebelled against the British officers. The event that sparked the famous Mutiny was the introduction of new cartridges, the end of which had to be bitten off before they could be used. Rumours spread that the cartridges were greased with the fat of pigs and cows which the Indians were forbidden by their religion to touch. Basically, however, the Mutiny was the result of the impact of Western culture on that of India. Over the previous century Britain had been slowly reforming India along Western lines. Many Indian customs could not be accepted by the English and were abolished. Upper-class Indian widows often burned themselves on their husband's funeral pyre, a practice that was known as suttee; some Indians ran elephants over children half buried in the sand; many made human sacrifices on a variety of occasions.

Although we can understand why the British stopped such behaviour, their action came as a rude shock to the Indians. We would feel the

India

The Mutiny of 1857

281

same if a conquerer abolished mass or communion in our churches, or prevented us from celebrating Christmas or New Year's. Other phases of British improvements, like the railway and the telegraph, frightened the Indians who saw in them embodiments of evil spirits. Only thirty years before, the same things had frightened Englishmen! Thus, while the Mutiny was largely confined to the army it reflected deep concern and serious alarm among the people.

During the Mutiny both sides committed horrible atrocities. Rebels overran the British garrisons, killing officers they had served under faithfully through years of hard campaigning, and slaughtered women and children with a cruelty that showed their hatred. The British dealt out fierce punishment to the guilty and blew mutinous soldiers from the mouths of cannons. Only after months of bitter fighting did the British finally restore the country to order.

The Mutiny showed Britain that she would have to alter her policy

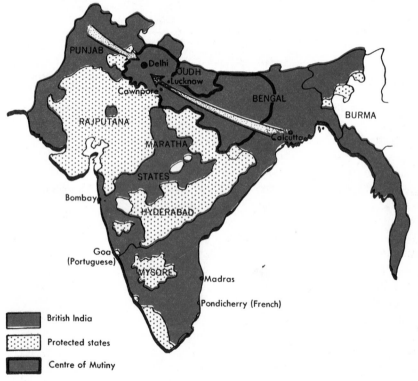

INDIA IN 1857

MUTINY OF THE INDIAN SEPOYS, 1857

The Mutiny began in May and for a time everything looked bleak for the British. Mutineers flocked to Delhi where a new government was to be established. British strongholds, garrisoned by the sepoys that remained loyal, were besieged. (The defenders at Lucknow were under attack for three months before relief came.) Slowly the British regrouped their forces. New troops were sent out from Britain. Two armies moved against the mutineers' centre at Delhi, one from Calcutta and one from the Punjab. Within six months order had been restored, but the cruelty shown by both sides created a rift between the English and the Indians which has never been bridged. Although it was not a national uprising, Indians look upon the Mutiny as the heroic beginning of the movement for national independence.

in India. The government of India was reformed and Indians were given a minor share in the government and civil service. India started on the long road from colony to nation, although she did not reach that milestone until 1947. At the same time, the Mutiny left bitterness and enmity on both sides which has never been entirely erased.

In the years between 1850 and 1870 the British people were not keenly interested in their Empire, for all their thoughts were concentrated on industrial progress and material success at home. The great imperial achievement was not expansion but reform. The first twenty years of Victoria's reign saw Britain find an answer to the problems of imperial government which it could not find in 1775. One empire had been lost; another was saved. In this period the idea of the Commonwealth of free and equal nations was born. That was an achievement great enough for any people at any time. After 1870 England experienced a new wave of imperialism. The colonies were drawn closer together and much of Africa was added to the Empire. But that is another story.

283

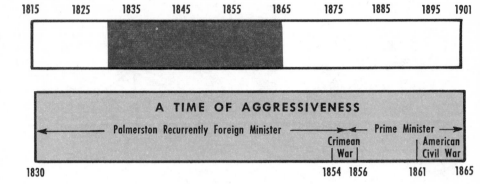

CHAPTER FORTY-ONE

THE AGE OF PALMERSTON

Just before the opening of Parliament in 1864 Lord Palmerston, the Prime Minister, was asked what his government planned to do about "domestic affairs and legislation". Rubbing his hands with an air of complete satisfaction, Palmerston replied, "Oh there's really nothing to be done. We cannot go on adding to the statute book *ad infinitum.* Perhaps we may have a little law reform or bankruptcy reform; but we cannot go on legislating forever."

Lord Palmerston With his dyed whiskers, his jovial air, and his boyish optimism, Palmerston embodied the bounce and confidence of mid-Victorian England. He was an ideal Prime Minister for a people who desired a minimum of change and government interference. The humorous magazine, *Punch,* expressed the sentiments of most Englishmen when it published a poem in 1861 to celebrate Palmerston's seventy-seventh birthday:

> An Irish lord my John was born
> Both dullness and dons he held in scorn
> But he stood for Cambridge at twenty-one,
> My gallant, gay Lord Palmerston.
>
> With his hat o'er his eyes and his nose in the air,
> So jaunty and genial and debonaire,
> Talk at him—to him—against him—none
> Can take a rise out of Palmerston.
>
> And suppose, his parish registers say,
> He's seventy-seven if he's a day;
> What's that if you're still all fire and fun
> Like Methuselah or John Palmerston?

THE SECOND BOMBARDMENT OF CANTON, 1856

For centuries China had been unwilling to trade with Western people, whom the Chinese regarded as barbarians. As the Emperor wrote to George III in 1793, "I set no value on objects strange or ingenious and have no use for your country's manufactures." But the West highly valued Chinese silks and tea. For a long time the East India Company carried on a limited trade with China through the port of Canton and found that opium would bring a good price. Chinese attempts to stop the opium trade and British determination to win greater trading concessions resulted in the "Opium War" from 1839 to 1842, during which British ships bombarded Canton. By the Treaty of Nanking in 1842 Britain got trading concessions in five ports and secured the island of Hong Kong. In 1856 came another crisis when the Chinese authorities boarded a British ship, "The Arrow", and imprisoned some of the crew. A British fleet again bombarded Canton, while the Chinese put a price on the head of every Englishman. Palmerston used the crisis as an excuse to send an expedition to China and exact greater commercial concessions for Britain and other Western powers. This method of "opening up China" was an unhappy beginning of China's relations with the West. The United States was "opening up" Japan at the same time in much the same way.

Lord Palmerston, who was Prime Minister of Britain from 1855 to 1865, represented an age that was passing away. He was one of the last representatives of the great aristocratic families who believed that by their noble birth they were entitled, indeed obliged, to rule Britain. Born in 1784, Palmerston entered Parliament as a young man of twenty-three and from 1830 on he acted as Foreign Secretary in most of the Whig Cabinets. His foreign policy was popular with the people of Britain, for it reflected their own feelings of confidence in themselves, in their country, and their Empire, and their unwillingness to take second place to any other people or nation. He defiantly asserted Britain's right to trade with China, whether the Chinese wanted to trade or not. When Belgium decided to break away from Holland in 1830, Palmerston championed the cause of Belgian independence. So audacious and aggressive was his foreign policy that one man said of him that the peace of Europe might well depend on which leg he put out of bed first.

Palmerston's Foreign Policy

285

Sometimes Palmerston went too far. Louis Napoleon, a nephew of the great French Emperor, had managed to have himself elected President of the Second French Republic. In 1851 he overthrew the Republic and set up the Second Empire with himself as Emperor. Without consulting the Queen or the Prime Minister, Palmerston sent his personal congratulations to Louis Napoleon. This action annoyed the Queen, who was no admirer of "that nasty old man", as she called Palmerston, and the Prime Minister was forced to dismiss him as Foreign Secretary. But Palmerston was back in office the next year. No government could long do without him.

Palmerston did not become Prime Minister until he was seventy years old, and it was the poor handling of the Crimean War by his predecessor that brought him to power. The causes of this war, which in 1854 broke a long period of peace for Britain, are important. Ever since the seventeenth century Russia had sought to expand westward and to gain a port on the Mediterranean. Turkey, or the Ottoman

The Crimean War 1854-1856

THE CRIMEAN WAR

286

Empire, as it was then known, alone stood in her way. Among the possessions of the Ottoman Empire was Palestine, the Holy Land of Christians. In 1853 Russia went to war with Turkey, using as an excuse her right to protect Christians in the Holy Land from oppression by the Turks. Britain and France had no desire to see a strong and aggressive Russia menacing their positions and security in the eastern Mediterranean. In 1854 these two countries entered the war against Russia, for it was clear that weak and impoverished Turkey was no match for the Russian Bear.

From the beginning Lord Aberdeen's government handled the war badly, so badly that the disgusted Palmerston resigned from the government. A British army was landed in the Crimean peninsula, but its commanders proved hopelessly inefficient and incompetent. The soldiers were badly provided for. As a result of poor planning they went

The Campaign in the Crimea

CHARGE OF THE LIGHT BRIGADE

A trooper of the Eighth Hussars who rode in the suicidal charge wrote: "I felt at that moment my blood thicken and crawl, as if my heart grew still and quiet like a lump of stone within me. I was a moment paralysed, but the snorting of the horse, the wild headlong gallop, the sight of the Russians before us, becoming more and more distinct, and the first horrible discharge with its still more horrible effects came upon us, and emptied saddles all about me. My heart now began to warm. . . . I longed to be at the guns." An English officer who watched the action from a height with a French general wrote: "We saw the Light Brigade . . . moving forward at a trot, in the face of the Russian army. 'Mon Dieu!' said the fine old French general, 'Que vont-ils faire?' They went steadily on, as Englishmen only go under heavy fire. Artillery in front, on the right and left. . . . I saw shells bursting in the midst of the squadrons and men and horses strewed the ground behind them; yet on they went, and the smoke of the murderous fire poured on them. . . . 'Pauvre garçon,' said the old French general, patting me on the shoulder, 'Je suis vieux, j'ai vu des batailles, mais ceci est trop.'" Another French officer is reported to have remarked, "C'est magnifique, mais ce n'est pas la guerre."

through a severe Russian winter wearing light summer uniforms; and one shipload of boots sent for the army proved to be all for the left foot.

The army fought with the outmoded tactics and weapons that had been used at Waterloo. The famous Charge of the Light Brigade, extolled as a glorious example of British courage and gallantry, was actually the result of mismanagement and incompetence on the part of the commanders, which resulted in the loss of more than two hundred lives within a few moments. Medical care for the troops and medical supplies were almost nonexistent. Cholera and scurvy spread among the soldiers and almost fifty per cent of the wounded and ill died. This state of affairs continued until the appearance in Crimea of a remarkable woman named Florence Nightingale. In an age when ladies of good family did not work, Miss Nightingale shocked her family by wanting to be a nurse. A hundred years ago nursing was not considered a respectable profession and there was no school in England that trained nurses. After she had overcome her family's opposition, Miss Nightingale had to go to Germany to receive her training.

When news of the frightful conditions among the wounded in the Crimea reached England, Florence Nightingale received permission to go there and to take with her thirty-four other nurses. They were not welcomed by army officials but, in spite of serious opposition from senior medical officers, Miss Nightingale, backed by public opinion at home, was able to establish clean, well-equipped, efficient hospitals in which the wounded received good care. So effective was the work of Florence Nightingale and her nurses that the death rate among the wounded was reduced from fifty to two per cent.

When the details of the mismanagement of the Crimean campaign became known in England, an aroused people forced the Aberdeen government to resign. Just as they had turned to Pitt in the Seven Years War, the English now turned to the man who was "never better than when the gales ride high". Though the Queen would have preferred another leader for the government, it was obvious that the people wanted Palmerston. To the nation's joy, he became Prime Minister in the spring of 1855.

Palmerston immediately reorganized the army and the supply systems. The Allied generals pressed forward the attack in the Crimea. Late in 1855 the great fortress of Sebastopol fell and the following year Russia retired from Turkey. With the war over, Britain happily returned to her peacetime task of industrial and commercial expansion.

Florence Nightingale (margin note)

FLORENCE NIGHTINGALE

The wretched conditions which led to the high mortality rate in the Crimean War were described vividly by the special correspondent of "The Times". "The whole plateau on which stands 'the camp before Sebastopol' . . . is a vast black dreary wilderness of mud, dotted with little locks of foul water, and seamed by dirty brownish and tawny-coloured streams running down to and along the ravines. On its surface everywhere are strewed the carcasses of horses and miserable animals torn by dogs and smothered in mud. Vultures sweep over the mounds in flocks; carrion crows and 'birds of prey obscene' hover over their prey, menace the hideous dogs who are feasting below, or sit in gloomy dyspepsia, with drooped head and drooping wing, on the remnants of their banquet." He reported later, "The 63rd Regiment had only seven men fit for duty yesterday. The 46th had only thirty men fit for duty at the same date. . . . The Scots Fusilier Guards, who have had out from beginning to end 1562 men, now muster, including servants and corporals, 210 men on parade."

Palmerston remained Prime Minister for ten years. His government did little in the way of legislation and hardly interfered with the people, believing firmly in the virtues of *laissez faire,* or a policy of doing nothing. The greatest crisis in foreign affairs came with the outbreak of the American Civil War in 1861. The causes of the Civil War are complicated and do not belong in this story, but one of them was the existence of a great number of Negro slaves in the Southern States and the insistence of the planters there that slavery must be continued. Several states therefore broke away from the Union and set up a separate country, called the Confederate States of America. As all civil wars are, it was a bitter struggle, and it lasted for four years. The sympathies of the British people were sharply divided between the two sides.

The American
Civil War
1861-1865

289

The British
Reaction

Palmerston, the upper classes whom he represented, and the middle class for the most part favoured the cause of the South, whose leaders had many close ties, both social and commercial, with Great Britain. The working class, on the whole, was for the North and for President Lincoln whom they believed to be dedicated to the abolition of slavery. The Northern States bitterly resented Palmerston's obvious sympathy for the Southern cause and feared that the British government might

The Threat
of War

recognize the Confederate States as a separate country. At one point in the struggle, the United States and Great Britain almost went to war. Two agents from the Confederate States were travelling to Britain in a British mail boat, the *Trent,* when the ship was stopped by a United States naval vessel and the Southern agents removed. Palmerston demanded an apology and the return of the agents and sent troops to Canada in case of war with the United States. The crisis was resolved when the Southern agents were released and sent to Halifax where they took ship for England, but anti-British feeling continued in the United States for the duration of the war and after.

The Americans were further exasperated when the British permitted ships to be built in English shipyards for the Southern States, which used them as raiders against Northern merchant vessels. One of these, the *Alabama,* sank many Northern ships before it was destroyed. American resentment was displayed in the threats to punish Britain by conquering Canada. This fear of a conquest of Canada by the United States was one of the most powerful influences in bringing about the confederation of the British North American colonies in 1867 to form the Dominion of Canada.

Domestic Policy

At home Palmerston's policy was conservative and almost barren of constructive measures. Beneath the surface of British life there were restless stirrings, however. The working class began once more to demand the share of political power withheld from them in 1832. Social critics and philosophers such as John Stuart Mill argued that the government should interfere in men's lives to help those who could not help themselves. Young political leaders like Gladstone and Disraeli, kept long in the background by men like Palmerston, sought political leadership and advocated reform.

Palmerston's death in 1865 marked the end of an era. In a sense he had been like the dam which holds back the flood. With his death the dam burst. Even Palmerston was aware of the new forces that were to change England and the new leaders who would control these forces. "Gladstone," he said, "will soon have it all his way and whenever he gets my place we shall have strange doings." When he heard of Palmerston's death Disraeli declared, "The truce is over. I foresee tempestuous times and great vicissitudes in public life." There were indeed to be tempestuous times and great storms in public life, and William Ewart Gladstone and Benjamin Disraeli were to be the men chiefly concerned with guiding Britain through the troubled waters.

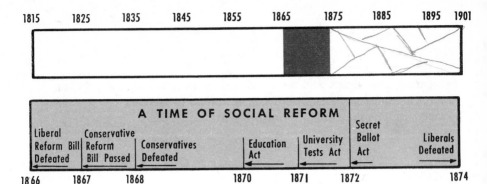

1815 1825 1835 1845 1855 1865 1875 1885 1895 1901

A TIME OF SOCIAL REFORM

Liberal Reform Bill Defeated	Conservative Reform Bill Passed	Conservatives Defeated	Education Act	University Tests Act	Secret Ballot Act	Liberals Defeated

1866   1867   1868   1870   1871   1872   1874

CHAPTER FORTY-TWO

GLADSTONE AND LIBERALISM: 1866-1874

Parliamentary Reform   By the time of Palmerston's death, the great issue agitating the British people was again that of parliamentary reform. In 1865 only one out of five adult males had the right to vote. In the years since 1848, when the Chartists made their final effort to have the franchise extended, the working class had become less radical and many people believed that the time had come to give them the vote. Throughout the 1850's and 1860's, the demand for an extension of the franchise grew in strength, but as long as Palmerston was Prime Minister, he opposed every attempt to grant it. After his death it was only a matter of time until another Reform Act was passed. The political leaders believed that the party which gave the working class the vote would in all probability have its support.

There were now two parties in Parliament, the Liberals, who were the successors of the Whigs, and the Conservatives, who were the Tories by another name. In 1866 William Gladstone, the leader of a Liberal **The Second** government, introduced a Reform Bill in the House of Commons. The **Reform Bill** Conservatives, led by Benjamin Disraeli, opposed it. Supported by some of Gladstone's more cautious followers, the Conservatives were able to defeat the Bill. Gladstone resigned and Disraeli took office. With that sure instinct that marks the successful politician, Disraeli set out to "dish" the Liberals by passing a Conservative Bill that would secure working-class support for his party. Many Conservatives objected to what they described as a "bold leap in the dark", but Disraeli convinced them that the people demanded the change. Moreover, he said, the Liberals had failed once to introduce a Reform Bill; they would not fail again. And then where would the Conservative Party be? The Conservative Bill, when introduced, proved to be more radical than that presented by the Liberals which had brought about Gladstone's defeat by Disraeli. During the debates the politicians made much of this turn-about on the part of Disraeli. A popular song of the day, sung to the tune of "Clementine" went:

> Oh my Dizzy, juggler-hearted! oh my Dizzy true no more,
> Oh the former Tory speeches; oh, the county members roar.

> Oh I see thee still in office (no Conservative indeed)
> With a hoard of clever sayings, preaching down the party's
> creed.

Disraeli's Act of 1867 gave the vote to almost all the urban working class, leaving only the agricultural workers and women without representation in Parliament. The number of voters in England was almost doubled. The Act also made representation in Parliament conform more closely to the distribution of people by taking more seats away from the sparsely populated South and giving them to the increasingly populous North. Old Chartists had seen at least part of their dream come true. *The Reform Act 1867*

Triumphant in Parliament, Disraeli confidently prepared for the election of 1868. He fully expected that the working class, grateful for the Second Reform Act, would support him. To his astonishment the Conservatives were badly defeated and Gladstone swept into power with a good majority. As Disraeli grudgingly admitted, more than one Act was necessary to convince the working class that the Conservatives really had its interests at heart.

With the election of 1868 the struggle between Gladstone and Disraeli commenced, a struggle which was to have a powerful effect on Parliament and on the course of British history. The two men, who overshadowed all their contemporaries, were worlds apart. They belonged to different races, had a different upbringing, and possessed different temperaments. Neither man ever understood the other and each regarded his opponent with faintly disguised contempt. Of Gladstone, who had won the first round, Disraeli once said that he was: *Gladstone and Disraeli*

> an unprincipled maniac . . . an extraordinary mixture of envy,
> vindictiveness, hypocrisy and superstition; and with one commanding characteristic—whether Prime Minister or leader
> of the opposition, whether preaching, praying, speechifying
> or scribbling, never a gentleman.

Disraeli, however, was hardly an impartial observer!

293

Gladstone was the son of a wealthy Liverpool merchant. After a brilliant career at Eton and Oxford he thought seriously of entering the Church, but decided, finally, on a career in politics. He was elected to the House of Commons in 1833 as a Tory and in his first speech opposed the abolition of slavery. Gradually his views became more liberal. He was a follower of Sir Robert Peel and supported his leader

GLADSTONE

Gladstone had great physical as well as mental energy. Visitors to his estate often watched in amazement as the great man chopped down a giant oak. One contemporary wrote: "His power of work and assimilation was amazing, his capacity to stand fatigue and long hours equally remarkable; he was endowed with unusual physical courage and unlimited assurance. . . . He was unquestionably the most efficient and eloquent speaker of his generation, his voice, elocution and gestures being almost faultless . . . with or without preparation Gladstone always spoke superbly well." Another man confessed: "Profoundly as I distrusted him . . . I have never listened to him even for a few minutes without ceasing to marvel at his influence over men. That white-hot face, stern as a Covenanter's yet mobile as a comedian's; those restless, flashing eyes; that wondrous voice . . . the masterly cadence of his elocution; the vivid energy of his attitudes; the fine animation of gestures;—sir, when I am assailed through eye and ear by this compacted phalanx of assailants . . . in defiance of my very will, I . . . exclaim, 'This is indeed the voice of truth and wisdom. This man is honest and sagacious beyond his fellows. He must be believed, he must be obeyed.' "

in 1846 when the Corn Laws were repealed. On Peel's death, Gladstone emerged as the leader of those men, the "Peelites", who, Disraeli charged, had "betrayed" the Tory Party. In 1859 he brought the "Peelites" into an alliance with the Whigs and Reformers to found the modern Liberal Party, of which he became leader soon after Palmerston's death.

Underlying Gladstone's political thought and actions was an intense **Gladstone's** religious conviction. He believed that politics was next only to the **Liberalism** Church as a spiritual force. The State, he argued, must have a conscience and help men obey the law of God. The belief that he was doing God's work gave him great moral fervour. On one occasion, when he was in the field against Disraeli, he wrote in his diary:

> I profess to believe it has been an occasion when the battle to be fought was a battle of justice, humanity, freedom, law . . . all on a gigantic scale. The word spoken was a word for millions, and for millions who themselves cannot speak. If I really believe this, then I should regard my having been morally forced into this work as a great and high election of God. . . . Why has my health and strength been so peculiarly sustained? . . . Was this not all for a purpose? And has it not all some connection with a process to which I have given myself? This appears to me to carry all the marks of the will of God.

With Gladstone doing God's work in politics, Disraeli found himself put in the unhappy position of working for the Devil!

Gladstone's political philosophy can best be described as a fervent belief in individual freedom and liberty. Only a free man, he believed, could possess the sense of worth and self-respect that made man a spiritual being. While he deplored the ills and evils in society and was at his best fighting privilege and injustice, Gladstone was not a social reformer. The function of government was not to reform society or people, he argued, but to make it possible for every man to have a free and equal opportunity to make the best of his own life. In many ways he was a typical Victorian, who believed in thrift, industry, and self-help. He once said, "It is the individual mind, the individual conscience; it is the individual character in which mainly human happiness or human misery depends, even though the government spends days and nights in your service."

Between 1868 and 1874 Gladstone's government passed Act after **Domestic** Act to abolish privilege and establish greater equality of opportunity **Reform**

295

for all classes. The field of education offers one example of his activities. In 1868, when he came to power, more than half the children in England Education were able to write little more than their own names. Such education as there was, was carried on largely by religious bodies in charity schools, or by a variety of private schools for the children of the well-to-do, which the English, for some obscure reason, call public schools. Gladstone's government passed an Education Act in 1870 which established a system of elementary schools supported by government grants. This made some education possible for almost everyone and ten years later there were over three million pupils in the new schools. He also made it possible for more people to attend the Universities of Oxford and Cambridge which at that time could be attended only by members of

EDUCATION

England in the early nineteenth century had no national system of education. Although there were hundreds of schools, most had a religious affiliation, and few were dedicated to educating the mass of the working class. There was little money available for education and there were few competent teachers. It was charged that the whole profession was made up of people with physical infirmities who could not perform any other kind of work. Teaching was often done by senior students or monitors who were taught first by teachers and who then passed on their knowledge to less advanced students. By the middle of the century the government was beginning to realize that the welfare of the community depended upon the level of education of its members. A parliamentary Commission appointed in 1858 found conditions to be deplorable and recommended that government grants to education be increased on the basis of "payment by results" of the examinations. "I cannot promise you either efficiency or cheapness," a member of the Commission reported to the Commons, "but if the system is not efficient it will be cheap, if it is not cheap it will be efficient." The system of payment by results failed and Gladstone's Act of 1870 marked the beginning of a modern education policy. But it was not until after the turn of the twentieth century that the government became responsible for free elementary and secondary education.

296

the Church of England. By his University Tests Act of 1871 university doors were thrown open to men of all faiths.

Gladstone followed up his work in education by reforming the civil service and the army. Competitive examinations were substituted for appointments in the civil service and thus merit, rather than family influence, became an important factor in securing a civil service position. In the army it was the custom for an officer to buy his commission and promotion often depended on his ability to purchase the rank above his. In this way the highest ranks in the army tended to be filled by the wealthiest, rather than the most competent, men; much of the mismanagement in the Crimean War was later blamed on the purchase system. Gladstone's government put an end to purchases, though only over the fierce opposition of the army authorities. *Civil Service and Army Reform*

Another of Gladstone's measures, the Secret Ballot Act of 1872, was of immense importance. Until this time, in an election, men voted by a show of hands, or by each individual mounting a platform and announcing the name of the candidate for whom he wished to cast his vote. Gladstone and the Liberals believed that there was little use in giving men the right to vote if they were prevented, by some means, from using it as they wished. Under the old system, factory owners could intimidate their workers and landowners their tenants by threatening to dismiss them from their jobs or their farms unless they voted as instructed. Moreover, it was possible for a candidate to buy an election vote and make sure that the voter delivered it. One very candid politician, commenting on the secret ballot, declared: "Suppose you give a man five pounds; he may receive the money and vote another way. Even if I purchase a man I may not be able to know how he is going to vote; he may vote against me after he has said he will vote for me." Although many echoed his sentiments and gave other reasons for their opposition, the Bill passed. With its passage, another step had been taken towards the modern democratic state. *The Secret Ballot*

For six years Gladstone's government investigated and legislated, yet with each reform measure some of his support vanished. Every reform displeased those who saw their special privileges taken away by it. For example, a well-meaning Act to restrict the sale of liquor bitterly offended the wealthy and powerful distillers, who supported the Conservatives in the election of 1874. Moreover, the government had become tired and Disraeli, with some truth, compared the Cabinet to a range of "extinct volcanoes". While the Liberals were bold and aggressive in their reform measures, they were hesitant and spineless in their *Defeat 1874*

297

AN ELECTION IN 1865

Before the secret ballot in 1872 elections had changed little for centuries. They were perhaps somewhat less violent than in the eighteenth century because of the establishment of police forces and the more restrained behaviour of the people. Yet at the same time they were much more spirited than in our own day. Jostling and huzzaing frequently burst forth into less gentlemanly behaviour. After the election it took the crowd only a few moments to reduce the platform, benches, and bunting to a shambles, in much the same spirit as football fans now converge upon the goal posts. The introduction of the secret ballot changed all this. Canada followed the British precedent and introduced the secret ballot in 1874.

foreign policy, and this was increasingly unpopular with a people accustomed to Palmerston's bravado. Bad harvests and hard times increased Gladstone's difficulties. Few people were surprised, then, when Disraeli, riding high on a crest of popularity, and with a newly-organized and efficient Conservative Party, swept Gladstone from power in the election of 1874.

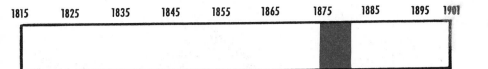

	A TIME OF IMPERIAL EXPANSION				
Social Reform Bills	Purchase of Suez Shares	Victoria "Empress of India"	Congress of Berlin	Cyprus Under British Control	Conservatives Defeated

1874   1875   1877   1878   1880

CHAPTER FORTY-THREE

DISRAELI AND TORY DEMOCRACY: 1874-1880

Benjamin Disraeli never ceased to astonish nineteenth-century Eng- Disraeli
land. He was born in 1804, the son of a Spanish Jew. He had never
been to a private school or to university and he was a member neither
of the aristocracy nor of the upper middle class. His first ambition was
to be a writer and he had published his first novel before he was
twenty-two. On the title page was the motto:

> Why, then, the world's mine oyster
> Which I with sword will open.

Disraeli's sword was his pen and his wit. The young man soon became
notorious in London society. He was an extraordinary figure, with his
long hair arranged in fancy ringlets and his extravagant dress. He
once went to a dinner party in a black velvet coat, purple trousers, a
scarlet waistcoat, and white gloves.

Although Disraeli continued all his life to be a writer, he had decided
by 1837 that politics would provide a great opportunity for his talents.
Proud and ambitious, self-confident and fearless, Disraeli believed that
he could achieve whatever he wished. His only problem, he felt, was to
decide which political party he should join. He had no great convictions
about either party and neither had a very strong appeal for him.

> Am I a Whig or a Tory? I forget. As for the Tories I admire
> antiquity, particularly a ruin. . . . I think I am a Tory. But
> then the Whigs give such good dinners, and are the most
> amusing. I think I am a Whig. But then the Tories are so
> moral and morality is my forte. I must be a Tory. But the
> Whigs dress so much better; and an ill-dressed party, like an
> ill-dressed man, must be wrong. Yes, I am decidedly a Whig!

DISRAELI

Disraeli's quick wit and his presence of mind in a crisis were much admired by his followers. A member of Parliament wrote the following account of an incident that occurred
while Disraeli was making a speech in the House. "In the most effective part of his
speech, Disraeli suddenly put up his right hand, in which was his handkerchief, to his
mouth, and turning round to his neighbour, Lord John Manners, apparently asked him a
question which he could not hear. 'What, what are you saying?' Disraeli then said
sotto voce: 'It is all right,' and he took up his speech at the exact word where he had
left off, and finished it amidst uproarious applause from the whole Tory benches. The
young men behind the Front Opposition Bench could not make out the purpose of this
bit of by-play. . . . Two days afterwards I sat next Alderman Lawrence, who sat exactly
opposite Disraeli in the House of Commons. He said to me, 'Your chief is a wonderful
fellow. . . . Would you like to know what happened the other night when he turned to
John Manners?' 'Very much', said I. 'Well,' he added, 'in the best part of his speech
and in the middle of a sentence his teeth fell out, and he caught them up with extraordinary rapidity in his right hand, turned round apparently to ask a question of his
neighbour, put them in, and resumed his speech at the exact word where he had left
it off'."

Disraeli's
"Tory
Democracy"

In the end he became a Tory, joining the party of the landowners, partly
because he was extremely critical of the middle-class leaders of industrial
England who were in the Whig camp. Disraeli was convinced that nineteenth-century industrial progress had divided England into two nations,
the rich and the poor—

> . . . between whom there is no intercourse and no sympathy;
> who are as ignorant of each other's habits, thoughts, feelings, as
> if they were . . . inhabitants of different planets; who are formed
> by different breeding, are fed by different food, are ordered by
> different manners, and are not governed by the same laws.

Unless this division were ended and the life of the poor improved,
argued Disraeli, the nation was doomed.

Disraeli's main object after 1846 was to turn the Tories away from
their futile opposition to free trade and convince them that only through

300

a policy of Tory democracy could they ever regain power. Day after day, year after year, he urged his party to adopt social reform as its platform. To the aristocratic and landed Tories he explained that:

While the feudal system may have worn out, its main principle —that the tenure of property should be the fulfilment of a duty—is the essence of good government. The divine right of kings may have been a plea for feeble tyrants, but the divine right of government is the keystone of human progress, and without it, government sinks into police, and a nation is degraded into a mob.

Under his intelligent and forceful leadership the Tories became the Conservative Party, with a more progressive programme than formerly.

SLUMS

As late as 1872 a visiting Frenchman could describe the sights of the slums in this way: "Street boys abound—bare-footed, dirty, and turning wheels in order to get alms. . . . Near them, leaning against the greasy walls, or inert on the steps, are men in astounding rags; it is impossible to imagine before seeing them how many layers of dirt an overcoat or a pair of trousers could hold. . . . It is in these localities that families have been discovered with no other bed than a heap of soot." Such conditions were exceptional, but the general level of working-class districts was very low. By this time most members of Parliament realized that the welfare, prosperity, and health of the nation as a whole could be improved by slum clearance and more effective sanitation laws and inspections. To this day, however, the large cities of Great Britain (and Canada) are hideous and squalid in many places, unplanned and dreary conglomerations of human beings.

301

When the Conservatives won the election of 1874, Disraeli finally had the chance to put his principles to the test of action.

Domestic Reforms By the time Parliament met in 1875, Disraeli's Cabinet had ready a wide variety of Bills, each designed to improve the condition of the working class. The Artisans Housing Act gave assistance to the towns in clearing away the dreadful slums in which so many of the workers were housed and in replacing them with new homes. Public Health Acts, a River Pollution Act, and water safety measures hit boldly at the lack of sanitation. Parks and playgrounds were to be built in English cities. Urged on by Samuel Plimsoll, the government passed the Merchant Shipping Act which protected seamen who had to sail in rotten and overloaded ships that were carefully insured by their owners in the expectation that they would sink. Trade unions were allowed to picket the factories of employers against whom they had grievances. Hours of work were reduced and regular safety inspections were ordered for dangerous machinery. Disraeli had not talked of Tory democracy in vain.

Foreign Policy After 1875, however, his attention was concentrated on foreign policy. Disraeli believed in the Empire and in imperial expansion, and by the 1870's most Englishmen shared his enthusiasm. In 1875 he purchased a majority of the shares in the Suez Canal from the Khedive of Egypt, a step which increased British power in the Middle East and later led to British control of Egypt. In 1876 he sought to glorify the British Empire in India by giving Queen Victoria the title "Empress of India". The Queen was delighted. She had always found the quick-witted and charming Disraeli much more attractive than Gladstone who, she said, always addressed her as if she were a public meeting.

Disraeli returned to the energetic and bold foreign policy of Palmerston. He was a political realist who thought only of the strength and interests of his country. To protect the Suez Canal and the eastern Mediterranean, Disraeli bolstered the weak Turkish Empire against the persistent Russian plan to advance south-westward to Constantinople and the Mediterranean. By 1878 Russia had forced the Turks to their knees and an aroused English people demanded that Britain should intervene against Russia. The streets echoed with the popular refrain:

We don't want to fight, but by Jingo if we do,
We've got the ships, we've got the men,
And got the money too.

The word "Jingo" entered the language to describe a policy of making threatening gestures to fight if a nation's wishes were not met. For

THE LIFELINE OF EMPIRE—THE SUEZ CANAL

some years, Britain's policy was Jingoistic. At the Congress of Berlin in 1878 Disraeli helped force Russia to back down. Thinking that it would be a useful base, he also secured the island of Cyprus for Britain. As Disraeli returned home from Berlin, claiming to bring "peace with honour", his popularity soared. "High and low," wrote Queen Victoria, "the country is delighted, except Mr. Gladstone who is frantic."

Thereafter Disraeli's stock fell. In 1879 Gladstone came out of semi-retirement to take the field and denounce Disraeli's foreign and imperial policy with fury. To Gladstone a moral question was involved in Disraeli's plans to expand the Empire. Imperial expansion had caused a war in Afghanistan and the death of many native tribesmen. "Remember the rights of the savage, as we call him," Gladstone warned. "Remember that the sanctity of life in the hill villages of Afghanistan, among the winter snows, is as inviolable in the eyes of Almighty God as can be your own." How could Disraeli support the Turks, he asked, when they had been guilty of butchering thousands of Bulgarian Christians? His eloquence kindled the flames of indignation which swept the country like wildfire.

As the election of 1880 approached, Gladstone was joined by a

303

new group of young Liberals led by Joseph Chamberlain. More radical than their leader, they pledged the Party to social reform and to the extension of the franchise to agricultural labourers. With a fury that recalled Bright's onslaught against the Corn Laws in the 1840's, Chamberlain, a Birmingham manufacturer, denounced the landowners and their leader. The Liberals, he told the working class, were the party of progress, prosperity, and social reform.

Defeat 1880 The combination of Gladstone and Chamberlain was irresistible; Disraeli went down to defeat in the election of 1880. Acute observers saw that the working class was trying one party after another and asked if it might not, in time, try a party of its own. There was a surprising result of the election that required immediate attention from the new government. In the new House of Commons sat sixty-five members from Ireland, known as Irish Nationalists. Led by Charles Stewart Parnell, they were pledged to home rule for Ireland. For six years, the activities of this group, and the efforts to find a settlement to the Irish question, dominated British politics.

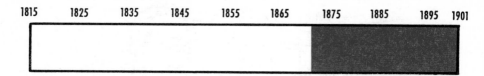

CHAPTER FORTY-FOUR

GLADSTONE AND IRELAND: 1868-1898

The history of the relations between England and Ireland is troubled and often tragic. Wars between the Irish and the English were continuous during the reigns of the Tudors and the Stuarts and it will be recalled that Cromwell put down a rising there with incredible savagery, garrisoned the country with English soldiers, and ruled Ireland from London. For a time after the Restoration, Ireland had its own government and Parliament. In 1800, however, the Act of Union united the two countries and thereafter Irish members sat in the British House of Lords and House of Commons. In 1829 Irish Catholics were granted the right to hold public office, which had been denied them since the sixteenth century. However, serious problems remained to plague generations of English statesmen in their efforts to arrive at a settlement of the Irish question. *Anglo-Irish Relations Before 1868*

These problems were religious, social, and economic. Most of the Irish were Roman Catholics, but they had to pay tithes, or taxes to support the Church of England. Moreover, much of the land in Ireland was owned by English landlords who lived in England and who rented land to Irish tenant farmers at high rents. The tenant could easily be evicted from his land if he did not pay his rent or if he displeased the landlord. Furthermore, if the tenant were evicted, he received no compensation for any improvements which he might have made to his land or buildings.

At the best of times the Irish peasant was close to starvation. One honest Englishman admitted that many Irish "were living on the verge of starvation, in places in which we would not keep our cattle." In the 1840's, these wretched conditions grew worse. A series of failures

305

PARNELL

Parnell was a young Protestant landlord, the son of an Anglo-Irish father and an American mother. Entering Parliament in 1875, he soon became the absolute master of his party and developed a plan of campaign which eventually changed the whole nature of British politics. Determined to prove to the English that Ireland could not be governed against its will, he mastered the techniques of parliamentary obstruction and almost brought government to a standstill.

of the potato crop, which was the principal article in the diet of the Irish, brought devastating famine to Ireland. Hundreds of thousands of Irishmen died and many others emigrated to the United States and Canada. Between 1841 and the end of the century, so many people died or left the country that Ireland's population declined from over eight million to under four and a half million.

Gladstone's Reforms   When Gladstone became Prime Minister in 1868, he immediately tried to improve conditions in Ireland. He had Acts passed to remove the special privileges of the Church of England in Ireland and to compel landlords to pay compensation to any evicted tenant who had improved his land or buildings. In spite of these measures, conditions in Ireland did not improve. In 1880 a member of Parliament reported:

> There are some 500,000 persons, at least at the moment, in Ireland, dependent for their means of subsistence, from day to day, upon charitable organizations. These persons receive a weekly dole of Indian meal, sufficient mostly to give them one meal each per day of that kind of sustenance which in England would scarcely be given to a gentleman's cat.

During his second ministry (1880-1885), Gladstone again tried to solve the problem of Ireland. A new Land Act, passed in 1881, granted what were known as the "Three F's": fair rent, fixed tenure, and free sale. To ensure obedience to the Act, a Land Court was established to which the Irish could appeal against the landlords. But the measure had come too late and it failed to satisfy the majority of inhabitants. Most Irishmen regarded themselves as a separate people from the English, with a history and culture of their own. They had

IRELAND, SHOWING THE NORTHERN COUNTIES THAT RESISTED HOME RULE

no desire to be British. Many had come to believe that only by gaining self-government or Home Rule could they solve their problems. They "Home Rule" began to agitate for Home Rule, and to reinforce their demands the more radical Irish started a systematic campaign of burning the homes of the absentee landlords or of their agents, killing representatives of the British government or Irishmen who supported them, and maiming cattle belonging to their opponents.

The movement for Home Rule was led by Charles Stewart Parnell. Charles Stewart Parnell hated all things English. To win his objectives, he devised a Parnell simple plan. His sixty-five fellow Irish members of Parliament were given clear-cut instructions: "Refuse all invitations, don't try to make yourselves popular, make yourself disliked, have no truck with the enemy, make him want to get rid of you, and above all else make it impossible for the Commons to transact business."

The Irish Nationalists responded whole-heartedly to these instructions. On many a famous "Irish night" in the House of Commons, they Irish spoke throughout the night and the following day on topics of no impor- "Filibustering" tance. By such tactics Parnell hoped to make parliamentary government impossible and force the English to establish a separate Irish Parliament in Dublin. One English politician remarked that dealing with him was like dealing with a foreign power. After the election of 1885 eighty-six Irish Nationalists, voting as a united group, virtually controlled Parliament, since neither the Liberals nor the Conservatives could govern

307

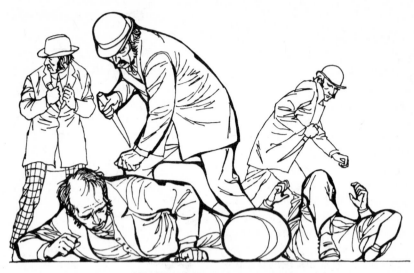

ASSASSINATION IN DUBLIN, 1882

In the spring of 1882 the British government passed an Arrears Bill, to strike off rents owed by Irish farmers, in return for which Parnell was to use his influence to end crime and disorder in Ireland. The sky looked brighter than it had for many years when, on May 6th, the newly-arrived Lord Cavendish, a young, amiable relation of the Gladstones, and Mr. Burke, an unpopular official, were attacked and murdered in Phoenix Park, Dublin. The assassins belonged to the "Invincibles", a small murder club which had escaped detection. The murder of Lord Cavendish, who had harmed no one, horrified even the most determined Irish nationalists. Parnell was dumbfounded and shaken, saying to a friend that he felt he had been stabbed in the back. In a public statement he wrote with anguish. "No act has ever been perpetrated in our country . . . that has so stained the name of hospitable Ireland as this cowardly and unprovoked assassination of a friendly stranger." He was also terror-stricken and believed the extremists might be after him. Even in Parliament he carried a revolver in his overcoat. The murders made a solution to the Irish problem much more difficult than ever before.

without their support. So influential did Parnell become that he was known as "The Uncrowned King". The Irish question had become the central issue of British politics.

Convinced that only Home Rule could solve the Anglo-Irish prob-
First Home lem, Gladstone introduced the first Home Rule Bill in 1886. This
Rule Bill measure, which would have ended the Act of Union of 1800 and estab-
1886 lished a separate Irish Parliament in Dublin to handle purely Irish affairs, aroused a storm of opposition from all sides. In the six northern counties of Ireland, together known as Ulster, Protestants were in the majority. These were, for the most part, the descendants of Scottish and English
The Ulster settlers placed in Ireland by James I and Cromwell. The Ulstermen
Problem threatened armed rebellion if they were put under the control of a Catholic Parliament in Dublin; and they were supported by the Conservative opposition. "Ulster will fight," cried the fiery Lord Randolph

308

Churchill, "and Ulster will be right." More serious than the Conservative stand was the opposition from within Gladstone's own party. Led by the brilliant Joseph Chamberlain, ninety-three Liberals voted against their leader, and the first Home Rule Bill was defeated. Gladstone lost the election which followed this defeat in 1886 and resigned.

Between 1886 and 1892 the Conservative government combined a policy of reform with repression, while maimings, burnings, and killings continued in Ireland. When the Liberals won the election of 1892, Gladstone, now over eighty, tried once again to pacify the Irish. In the following year his second Home Rule Bill passed through the Commons only to be defeated in the House of Lords. When Gladstone died in 1898, the Irish question was still unsolved. It was to distract England for many years.

Ireland represents one of the greatest failures of British statesmanship. Gladstone's efforts had been honest, humanitarian, and realistic, but they were not sufficient to overcome the desire of the Irish to rule their own country and to develop their own traditions and culture.

Gladstone's
Failure

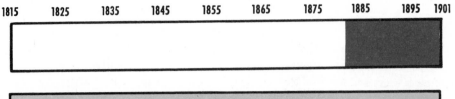

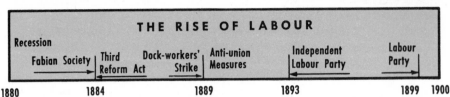

CHAPTER FORTY-FIVE

LABOUR ENTERS POLITICS

In 1886 Charles Booth, a social scientist, stated that one-third of the people in London still lived below "the poverty line". It was not a surprising discovery, but it sharply contradicted the Victorian belief that material progress would soon banish poverty from the earth. People were forced to ask whether the optimistic hopes that had inspired England at the time of the opening of the Great Exhibition of 1851 ought not to be revised. Not only was there poverty and hunger in the land, but there were also signs that the pace of the expansion of industry was slowing down and that growth might stop altogether. British capital had been invested in the industrial and railway systems of other countries, particularly those of Germany and the United States. By 1880 these fields for profitable investment disappeared and, what was worse, manufactured products from other countries were now competing with those manufactured in Britain. British investors and merchants both became alarmed. Their factories were working steadily, but falling prices meant a loss in profits. Their old confidence in the rightness of the Victorian world began to disappear. When workers demanded higher wages, they were told that they would be lucky if wages were not cut.

British agriculture was also badly affected by foreign competition. Railways, faster sea transportation, and the development of refrigeration made it possible for American and Canadian wheat, South American cattle, and frozen meats and butter from Australia and New Zealand to compete with British products in the British market. Many British farmers cut down the acreage under cultivation. Farm labourers were dismissed and moved to the cities or overseas to the colonies.

As long as the economic system was expanding and times were good,

KARL MARX AT WORK

Marx was born in Prussia in 1818, the son of a Jewish lawyer, and studied law, history, and philosophy at the Universities of Bonn and Berlin. In 1849 he settled in London and soon became intimate with leading Chartists. In London he lived in poverty in a few small rooms, repeatedly saddened by the death of three of his six children. Most of his days were spent in the British Museum, where he studied the history and economic organization of the country. The results of his work were published in 1867 in a book, "Das Kapital". In this and other works Marx attacked the capitalist system and argued that it would in time decay and fall apart. Most socialist and communist philosophy has its origin in the theories of Karl Marx, who died in London in 1883.

few people listened to the social reformers. In 1867 Karl Marx had written a book called *Das Kapital* in which he criticized the British economic system and prophesied that it was doomed to collapse. Few Englishmen read *Das Kapital* and those who did scoffed at its predictions. Now however, when the economic system began to show signs of weakness, radicals charged that fundamental economic and social changes were necessary. Liberals and Conservatives, the reformers argued, accepted poverty and unemployment as a fact and tried only to apply salves and medicines. What the patient needed was surgery. Those who advocated radical changes were generally described as *socialists*.

Two socialist organizations appeared in the 1880's. H. M. Hyndman formed the Social Democratic Federation in 1881, which advocated The S.D.F. a working-class revolution to overthrow the governing class. Hyndman 1881 gained very few supporters, however, for Englishmen were too firmly attached to the rule of law to be attracted to the idea of a revolution. Far more important than the Social Democratic Federation was the Fabian Society, founded in 1884. It was an organization started by The Fabians middle-class intellectuals and reformers like H. G. Wells, the brilliant 1884 novelist; George Bernard Shaw, the playwright; and Sidney and Beatrice

311

Webb, socialist writers. The society took its name from Fabius, a Roman general who, when Rome was at war with Carthage, had advocated a cautious policy rather than a pitched battle. "One must wait," he said, "until the time is ripe to strike." The Fabians believed it was inevitable that socialism should come to Great Britain, but they also argued that it should come gradually and peacefully through democratic and parliamentary methods. Ever since 1884 the Fabians have had a very important influence on the history of social reform and labour politics.

But the Fabian Society was a middle-class movement, and the working class had been following a different path. Since the failure of the Chartists, working-class leaders had turned their energies to the organization of trade unions. They believed that while one worker in a trade would have little chance of winning higher wages and improving working conditions, a union of all the workers in the same trade would be much more successful. Soon, each of the trades had a well-organized union and in 1868 the Trade Union Congress had been formed to provide an organization through which all the unions might work together. Through the power of the Congress the unions had won important improvements in wages, hours, and conditions of work.

The Growth of Trade Unions

In 1889 there was a striking demonstration of the power of the new trade unions. Led by the fiery and intelligent John Burns, the London dock-workers struck for higher wages. For a month English shipping was paralyzed. The strike was bitter and hard-fought, but support from the working class flooded in from all over the country. Finally, the employers gave in and accepted almost all the union's demands. The dockers were not skilled tradesmen, and their success in this strike led to the rapid organization of other unskilled workers into huge unions.

By this time many of the working-class leaders were beginning to think of organizing a political party to represent their class in Parliament. Workers in the town and cities had received the vote in 1867. By the Third Reform Act, passed by Gladstone's administration in 1884, almost three million people, mostly agricultural labourers and miners, were given the vote. In the election of 1892 Keir Hardie, a Scottish miner, John Burns, a trade union organizer, and thirteen other Labour or Liberal-Labour candidates had been elected to Parliament. This success convinced Hardie that the time was ripe to start a new party. John Burns agreed. As he said:

Third Reform Act 1884

> The world moves on its belly; and politicians will find that the people have longer memories than formerly, especially

KEIR HARDIE ENTERS PARLIAMENT

Hardie was born in 1856 and went to work in the mines when only ten years old. In 1887 he started a socialist paper with some friends and in 1888 fought and lost his first election. Four years later he was elected to Parliament and in 1893 was a leading figure in the creation of the Independent Labour Party, forerunner of the modern Labour Party. Many members of Parliament mocked the miner, with his rough clothes and rustic talk, but they soon learned to respect his honesty, integrity, and genial and lovable nature.

when the possessors of the empty bellies have votes . . . for the first time in the history of the human race the working people possess the power, through elective institutions, to embody in law their economic and material desires.

In 1893 Hardie formed the Independent Labour Party, or the I.L.P. as it was called. At first the party did not flourish, but it marked an extremely important beginning. In Parliament, Hardie's rough tweeds and miner's cloth cap stood out sharply among the frock coats and top hats of other members and served as a continual reminder to both Liberals and Conservatives that a new political force had arrived. What the Independent Labour Party lacked was the organized support of the trade unions, which would mean mass voting power and, perhaps, financial assistance.

The I.L.P.
1893

The late 1890's were increasingly difficult years for the working class, as the employers fought bitterly against the growing power of organized labour. To counter the strike weapon of the working class, the employers used the lockout; they simply closed their factories and denied their employees work and wages. Lockouts against engineers and miners ended in victories for their employers. As Beatrice Webb, the Fabian writer, said:

313

> The employers have, as regards immediate victory, played their cards with remarkable astuteness. . . . But they are over-reaching themselves. . . . It is childish to expect good results from a consent wrung from thousands of men by threats of absolute starvation. . . . And they forget the polling booth.

The failure of the strike weapon turned labour's thoughts more definitely towards securing their aims by political action. In 1899 the Trade Union Congress took a fateful decision to invite delegates from all working-class radical reform and socialist organizations to meet together and discuss the formation of a united Labour Party. After lengthy discussions the delegates decided to organize the Labour Representation Committee, later known as the Labour Party. In the election of 1906 the Party sent twenty-nine members to Parliament and by 1929 the Labour Party was strong enough to form the government.

The rise of the Labour Party marked the decline of nineteenth-century beliefs in self-help and *laissez-faire*, the policy which implied that if no action were taken everything would work out well in the long run. To gain the support of the working class, Liberals and Conservatives moved increasingly towards reform measures that would have terrified Gladstone and astounded Disraeli. Old-age pensions, hospital insurance, workmen's compensation for accidents, were only a few of these measures. Political democracy and industrialism had killed *laissez-faire* and had brought in the age of state action, just as nineteenth-century England was coming to an end.

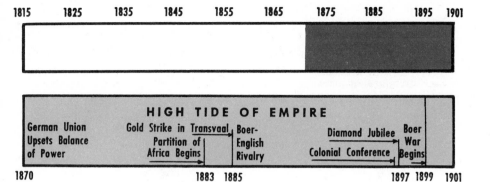

| 1815 | 1825 | 1835 | 1845 | 1855 | 1865 | 1875 | 1885 | 1895 | 1901 |

HIGH TIDE OF EMPIRE

German Union Upsets Balance of Power

Gold Strike in Transvaal, Partition of Africa Begins

Boer-English Rivalry

Diamond Jubilee

Colonial Conference

Boer War Begins

1870   1883 1885   1897 1899 1901

CHAPTER FORTY-SIX

THE CLIMAX OF BRITISH IMPERIALISM

In June 1897 five million Londoners lined the streets to watch a gigantic parade. Passing before their eyes were Mounted Police from Canada, splendid in their red coats, turbanned Sikhs from India, Dyaks of Borneo, Jamaican cavalrymen, troops from Australia and New Zealand, African tribesmen, and crack British regiments in dress uniforms. The occasion was the sixtieth anniversary of Queen Victoria's accession to the throne of Great Britain. At the end of the parade came the great ornate carriage drawn by eight cream-coloured horses, bearing the frail old Queen, now seventy-seven years old, the head of the greatest empire the world had ever seen. The Diamond Jubilee 1897

It was a moving moment, a stupendous spectacle, and it marked the climax of Britain's imperial adventure. The British people were proud of their achievement. Fifty years before, their fathers had questioned the value of an empire, but there were few who questioned it in 1897.

There were a number of reasons why the mid-century indifference had given way to an exuberant enthusiasm for the Empire. As long as England felt herself to be economically and commercially supreme there seemed to be little need for colonial possessions which had to be defended and governed. As the century neared its end, however, Britain's economic supremacy was being rudely challenged. British merchants were meeting stiff competition from other industrial countries, and markets were increasingly difficult to find. British manufacturers worried lest other nations secure the raw materials which had previously come naturally to them; and British investors were finding it harder to invest their money profitably. The New Imperialism The Economic Challenge

The rapidly changing nature of international politics was another

315

factor which caused the British to recognize the importance of their Empire. In 1870 a well-armed and powerful Germany under the leadership of Bismarck had defeated the French army and united the German states into a new empire. This event ended the balance of power which had been established in Europe in 1815 after the Napoleonic wars. At the same time the United States had emerged from the Civil War as a mighty nation, and Italy, which had consisted of a number of independent states, was united under the rule of one king. A united Italy, an expanding Russia, a strong Germany, and a revived France set out to increase their strength and their territory. Britain was no longer supreme. The age of power politics, when each country tried to add to its own strength, had begun and was to end only in the catastrophe of the first World War.

The Struggle for Power

All of these countries sought empires of their own. Areas where Britain had traded freely now began to fall under the control of other powers. Strategic islands on the sea-lanes had to be secured by Britain before they were taken by someone else. The vast continent of Africa, only recently opened up by explorers, offered a rich and tempting prize, and Germany, France, Italy, and Britain began to divide it up among themselves, each trying desperately to get his share.

In this age of imperial rivalry and power politics Britain was determined to be strong. Charles Darwin had argued that in the animal world the strongest or fittest species survived and the weak became extinct. It this were true of human society as well, as seemed likely to many men in the late nineteenth century, it followed that if a nation were to survive it must be strong and its armies powerful. In most books of the day, there was a new emphasis on adventure, heroism, and glory.

Rudyard Kipling

The most famous writer of the period was Rudyard Kipling who became for millions the spokesman of imperialism. In his poems and stories he glorified the life of the soldier. Patriotism and courage were the qualities Kipling demanded of the British people. War was not a catastrophe; it was a glorious necessity. The English had a mission; they must assume the "white man's burden" and bring British civilization to the far corners of the earth for the glory of the race and the improvement of the conquered peoples.

Popular Imperialism

This new imperialism quickly became a mass emotion. By the 1890's cheap daily papers, with sensational headlines, were to be found in every home. These papers encouraged the imperialistic outlook of the people by emphasizing the daring exploits of the Empire-builders in Africa and Asia. The music halls shook to the rafters as the audience joined in

316

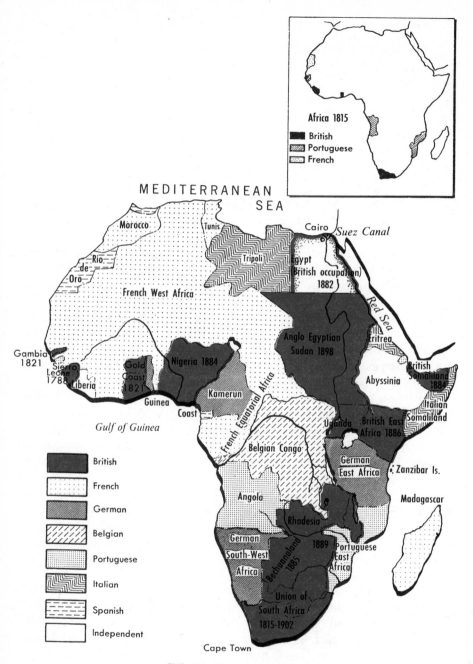

Africa 1815

British
Portuguese
French

MEDITERRANEAN SEA

Morocco
Tunis
Cairo
Suez Canal
Rio
de
Oro
Tripoli
Egypt
(British occupation)
1882
French West Africa
Red Sea
Gambia 1821
Anglo Egyptian Sudan 1898
Eritrea
Sierra Leone 1788
Gold Coast 1821
Nigeria 1884
British Somaliland 1884
Liberia
Abyssinia
Guinea Coast
Kamerun
Italian Somaliland
Gulf of Guinea
French Equatorial Africa
Uganda
British East Africa 1886
Belgian Congo
German East Africa
Zanzibar Is.
British
Angola
Madagascar
French
Rhodesia
German
German South-West Africa
Bethuanaland 1885
1889
Portuguese East Africa
Belgian
Portuguese
Italian
Union of South Africa 1815-1902
Spanish
Independent
Cape Town

THE PARTITION OF AFRICA

the chorus of "The Soldiers of the Queen":

> It's the Soldiers of the Queen, my lads,
> Who've been, my lads,
> Who're seen, my lads,
> In the fight for England's glory, lads;
> Of its world-wide glory let us sing,
> And when we say we've always won,
> And when they ask us how it's done,
> We'll proudly point to every one
> Of England's Soldiers of the Queen!

The first stirrings of imperialism were evident in Disraeli's time, but the peak of the movement was not reached until the 1890's. The new imperialism took two forms. One was the expansion of the Empire, the other was the consolidating and strengthening of the relations between Britain and the self-governing colonies like Canada. The chief architect of both movements was Joseph Chamberlain who in 1895 became Colonial Secretary in a Conservative government.

Imperial Centralization

Joseph Chamberlain

Chamberlain believed that the young daughters of the Empire, like Canada, Australia, and New Zealand, could be a great source of military and economic strength to Great Britain. He asked the Prime Ministers, who were in London in 1897 to attend Queen Victoria's Diamond Jubilee, to attend a Colonial Conference where he put before them his plans for a form of imperial union or federation. He was particularly anxious to see the whole Empire united for defence and to have the younger countries support Britain in case of war. The closest rival of Britain was the new German Empire, which was engaged in building up a navy to equal or excel Britain's Royal Navy, and Chamberlain wished the colonial Prime Ministers to help Britain add to her navy. He also felt that, politically and economically, the colonies and the Mother Country should be bound together more closely.

Wilfrid Laurier

Chamberlain's imperialist views were sharply challenged by Sir Wilfrid Laurier, the Prime Minister of Canada, who bluntly refused to consider submerging Canada's identity as a nation in any imperial federation. He was sympathetic to Chamberlain's arguments about the need for imperial defence, but he refused to have Canada make any contribution, on the grounds that Canada might be drawn into British imperial wars that did not concern her. Yet the Colonial Conference of 1897 did emphasize that Britain and the colonies were part of one family of nations. At this meeting the idea of a Commonwealth of Nations began to take the shape it was to have in the twentieth century.

318

SIR WILFRID LAURIER AND QUEEN VICTORIA

In 1897 the British government called a Colonial Conference in London, as part of the Diamond Jubilee celebrations. Chamberlain hoped to make some progress towards his ideal of a political, military, and economic federation of the Empire. His proposals were resisted by the Canadian Prime Minister, Wilfrid Laurier, a determined nationalist. Laurier was wined, dined, and knighted by the aged Queen; but the man who boasted, "The twentieth century belongs to Canada" was deaf to Chamberlain's appeals.

Meanwhile in South Africa events were leading rapidly towards a disaster for British imperialism. Since 1836, when the Boer farmers had trekked north from the Cape Colony beyond the Orange and Vaal Rivers to form their new republics, Boers and British had regarded each other with much hostility. When gold was discovered in Johannesburg in 1885, the British flooded into the Transvaal. The Boers, now in a minority, resented British newcomers whom they called Uitlanders, or Outsiders. They refused the Uitlanders the right to vote, denied them the privileges of a citizen of the Transvaal, and taxed them heavily. *The South African Problem*

The Uitlanders found a champion in Cecil Rhodes, Prime Minister of Cape Colony. Rhodes had become a multi-millionaire at twenty because of wise investments in diamond mines. He was deeply attached to both Africa and the British Empire and his great dream was of a British state in Africa which would stretch from the Cape of Good Hope to Cairo in Egypt. After 1890 his political and economical interests extended into Rhodesia, far to the north and west of the Transvaal. *Cecil Rhodes*

The Boers of the Transvaal, under their President, Paul Kruger, had no intention of retreating before this British expansion. Theirs was a society based on agriculture and they were afraid that their way of life would be dominated by the Uitlanders' passion for money and progress if the British annexed them. They had reasons for their fear of annexation. In 1895 a man named Dr. Jameson led a raiding party into the Transvaal with the obvious intention of stirring up trouble and *Paul Kruger* *Jameson*

319

BOER COMMANDOS

When war broke out in the fall of 1899 Boer commandos struck quickly and threatened, as President Kruger said, to drive the British into the sea. Fifty thousand new soldiers from Britain, soon to be joined by 8,000 Canadians as well as Australians and New Zealanders, barely stemmed the advancing tide. By the summer of 1900, however, the British had regained the initiative from the heroic, outnumbered, and outgunned Boers. Yet the Boers were far from finished. Boer armies were dissolved and countless small, highly mobile commando bands waged guerilla war for over a year. Only when their families were placed in barbed-wire camps, the railroads lined with blockhouses and trains protected by armoured cars, and the elusive commandos captured by specially-trained British cavalry, did the Boers accept the Peace of Vereeniging in May, 1902. At the war's end the British had used almost a half million men and a billion dollars to crush the Boer population. It was an abrupt end to the more bellicose type of imperialism.

starting a revolution there. Jameson's raid was a failure, for his plan was discovered and his party captured by the Boers. It was well known that Rhodes was a close friend of Dr. Jameson, and many people rightly believed that it was Rhodes who had inspired Jameson's raid. The Boers became more stubborn than ever in their relations with Britain and in this they were encouraged by Britain's rival, Germany. Conditions became so bad for the Uitlanders that in 1899 they petitioned the British government to intervene in the Transvaal on their behalf. Conferences between the British and Boer leaders failed to reach a solution and in the end, uncompromising opinion on both sides brought war in 1899.

320

The South African War was to last until 1902. The Boers were expert riders and marksmen, perfectly at home on the South African plains. At first they enjoyed a great success, even invading British territory and besieging Kimberley, Ladysmith, and Mafeking. In December 1899, the British sent three relief forces to raise these sieges, but each failed miserably. This "Black Week" in December made Britain take the war more seriously. Reinforcements were sent from Britain, and Australia, New Zealand, and Canada sent volunteers. In 1900 these enlarged forces, under Lord Roberts, quickly moved north. Mafeking was relieved and the major Boer cities, Pretoria and Johannesburg, were captured. President Kruger fled to Europe. For two more years the great Boer generals, Botha and Smuts, continued to wage guerilla warfare against the British. Only after General Kitchener had rounded up all the Boer farmers and their families and confined them to camps was resistance wiped out.

In the British Parliament, many Liberals had opposed the war and their influence now helped to secure generous peace terms for the Boers. The Boer farmers were given money compensation for their losses and the Boers in the Transvaal and Orange Free States, once again colonists of Britain, were promised self-government. This promise was kept in 1907 and was followed in 1910 by the creation of a new Dominion, the Union of South Africa. Consisting of Cape Colony, Natal, the Orange Free state, and the Transvaal, the new Dominion was to have the same freedom as the older Dominions, such as Canada. The first Prime Minister of this new Dominion was General Botha who had fought the British so heroically during the Boer War.

The Boer War was a turning point for British imperial policy. It had shown that imperialism might go too far and many Englishmen were appalled by the hysteria of the Jingos and the brutality of the war itself. Moreover, the war had revealed weaknesses in the British army which were all the more serious in the face of the hostility of Germany, France, and even the United States; for Britain at the turn of the century stood alone, friendless and isolated. Henceforth Britain's programme of imperialism became more subdued.

As the twentieth century dawned, Britain saw that no country could stand alone in the international rivalries of the time. She was determined to end her isolation and to find friends, and soon she sought these among the countries threatened by the rise of imperialist Germany.

The Home of Liberty	The Cradle of a Universal Language	A Great Empire An Emerging Commonwealth
A Monarchy	Chaucer	Canada
↓	Shakespeare	Australia
A Parliamentary Monarchy	Milton	New Zealand
↓	Tennyson	South Africa
A Democratic Parliamentary Monarchy		

1901

CHAPTER FORTY-SEVEN

THE END OF AN ERA

On January 22, 1901, Queen Victoria died. Few of her subjects could remember that day, sixty-four years before, when the eighteen-year-old girl had become their Queen. During her long reign, and particularly in her last years when she was almost a symbol of Britain's imperial achievement, she had gained a great hold on the affections of her people. With her death the entire nation and Empire was plunged into heart-felt mourning. Many sensed that not only Queen Victoria, but Victorian England, had died. The Queen's death marked the end of an era.

Already the strong winds of socialism and imperialism gave promise of the great storms that would rock the new century. As the twentieth century began, doubt and uncertainty were replacing the Victorian beliefs in inevitable progress and unending material prosperity. Old Victorians shook their heads in horror as they read of the gigantic labour strikes, watched the exploits of the younger generation of imperialists, and saw their grandchildren reading books that would never have been allowed inside a mid-Victorian home. What would happen to a country, they wondered, whose young people spent their time on bicycles and at soccer matches, who preferred Kipling to Lord Tennyson, and whose favourite song was "Ta-ra-ra-boom-dee-ay"? The world of the twentieth century seemed to them a strange new world indeed. It was, in fact, to be stranger and more calamitous in many ways than even the most pessimistic ever imagined.

But this lay in the future. The Englishman who watched Victoria's funeral procession move slowly through the London streets to Westminster Abbey had much of which he could be proud. In his own life-

DEVELOPMENT OF DEMOCRATIC
PARLIAMENTARY GOVERNMENT

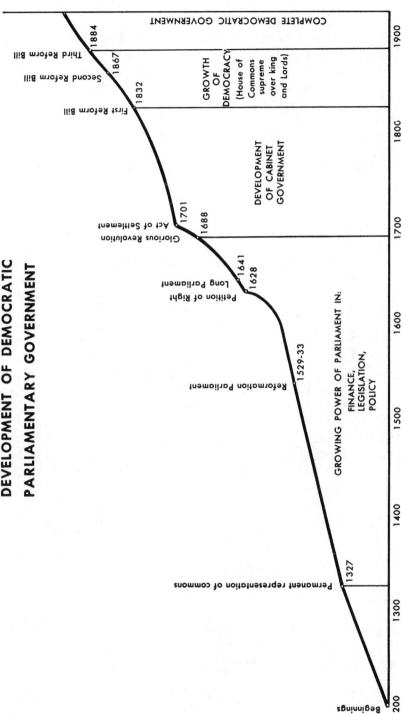

COMPLETE DEMOCRATIC GOVERNMENT

GROWTH OF DEMOCRACY (House of Commons supreme over king and Lords)

DEVELOPMENT OF CABINET GOVERNMENT

GROWING POWER OF PARLIAMENT IN: FINANCE, LEGISLATION, POLICY

1884 Third Reform Bill
1867 Second Reform Bill
1832 First Reform Bill
1701 Act of Settlement
1688 Glorious Revolution
1641 Long Parliament
1628 Petition of Right
1529-33 Reformation Parliament
1327 Permanent representation of commons
1200 Beginnings

1200 1300 1400 1500 1600 1700 1800 1900

time he had seen the development of parliamentary democracy reach almost its completion. Mediæval kings had brought Parliament into being to assist in the government of the land. By Tudor times Parliament was beginning to be regarded as an instrument of the people, as well as an instrument of the king. In the seventeenth century it had dared to oppose the Stuart monarchs and by 1688 it had created a form of government that may be called parliamentary monarchy. The great economic and social changes of the eighteenth and nineteenth centuries had made it inevitable that Parliament in time would come to represent the interests of all the people, not only those of the landed aristocracy who had ruled the country for so long. With the great Reform Acts of 1832, 1867, and 1884 political democracy had finally triumphed. At the Queen's death women were the only large group that remained without the right to vote.

This advance towards democracy meant that the British people in the new century were going to demand more of their government. The old idea of *laissez-faire* was to be swept aside in favour of more state intervention in the lives of the people. The Queen and such eminent Victorians as William Ewart Gladstone had little sympathy for such ideas, but theirs were the voices of the past. The voices of the future, many of which could already be heard in 1901, were those of labour leaders, socialists, Conservative humanitarians, and radical Liberals, and it was their activities that were vitally to affect the lives of the British people in the twentieth century.

As he watched the kings, the princes, the generals, and the admirals follow the Queen's body through the streets of London, the Englishman might also reflect that England was the home of liberty. The legal system which had begun in Anglo-Saxon and Norman times and had been fashioned by the genius of Henry II, had established the principle that all Englishmen were equal before the law. Neither kings nor subjects, in the centuries that followed, were to be permitted to stand above or to break the law. While other peoples were still subject to the will of an arbitrary ruler, the Englishman had come to expect as his right that he would not be imprisoned without just cause and that if by mischance he were imprisoned, he would receive a quick and a fair trial before a jury of his peers. He also possessed as his right freedom of association—the right to gather together with his fellows for discussion or action—, freedom of speech, and freedom to act as he wished as long as his actions did not affect the welfare of his fellow-citizens. This passionate belief in the rule of law and in the existence of fundamental

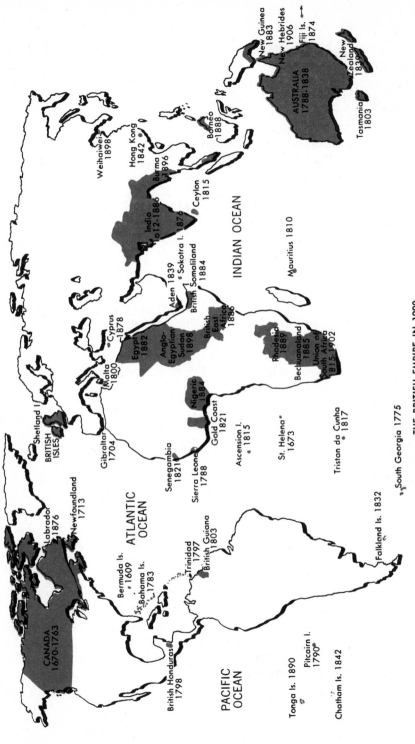

New Guinea 1883
New Hebrides 1906
Fiji Is. 1874
New Zealand 1839
AUSTRALIA 1788-1838
Tasmania 1803

Weihaiwei 1898
Hong Kong 1842
Burma 1896
Borneo 1888
Ceylon 1815
India No.12-1886

INDIAN OCEAN

Aden 1839
Sokotra I. 1879
British Somaliland 1884
Mauritius 1810

Cyprus 1878
Egypt 1882
Anglo-Egyptian Sudan 1898
British East Africa 1886
Rhodesia 1889
Bechuanaland 1885
Union of South Africa 1815-1902

Malta 1800

Shetland I
BRITISH ISLES
Gibraltar 1704
Senegambia 1821
Sierra Leone 1788
Nigeria 1884
Gold Coast 1821
Ascension I. 1815
St. Helena 1673
Tristan da Cunha 1817
South Georgia 1775

ATLANTIC OCEAN

Labrador 1876
Newfoundland 1713
Bermuda Is. 1609
Bahama Is. 1783
Trinidad 1797
British Guiana 1803
Falkland Is. 1832

CANADA 1670-1763
British Honduras 1798

PACIFIC OCEAN

Tonga Is. 1890
Pitcairn I. 1790
Chatham Is. 1842

THE BRITISH EMPIRE IN 1900

human rights was one of Britain's most important exports to the lands into which British people and British ideas penetrated.

If there was any universal language in 1901 it was English. Few countries since ancient Greece had contributed more to the culture of the modern world. The works of England's great writers, from Chaucer to Shakespeare, to Tennyson, Dickens, and Kipling, had been translated into almost every language and studied in every university and school. Wherever educated men gathered, English was likely to be the language of communication.

In spite of the sobering effect of the Boer War, the English had every reason to take pride in their Empire. It was, indeed, a remarkable achievement that this small island power should have become the centre of the greatest empire the world has ever seen. Even Oscar Wilde, who usually did not care about such matters, was moved to write the poem, "Ave Imperatrix" in praise of the British Empire:

> Set in this stormy Northern sea,
>> Queen of these restless fields of tide,
> England! what shall men say of thee,
>> Before whose feet the worlds divide?
>
> The earth, a brittle globe of glass,
>> Lies in the hollow of thy hand,
> And through its heart of crystal pass,
>> Like shadows through a twilight land,
>
> The spears of crimson-suited war,
>> The long white-crested waves of fight,
> And all the deadly fires which are
>> The torches of the lords of Night.

Yet there was more to the Empire than conquest. Its real glory lay in the fact that Britain, after the American Revolution, had found a means whereby colonies could become self-governing and yet remain within the Empire. The path blazed by Canada, Australia, and New Zealand was to be followed in time by India, Pakistan, Ghana, and others, until the Commonwealth of Nations included independent countries on every continent and members of almost every race, religion, and language.

The Englishman in 1901 was living on the threshold of revolutionary changes in transportation. During his own lifetime he had seen the world shrink in size as improvements in land and ocean travel and the development of the telegraph and the trans-Atlantic cable made communication more rapid and efficient. But these changes were nothing compared to those that were to follow in the twentieth century and were to bring the nations and peoples of the world into even closer contact with one another. Victoria's subjects who could remember the great days of the Crystal Palace and the wonders displayed in the Great Exhibition, could never have pictured the existence of such modern marvels as radio and television. Nor in their wildest flight of fancy would they have imagined that little more than fifty years after the death of the great Queen men would be making plans to travel to the moon, or that great nations would be soberly discussing the division of interplanetary space, as once they had discussed how Africa should be divided among them.

The Victorians sensed that a new era in international politics was beginning, but they could not have foreseen the effect it was to have on Britain. They had been accustomed to think of Britain as standing alone and supreme, safely entrenched behind the iron-clad wall of the British navy. As they looked about them in 1901, however, they could see that this period had come to an end and that Britain could no longer stand alone. Thirteen years after the Queen's death Britain was to find herself engaged in the greatest war in her history, a war in which more men were killed in a week than in the twenty-five years of the Napoleonic wars.

All of this was far in the future on that sad January day in 1901 when the Queen died. But most of the forces that were to determine the course of the twentieth century were already present. Fortunately for the history of the modern world, so too were the forces that were to enable Britain to survive: a sturdy, intelligent, and courageous people, a strong democratic government, and an Empire tied so closely by affection that it was to come to her assistance in the two great crises of her modern life. She had been great in the past; she was to be great in the future. Hers is indeed a glorious history.

TIME CHART

IN THE BRITISH ISLES		ELSEWHERE
POLITICAL	**OTHER**	
	1815 New Corn Law	
1819 Peterloo and repressive Acts		1818 49th Parallel to Rockies recognized as Canadian border 1819 Singapore founded 1821 Union of North West Company and Hudson's Bay Company 1823 U.S. adopts Monroe Doctrine
1829 Catholic Emancipation 1830 Grey's Reform Ministry 1832 First Reform Act 1833 Factory Act 1834 Poor Law	1830 Opening of Liverpool and Manchester Railroad 1833 Owen's Grand National Consolidated Trade Union	1833 Abolition of slavery in British Empire 1837 Boer Trek in South Africa Rebellion in Upper and Lower Canada
	1838-46 Free trade movement 1838-48 Chartism 1839 Guarantee of Belgium's neutrality	1838-9 Durham's Report 1840 Establishment of colony in New Zealand 1841 Union of two Canadas
1844 Factory Act 1846 Repeal of the Corn Laws 1847 Ten Hours Act		1848 "Communist Manifesto" Revolution in Europe California Gold Rush Responsible Government in Canada
	1849 Repeal of Navigation Acts	
	1851 Crystal Palace Exhibition 1854-56 Crimean War 1859 Darwin's "Origin of Species"	1851 Australian Gold Rush 1860 Lincoln elected President of the United States 1861-5 American Civil War 1865 Lincoln murdered

TIME CHART

IN THE BRITISH ISLES		ELSEWHERE
POLITICAL	OTHER	
1867 Second Reform Act		1867 Confederation of Canada Sir John A. Macdonald first Prime Minister
1868-74 Reforms of Gladstone government		
		1870 Manitoba enters Canadian Confederation Germany defeats France 1871 Britain, Canada and the United States sign Treaty of Washington British Columbia enters Canadian Confederation 1873 Prince Edward Island enters Canadian Confederation
1874-80 Social reforms of Disraeli's administration		
		1875 Purchase of Suez Canal shares
		1876 Queen Victoria Empress of India 1878 Congress of Berlin 1879 National Policy adopted by Conservative Party in Canada
1880 Liberal victory		
1884 Third Reform Act	1881 Social Democratic Federation formed	
		1885 North-West Rebellion in Canada Canadian Pacific Railway completed
1886 First Home Rule Bill		
1893 Gladstone's Second Home Rule Bill 1895 Chamberlain becomes Colonial Secretary	1887 First Colonial Conference 1889 Dock strike 1893 Independent Labour Party formed	
		1896 Laurier becomes Prime Minister of Canada
	1897 Queen Victoria's Diamond Jubilee Second Colonial Conference 1899 British Labour Party formed 1901 Death of Queen Victoria	1899 Outbreak of Boer War

THE ROYAL HOUSES
OF BRITAIN

THE NORMAN KINGS

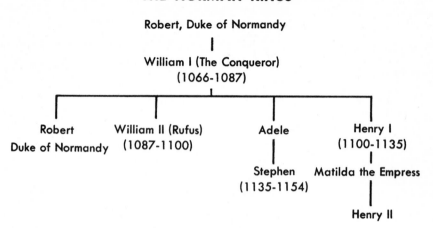

Robert, Duke of Normandy
|
William I (The Conqueror)
(1066-1087)

Robert, Duke of Normandy

William II (Rufus)
(1087-1100)

Adele
|
Stephen
(1135-1154)

Henry I
(1100-1135)
|
Matilda the Empress
|
Henry II

THE HOUSE OF ANJOU (PLANTAGENET)

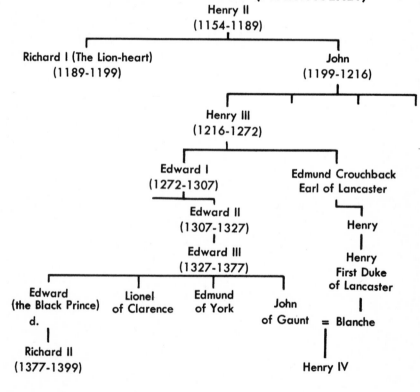

Henry II
(1154-1189)

Richard I (The Lion-heart)
(1189-1199)

John
(1199-1216)

Henry III
(1216-1272)

Edward I
(1272-1307)

Edmund Crouchback
Earl of Lancaster

Edward II
(1307-1327)

Henry

Edward III
(1327-1377)

Henry
First Duke
of Lancaster

Edward
(the Black Prince)
d.
|
Richard II
(1377-1399)

Lionel
of Clarence

Edmund
of York

John
of Gaunt = Blanche
|
Henry IV

THE HOUSES OF LANCASTER AND YORK

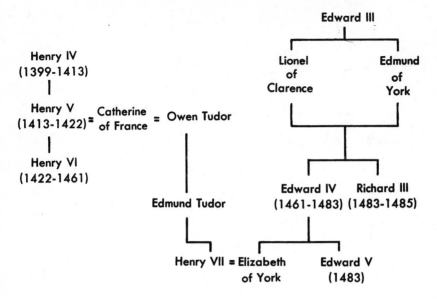

Edward III

Henry IV
(1399-1413)

Henry V
(1413-1422) = Catherine of France = Owen Tudor

Henry VI
(1422-1461)

Lionel
of
Clarence

Edmund
of
York

Edmund Tudor

Edward IV
(1461-1483)

Richard III
(1483-1485)

Henry VII = Elizabeth
of York

Edward V
(1483)

THE HOUSE OF TUDOR

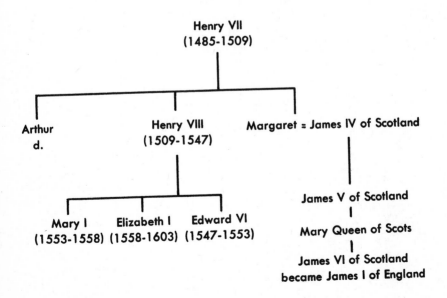

Henry VII
(1485-1509)

Arthur
d.

Henry VIII
(1509-1547)

Margaret = James IV of Scotland

Mary I
(1553-1558)

Elizabeth I
(1558-1603)

Edward VI
(1547-1553)

James V of Scotland

Mary Queen of Scots

James VI of Scotland
became James I of England

THE HOUSE OF STUART

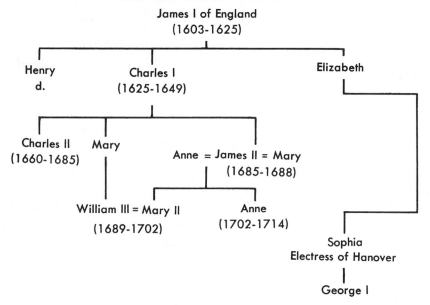

James I of England
(1603-1625)

Henry
d.

Charles I
(1625-1649)

Elizabeth

Charles II
(1660-1685)

Mary

Anne = James II = Mary
(1685-1688)

William III = Mary II
(1689-1702)

Anne
(1702-1714)

Sophia
Electress of Hanover

George I

THE HOUSE OF HANOVER

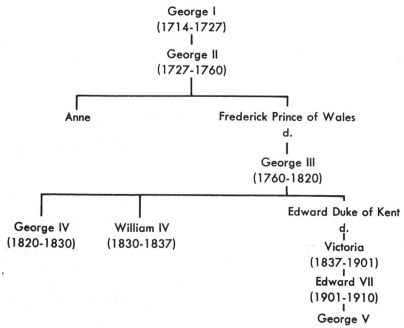

George I
(1714-1727)

George II
(1727-1760)

Anne

Frederick Prince of Wales
d.

George III
(1760-1820)

George IV
(1820-1830)

William IV
(1830-1837)

Edward Duke of Kent
d.

Victoria
(1837-1901)

Edward VII
(1901-1910)

George V

THE HOUSE OF WINDSOR

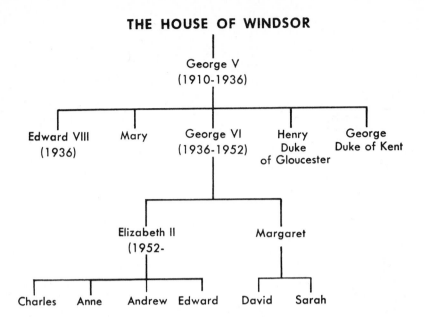

INDEX

337

Economic depression, 223, 231, 261, 310, 315
Economic prosperity, 100, 104, 220, 222
Edinburgh, 109
Education, 18, 20, 72-3, 296
Education Act, 296
Edward the Confessor, 15, 25
Edward the Elder, 23
Edward I, 51-2, 53-4
Edward II, 52
Edward III, 53, 54, 55-6, 57, 59, 60, 71
Edward IV, 74, 80
Edward VI, 89
Egbert, King, 12
Egypt, 231, 302
Elba, island of, 236
Eldon, Lord, 228-9
Elgin, Lord, 277
Eliot, John, 116
Elizabeth I, 91-9, 106-7, 108
Elizabeth II, 21
Elizabeth of York, 80
"Empress of India", 302
Empson, Richard, 82
Enclosures, 101, 102-3, 219
Engels, Frederick, 264
English language, 55-6, 71-2, 74, 326
Ethelred the Unready, 14, 15
Evangelicals, 215
Evelyn, John, 149
Evesham, Battle of, 50, 51
Evolution, theory of, 274
Exchequer, 31-2
Excise Bill, 181

Fabian Society, 311-12
Factories and factory legislation, 222, 223, 258-60, 264, 302
Factory Acts, 260, 264
Fairfax, Sir Thomas, 129
Falkirk, Battle of, 52
Family Compact, 277
Faversham, 155
Fawkes, Guy, 112
Fealty, 30

Feudal system, 29-30, 71
Fief, 29
Fielding, Henry, 171
Fifth Monarchy, 138
Finance, 225
Fire of London, 148-9
Fisher, Bishop, 87
Flodden, 89
Foreign policy:
    Palmerston, 285
    Gladstone, 297-8
    Disraeli, 302-3
France: 225, 226-8, 286, 287, 316; war with, 158-63, 186-8, 204, 230-8; see also North America, India, West Indies
Franchise, 179, 252, 256, 292, 293, 312, 324
Frederick the Great of Prussia, 190, 193, 194
Free trade and protection, 225, 265-9, 300
Freedom:
    Of association, 246, 324
    From unlawful arrest, 209-11
    Of the press, 209-11, 246
    Of speech, 209-11, 324
Freeholders, 250, 252, 256
French Revolution, 226-8
Frobisher, Martin, 104
Frontenac, Count de, 159-60
Fyrd, 21, 27, 32, 35

Gage, General, 198, 203
Gambling, 170, 172
Gatton, 252
General warrant, 210
George I, 163, 169, 177, 180, 208
George II, 180, 208
George III, 196, 198, 207-9, 210, 224, 226, 285
George IV, 253
Georgian outlook, 169-76
Germany, 316, 320
Gibraltar, 161, 163, 204
Gilbert, Sir Humphrey, 104
Gin, 174, 218